Lucien Bonaparte Maxwell

Lucien B. Maxwell, the Napoleon of the Southwest. This oil portrait hangs in the Board Room of the First National Bank of Santa Fe, through whose courtesy it is reproduced.

Lucien Bonaparte MAXWELL

Napoleon of the Southwest

By Lawrence R. Murphy

University of Oklahoma Press
Norman

Other books by Lawrence R. Murphy

Indian Agent in New Mexico (Santa Fe, 1967)

Out in God's Country: A History of Colfax County, New Mexico (Springer, N.M., 1969)

Philmont: A History of New Mexico's Cimarron Country (Albuquerque, 1972)

Frontier Crusader: William F. M. Arny (Tucson, 1973)

The Slave Narratives of Texas (with Ron C. Tyler) (Austin, 1974)

Anti-Slavery in the Southwest (El Paso, 1978)

The World of John Muir (with Dan Collins) (Stockton, 1981)

For R. L. G.
With love and thanks

Library of Congress Cataloging in Publication Data

Murphy, Lawrence R., 1942–
    Lucien Bonaparte Maxwell, Napoleon of the Southwest.

    Bibliography: p. 253.
    Includes index.
    1. Maxwell, Lucien Bonaparte, 1818–1875.   2. New Mexico—
History—1848–   .   3. Ranchers—New Mexico—Biography.
4. Ranch life—New Mexico—History—19th century.   5. Pio-
neers—New Mexico—Biography.   6. New Mexico—Biography.
I. Title.
F801.M39M87   1983   978.9'04'0924   82-40454

Contents

Illustrations

LUCIEN BONAPARTE MAXWELL

Preface

F EW nineteenth-century frontiersmen achieved the lasting renown of New Mexico rancher Lucien Bonaparte Maxwell. Born on the Illinois frontier at a time when the nation was beginning to push westward across the continent, Maxwell shared in the pioneering activities of such mountain men as Charles and William Bent, Tom ("Broken Hand") Fitzpatrick, Jim Bridger, and Milton Sublette. With his boon companion Kit Carson he accompanied pathfinder John C. Frémont on three transcontinental expeditions. What ultimately made Maxwell famous, however, were his successful settlements along the northeastern frontier of New Mexico. Marriage to a daughter of Taos merchant and landowner Charles Beaubien enabled him to establish ranches along first the Rayado and later the Cimarron rivers. He gained fame as an Indian fighter, farmer, and stockman. Sales of foodstuffs to the United States Army and the Office of Indian Affairs made him prosperous enough to purchase nearly all of the Beaubien and Miranda land grant. The discovery of gold at Maxwell's ranch and the sale of the grant to foreign investors made Lucien one of the richest men in the West.

Maxwell's colorful and sometimes enigmatic personality fascinated both his contemporaries and subsequent historians. Exposed to only limited formal education, he grew to maturity among the hardy, crafty pioneers who first traversed the West. He learned to be loyal and dependable to his friends. Anglo mountaineers, Indian chiefs, and impoverished Mexican farmers turned to him for help and advice. Lucien's Cimarron home became famous for the hospitality he dispensed; visitors could always expect to be housed, fed, and entertained as Maxwell's guests. On the other hand, Maxwell could be arrogant, stubborn, and even cruel to those who challenged his authority, especially if they were Mexican. His hot temper was as famous as his generosity. He was, in short, one of a handful of men around whom the history and legend of the American West have been built.

In tracing the life of Lucien Maxwell, I have accumulated a storehouse of debts, both personal and professional. Several of the persons who were most instrumental in stimulating my interest in the history of New Mexico in general and of Lucien Maxwell in particular are now deceased: William Morrison, of El Paso, Texas, a descendant both of the Ferdinand Maxwell and William Morrison families, aroused my interest in Lucien and provided invaluable information about his life, especially the early days in Illinois; historian Morris Taylor, who devoted his life to teaching and writing about southern Colorado and northern New Mexico, generously shared his knowledge of the subject on many occasions; and Harry G. McGavran, M.D., provided assistance during my early research efforts. My gratitude to individuals with whom I have lived and worked in Cimarron and Taos is also immense. In particular, Jerry Traut and Nick Pisor first introduced me to the glory of northern New Mexico, while the late J. W. ("Doc") Leitzell and his wife Vivian, whose home occupies the exact spot where Lucien Maxwell's mansion once stood, shared much of their knowledge and understanding of the early history of the area. Steve Zimmer, curator of the Ernest Thompson Seton Memorial Library, and Victor Grant, a young Cimarron historian who is now curator of the Mariano Martínez home in Taos, have also been exceptionally helpful, especially in providing pictures. In Taos, Kit Carson's biographer M. Morgan Estergreen and Major Jack Boyer, of the Kit Carson Museum, assisted during early stages of my work, while Myra Ellen Jenkins, now retired as New Mexico's state historian, shared not only her keen insight and invaluable archival materials but also her zest for the history of the Southwest.

Many libraries, archives, and museums accommodated my need for information about Maxwell. In Illinois, the State Historical Library, the Historical Survey at the University of Illinois, Western Illinois University, and the Pierre Menard Home State Park provided assistance; Maxwell's Missouri antecedents were developed from collections in the Missouri Historical Society and the Saint Louis University library. The Colorado Historical Society and, especially, the Pioneers' Museum, in Colorado Springs, shared their unique resources, as did, in Santa Fe, the library at the Palace of the Governors, the officers of the First National Bank, and the State Historic Records Center. While in California, I depended heavily on the resources of the Holt-Atherton Pacific Center for Western Studies of the University of the Pacific and the kindnesses of Katherine Kemp, Bart Harloe, and other capable librarians. Like all other historians, I continue to be grateful for the existence of the National Archives and Library of Congress, and I extend my thanks to their kind and helpful staff members. John Porter Bloom, formerly with the National Archives, has been especially helpful.

Several sections of this manuscript have appeared elsewhere in modified form. Portions of chapter 3 have appeared in volume 4 of *Valley Trails,* the occasional publication of the Stockton Corral of Westerners. For the use of those sections of chapter 5 that originally appeared in the *New Mexico Historical Review,* I am grateful to editor Richard W. Etulain. Bruce Dinges, acting editor, has kindly granted to me permission to use the portions of chapter 10 that first appeared in *Arizona and the West.*

For assisting with final revisions on the manuscript and the collection of illustrations — as well as tolerating me in general — I am grateful to my long-suffering secretary, Arlene McNeal, my assistant Dan Collins, and Russell Griffin. I, of course, bear full responsibility for all information and interpretations.

LAWRENCE R. MURPHY

Mount Pleasant, Michigan

Lucien Bonaparte Maxwell

1

A Frontier Boyhood

Lucien Maxwell was born on September 14, 1818, during a crucial period in the history of the frontier. Only weeks before, on August 26, crowds had gathered in his hometown, Kaskaskia, to celebrate the creation of the state of Illinois. From the wood-frame houses that gave the town the look of a French provincial village advanced the independent militia company carrying the new twenty-star flag recently adopted by Congress. The company field officers, members of the regular army, and officials from the territorial government gathered near the small building that served as a temporary capitol. The onlookers included men in black frock coats and women in fine, colorful bonnets and long dresses imported from Philadelphia or New York. Many of those present spoke French, which was still the language of most Kaskaskians. Others revealed their southern origins by their heavy accents and the presence of black servants. Spanish, a language more familiar across the Mississippi in what had been Spanish territory until less than two decades before, could also be heard. There may even have been a few Kaskaskia Indians from the nearby village. Soon twenty rounds boomed across the surrounding countryside; then came one more for the new state of Illinois.

"This was truly a proud day for the citizens of Illinois," proclaimed the bombastic editor of the town's weekly *Illinois Intelligencer* in his next issue. Upon the new constitution, he and many others were convinced, "hung the prosperity and hopes of tens of thousands yet to follow." It was "justly the basis of our future greatness."[1]

No other season could have been more appropriate for the birth of a child who would be important not only in developing the greatness of a single state but also in the movement of the entire nation westward toward the Pacific. The spirit of the times may well have affected Hugh and Odile Maxwell, because they named their boy Lucien Bonaparte, after Napoleon's flamboyant younger brother.[2] Even though Lucien never used his full name, preferring the initials L. B., the named proved appropriate; for his work in exploring, settling, and taming the American frontier he would one day be known as the Napoleon of the Southwest.

The family into which Lucien Maxwell was born was every bit as impressive as the time and place of his nativity. His best-known relative undoubtedly was his maternal grandfather Pierre Menard, who had played a major part in events leading to Illinois statehood and was one of the most distinguished citizens of Kaskaskia and the entire Northwest. A Canadian by birth, he had moved to Vincennes on the Wabash River the year Americans drafted their constitution in Philadelphia. He engaged in the lucrative Indian trade for several years before moving farther west to Kaskaskia. As the Mississippi River town's principal merchant, an Indian trader with depots throughout the Middle West, and a buyer of fur pelts from the upper Mississippi and Missouri, Menard enlarged his wealth and his prestige.

He also found time for public service. He had served as a militia commander, had been chosen by Indiana Governor William Henry Harrison to be a local judge, and had been elected to both the Illinois and Indiana territorial legislatures. In all, he was one of the most powerful and influential men on the frontier. So respected was Menard that his colleagues inserted a special provision in the Illinois Constitution of 1818 stating that, although only recently granted United States citizenship, Menard

Pierre Menard, Lucien Maxwell's grandfather and the first lieutenant governor of Illinois. Courtesy Illinois State Historical Library.

could stand for lieutenant governor. He announced almost immediately, and the week his grandson Lucien was born, Menard received an overwhelming majority of votes. In Randolph County, where Kaskaskia was located, Menard received 376 votes to his two opponents' 18.[3] "He was endowed with a strong, vigorous intellect," reported pioneer historian John Reynolds, who knew Menard, "and [was] also blessed with an energy that never ceased exertion . . . ."[4]

The mansion Menard completed about 1802 reflected the status and wealth he had achieved. Sometimes termed the "Mount Vernon of Illinois," it overlooked Kaskaskia from the east side of the Kaskaskia River. Traditional French colonial design, a sturdy frame construction, dormered windows to light the attic, and a broad columned porch along the entire front of the building combined to give it, in the view of one architectural historian, a "high place on any list of historic homes in the United States."[5] Spacious but plainly decorated rooms with beautiful mahagony woodwork reflected the prosperity and dignity of its owner, his French heritage, and the frontier society in which he lived.[6] The mansion has been restored by the State of Illinois and is one of the sites at Kaskaskia State Park visited annually by thousands of tourists.[7] Young Lucien must have found his grandfather's house impressive, for years later in the New Mexico wilderness he incorporated elements of its architecture into two of his own residences.

On June 13, 1792, about a year after he settled at Kaskaskia, Pierre Menard married nineteen-year-old Marie-Thérèse-Michelle Godin, the daughter of a prominent French resident of the community.[8] Their first daughter, Marie-Odile, born the next year, would one day be Lucien Maxwell's mother. The couple had five other children, but only three of them, Pierre, Jr., Thérèse-Bérénice, and Modeste-Alzire, lived beyond early childhood.[9] Mrs. Menard died in late July, 1804. With such a large family and so many other responsibilities, Pierre could not long remain a widower. In September, 1806, he married Angé-

*Pierre Menard's mansion overlooking the Mississippi contained
architectural elements used in several of Maxwell's frontier homes.
Courtesy Illinois State Historical Library.*

lique Saucier, granddaughter of the French engineer who
had designed and built Fort de Chartres north of Kaskaskia.[10] What was perhaps more important, Angélique's
sister had married Jean Pierre Chouteau, the Saint Louis
businessman whose Missouri Fur Company controlled the
Indian and fur trade on the western frontier. Menard's
interest in the fur trade subsequently increased as a result
of his association with the powerful Chouteau family.[11]
Angélique was noted for her "generous hospitality" and
"elegant and refined manner." "Her charities were the
gifts of silence," a family friend recalled; "unknown to
the world, they were dispensed with a loving hand to the
poor and unfortunate."[12] Young Odile and her future son
Lucien showed many of the same characteristics, perhaps
demonstrating the influence of the second Mrs. Menard
on her children and grandchildren. Angélique and Pierre

had eight children, six of whom survived to adulthood: François-Xavier, Jean-Baptiste-Edmond, Matthieu-Saucier, Louis-Cyprien, Joseph-Amédée, and Sophie-Angelique. The three youngest were contemporaries of Menard's grandchildren, including Lucien Maxwell.[13]

The Menards were only slightly more prominent on the Illinois side of the Mississippi Valley than the Maxwells were in Missouri. The first of that family in the area was a priest, the Reverend James Maxwell. An Irishman, probably born in or near Dublin about 1742, he studied at the famed University of Salamanca, where he took his priestly vows. In 1794 the Spanish court identified Father Maxwell as the ideal candidate to work with the many settlers from Ireland and the United States taking up farms on the Spanish side of the Mississippi. Appointed Vicar General of Upper Louisiana, he arrived at the French town of Sainte Genevieve, just across the Mississippi from Kaskaskia, in 1796. There he gained popularity among the local citizens and earned a reputation as a "learned and practical Irish priest" among the hierarchy.[14]

Like Menard, Maxwell had interests that extended beyond his church work. In 1799, just before Spain relinquished its ownership of the Trans-Mississippi West, first to France and then through the Louisiana Purchase to the United States, Maxwell petitioned for three grants of land. The largest, encompassing more than 95,000 acres, was located at the forks of the Black River in what became southeastern Missouri. Smaller tracts were nearer Sainte Genevieve. In his request, Father Maxwell explained that he planned to establish an Irish Catholic settlement for immigrants "rescued from British tyranny and persecution to which they are exposed on account of their religion . . . ." The Spanish governor, Carlos Dehault Delassus, agreed that the project would encourage the immigration of "a class of laborious inhabitants," and on November 3, 1799, approved the grant.[15]

The first party of Irish immigrants to arrive in New Orleans late in 1799 brought two of Father Maxwell's nephews, eight-year-old Hugh and his older brother John. Along with other Irishmen, they moved to the forks of the Black River where their ignorance of how to get along in the "new country" amused the local frontiersmen. Father Maxwell built a stone trading post for the newcomers, and there his nephew Hugh learned the rudiments of running a store.[16]

Within a few years, the American takeover of Louisiana generated disputes about the validity of Spanish land grants not unlike those which arose in the Southwest after the Mexican War. Like other claimants, Father Maxwell appeared before a board of commissioners to have his title reviewed; despite pleas that the founding of a large settlement had been made impossible by wars and British prohibitions against emigration from Ireland, the commission ruled that he had failed to fulfill the conditions of the grant and rejected his claim.[17] Legal appeals continued for another sixty years, by which time another Maxwell Land Grant in the Southwest had attracted widespread publicity.

Father Maxwell was a public-spirited man who frequently engaged in politics. In 1805, General James Wilkinson, the American governor of Louisiana Territory whose fame resulted from his association with Aaron Burr's attempts to establish an independent regime in the Southwest, appointed Maxwell as a justice of peace.[18] Later he served as president of the Missouri Territorial Council[19] and helped found the first secondary school in Missouri at Sainte Genevieve.[20] He died in 1814 at age 72, after a fall from his horse.[21]

Meanwhile, nephew Hugh Maxwell had become a prominent resident of the Sainte Genevieve–Kaskaskia community. He was known as "an extensive merchant and planter,"[22] who operated a Kaskaskia store in partnership with William Shannon for several years. Often the two provided supplies, wood, and other goods to the Illinois territorial legislature.[23] After the partnership dissolved in 1817, Maxwell reopened a business of his own in a "new house" offering a "very general assortment of MERCANDIZE [*sic*] lately purchased from Philadelphia and Baltimore . . . upon the most modest terms."[24] During the War of 1812, Maxwell served as aide-de-camp to the commander of the Illinois militia; later he was named auditor of Illinois public accounts and private secretary to territorial governor Ninian Edwards.[25] In 1819, the year after Maxwell's son Lucien was born, one Kaskaskia resident thought enough of Hugh Maxwell to write in his name on the ballot for Illinois's first voting representative to Congress, even though he was not a candidate.[26]

Despite his government service, Hugh apparently never became an American citizen. This situation gave rise to a problem when, after the death of Father Maxwell, Hugh and his brother John took charge of their uncle's estate. Two tracts of land had to be sold at public auction in order to satisfy the priest's debts, and additional property was advertised for sale in the Kaskaskia newspaper.[27] The brothers worried for fear that because federal law prohibited foreigners from inheriting land, they would be unable to secure any claim to the disputed land grant on the Black River. In a petition to Congress, November 18, 1815, they asked to be naturalized retroactively to a date before Father Maxwell's death so that they could "not only inherit the property left thus vacant, but be entitled hereafter to all the privileges of citizens of the United States, it being their country of choice." Washington officials were unwilling to grant their request, but in a private act approved the following year and signed by President James Madison in April, the nephews were granted the right to inherit their uncle's lands "as fully as if they had been citizens" before his death, avoiding the more important question of whether his original title had been valid.[28]

Hugh Maxwell's social and business prominence was further boosted by his marriage to Pierre Menard's eldest daughter, Odile, in 1811. Thereafter his business interests frequently coincided with those of his famous father-in-

Hugh H. Maxwell, Lucien's father.
Courtesy of Victor Grant,
Taos, New Mexico.

Odile Menard Maxwell,
Lucien's mother. Courtesy
of Victor Grant,
Taos, New Mexico.

law. When local businessmen organized a Bank of Kaskaskia in 1819, for example, the commissioners included both Menard and Maxwell, as well as many other prominent citizens. Stock was available for purchase at the Maxwell store.[29]

Hugh Maxwell's family grew quickly. The first child born was Ferdinand, who remained in Kaskaskia for many years, occasionally in Menard's employ, served as clerk of the Randolph County court, and moved to New Mexico in the 1850s to join his younger brother Lucien. Pierre Menard Maxwell, just over a year younger than Ferdinand, emigrated to Texas, where he helped found the city of Galveston. Catherine, born in 1815, and Maria-Thérèse, a year older, died young, the latter only two weeks before Lucien's birth in September, 1818. The precariousness of life on the Illinois frontier was demonstrated by the fact that four of Lucien's younger brothers and sisters died during childhood. Émilie-Alegerie lived to be twelve, Joseph Edward to be thirteen, George less than a year, and the youngest, Jean François, to be twelve. Another sister, Odile-Adeline, died when she was twenty-six, and besides Lucien, Pierre Menard, and Ferdinand, only younger sisters Berenice (born in 1826) and Sophie (born in 1831) lived to old age.[30] It should not be surprising that Lucien, after witnessing the deaths of so many brothers and sisters was excessively protective of his own children.

Except for frequent deaths within the Maxwell family, life in Kaskaskia must have been happy for Lucien. The Maxwell house, erected in 1808, was a plain, one-story frame structure with a French architectural style that resembled many residences in both Kaskaskia and Sainte Genevieve. A broad front porch provided ample space for children to play.[31] The home was close enough to the river that it was subject to flooding during high water, and years later, during a rampage which destroyed all the crops in the bottomland, six feet of water in the Maxwell house forced its inhabitants to seek shelter in the safer Menard mansion.[32] Hugh Maxwell's prosperous store enabled his family to live well, although not in the style of the Menards or other wealthy families. In 1820, for example, the home sheltered a total of thirteen persons, five of whom were servants, probably indentured blacks.[33]

Securing an education was never easy on the frontier, and locating a school in Kaskaskia proved to be typically difficult. Lucien was only five when the Reverend S. Wylie and G. T. Ewing opened an academy to teach Latin, Greek, Hebrew, mathematics, spelling, reading, writing, and geography, besides bookkeeping, the use of globes, and astronomy.[34] Apparently the school closed within a few months, for the next year the local newspaper advertised for a teacher to provide instruction in reading, writing, arithmetic, grammar, and geography. "A large school may be had by a gentleman of good morals, industry, capability, and respectable deportment," the notice added. "No other need apply."[35] The school which Lucien's great-uncle, Father James Maxwell, had organized in Sainte Genevieve apparently failed to survive his death, and it was several years before classes again commenced in the Missouri town.[36] A number of other itinerant schoolmasters tried to open academies in Kaskaskia, and it is likely that young Lucien and his brothers and sisters studied for a short time in one or more of them.

The absence of local schools left most families who wanted their children properly instructed no choice but to send them away to boarding school. The one nearest Kaskaskia was in Perry County, south of Sainte Genevieve, at what became Perryville. It had been established in 1815, when Father Louis DuBourg, administrator of the Diocese of Louisiana, brought thirteen priests from Rome. He had originally planned to go to Saint Louis, but moved the school south when a site known as "the Barrens" was donated by local residents. It was mid-1819 before students first enrolled at the new Saint Mary's of the Barrens Seminary, the first collegiate-level institution in Missouri. Even after the completion of a residence hall, classroom building, and other facilities, the school was poor and spartan. One priest complained that the main building was a "miserable log cabin," that there was little to eat except "ill-baked bread," potatoes, and cabbage, and that ten different varieties of insects attacked him during the night. Nevertheless, an early-day observer reported that "such was the piety and the resignation of the inmates of the seminary . . . that all seemed to feel happy and advanced in the way of salvation."[37]

In addition to training priests, in an adjacent unfinished house Saint Mary's offered secondary training for area children.[38] Many prominent families in southeastern Missouri and southwestern Illinois, including the Menards, sent their boys and girls.[39] It is certain that Lucien Maxwell attended, for in September, 1834, Louis-Cyprien Menard wrote to his father: "We learn by a letter which Lucian [sic] received from his brother that you are all well. . . ."[40] How long he stayed or what he studied are unknown. The curriculum probably resembled what was offered in most Catholic schools of the era. In addition to a thorough indoctrination in Catholic dogma and liturgy, young people learned to read and write in both English and French; to do simple mathematical calculations; and the rudiments of history, geography, and philosophy. It seems unlikely that such a school would have appealed to Lucien, whose propensity for the out-of-doors was probably established at an early age. Years later his penmanship, grammar, and spelling were noticeably poorer than those of his brother or cousins. Yet Lucien's education was, as has often been said, good "for the time," and he was definitely not the illiterate barbarian portrayed by some writers.[41]

Of greater value to Lucien was the kind of schooling that occurred outside classrooms and without teachers. No doubt much of his time was spent at his father's store, located at the corner of Poplar and Elm streets across from William Morrison's two-storied mansion.[42] When Lucien was growing up, Illinois merchants were in the midst of an important commercial transition. The earliest traders, like Pierre Menard and William Morrison, had engaged primarily in the Indian trade, exchanging iron pots, blankets, and trinkets for furs and skins. The first generation of white settlers had been largely self-reliant, producing their own clothing, food, and tools. They bought as little as possible from stores. By the 1820s, however, the Indian trade had largely ended, and merchants began to import cloth, glassware, metal utensils, and other goods from the east and even overseas for sale to increasingly prosperous settlers. Especially in Kaskaskia, where six stores competed for the available business, merchants urged farmers to abandon their home-produced goods in favor of what the tradesmen had for sale.[43]

Hugh Maxwell was a good example of the new breed of storekeeper. In 1824, for example, he advertised "great bargains" in calicoes, ginghams, flannels, muslins, silk shawls, hose, and shoes. His grocery department stocked wines, brandies, tea, coffee, sugar, pepper, spices, shaving soap, snuff, and rifle powder; while the hardware list included knives, hinges, files, knitting needles, curry combs, and candlesticks.[44] Purchasing such a variety of goods from several distant suppliers, arranging their shipment down the Ohio or overland to Kaskaskia, recording purchases and sales, and maintaining a competitive edge against larger, better-financed merchants was no easy task.[45] Lucien and his brothers doubtless learned many trading secrets from their father, and not surprisingly, years later, Lucien gained renown as a shrewd and successful businessman in his own right.

Other businessmen looked farther west for new sources of income. Among the first to take advantage of new opportunities was Lucien's grandfather Menard. As early as 1807, he, William Morrison, and Manuel Lisa organized a trapping and trading expedition up the Missouri River. The profits they made the first year persuaded them to join with Saint Louis entrepreneurs including distant relatives of Menard, Pierre and Auguste Chouteau, to organize the Missouri Fur Company. Menard himself led one expedition to Fort Mandan and maintained an active interest in the company until its dissolution in 1814.[46] His interest in the West persisted, and the Chouteaus and others engaged in frontier trade frequently visited Kaskaskia to report on their activities. The stories of their adventures and of the money which could be made in the distant West would have thrilled any boy. There can be little doubt that such conversations sparked young Lucien's interest in the frontier.

Even the far-away settlement of Santa Fe interested the Kaskaskia merchants. In 1804, William Morrison supplied trade goods for a French Creole named Baptiste La Lande to take to New Mexico. La Lande completed the journey and sold his wares, but he liked the Southwest so much that he never returned or repaid Morrison.[47] Years later, when the Santa Fe Trail had developed into a major commercial artery, the *Kaskaskia Republican* urged Illinois businessmen to take advantage of its opportunities as had the Missourians. "Are the young men of Illinois less enterprising than those of Missouri or other states?" asked the editor in 1825. "Let them embrace this opportunity not only by pushing their fortunes but of gratifying that spirit of adventure which is the distinguishing trait in the character of the citizens of the West." Here, he concluded, was a chance for "immense gain, with but little risk; here may be realized the fabled treasures of El Dorado."[48] Such a challenge fell on responsive ears, for besides Lucien Maxwell other Kaskaskians such as Céran St. Vrain, Nathaniel Pope, and Ferdinand Maxwell took their places among those who settled the Southwest.

Kaskaskia also provided young Lucien with opportunities to encounter Indians in a region where the frontier was rapidly giving way to civilization. Only sixty Kaskaskia Indians remained on a 350-acre reservation in a valley near the town.[49] The remnants of a once-powerful tribe, they had become curiosities, as visitors traipsed through their encampment, gawking at the old women cooking or sewing and peering into bark huts.[50] Other tribes, wishing to trade furs with town merchants, also visited Kaskaskia, often camping on the outskirts and wandering the streets of the village. The Menard family—like Lucien Maxwell years later—adopted an Indian girl, named Maria, who was treated as a member of the family and frequently played with the children and grandchildren.[51]

Pierre Menard's experience as a fur trader earned him a reputation as an expert regarding Indians. In 1818 he was appointed a federal Indian sub-agent for southern Illinois, with responsibility for distributing the annuity payments due the tribes in that area and for maintaining peace between them and their white neighbors. Menard saw himself as an advocate for the Indians and protested vigorously when their annuities failed to arrive. The meager amounts due the Kaskaskias proved so inadequate that he supported the tribe with his own funds, just as his grandson did years later.[52] Frequently Menard entertained bands of visiting Indians in his mansion. In 1820, for example, he submitted receipts for ferrying thirteen Delawares across the Mississippi, feeding them and their horses, and providing a coffin for one chief who was killed.[53] Several years later the chief of the Cherokees of the Arkansas died in the Menard home on his way to a Washington meeting.[54]

In 1828, when Lucien was ten, President John Quincy Adams appointed his grandfather to organize an Indian conference at Prairie du Chien, Wisconsin. It was during the trip to this conference that Menard honored the famed Sac chief Keokuk by naming a new settlement in southern Iowa in his honor. Menard's ability to mediate Indian-white disputes was so respected that during an Indian uprising in Shelby County, Illinois, in 1831, Governor John Reynolds summoned him to prevent bloodshed.[55] The knowledge of such experiences proved extremely valuable to Lucien, who drew on them in later years as he faced many of the same problems with Indians on his New Mexican ranch. In large measure, his policies coincided with those of his grandfather, and many of his ideas about Indians no doubt grew out of his boyhood experiences in Kaskaskia.

Despite the practical education Lucien received in Kaskaskia, it must have been as clear to him as to others that this was no place for an ambitious young man to build an empire. No sooner had Illinois achieved statehood than the capitol moved to the better-located town of Vandalia, depriving Kaskaskia of the income provided by visiting legislators, state jobs, and lucrative contracts. Other state and federal offices also left, as well as many industrious and successful residents. New towns took away business once monopolized by Kaskaskia merchants. The growth of Saint Louis, which was rapidly becoming the major trading center in the Mississippi Valley, was especially damaging, as was the development of Cairo on the Ohio River. Already in 1819 a visitor noted that despite its having been the capital, Kaskaskia was "not very important." "The dullness of the times," reported the *Kaskaskia Republican* in 1825, had become the "common theme of conversation."[56]

In part, location was responsible for Kaskaskia's decline. The bottomlands on which most of the town was located were subject to frequent flooding, either when the Kaskaskia River overflowed its banks or when high water on the Mississippi blocked the Kaskaskia from entering its channel, causing a backup of water from the smaller river. Floods not only destroyed property and crops, but also frequently left the area so damp that mosquitoes bred by the millions, and disease spread easily. Town leaders, obviously worried about stories that Kaskaskia was an unhealthful place in which to live, argued that people elsewhere were just as subject to "the prevalent diseases of the country," and even stated that it was the "healthiest town in the state, and in fact as healthy as any town west of the Ohio River."[57]

The inaccuracy of such statements was clearly evident to the Maxwell family. In 1833, cholera once again ravaged the town, striking down a number of Kaskaskia residents, one of whom was Lucien Maxwell's father, Hugh, who died of the disease September 4, 1833.[58] The death of his father must have been traumatic for Lucien. His mother, according to later, perhaps exaggerated, reports, was left in "straitened circumstances with a large family to rear." Her eldest son, Ferdinand, took over the family store and gave her some assistance. The Menards provided money when it was needed and helped out with legal affairs, though there is no evidence that the Maxwells moved in with the Menards.[59] Lucien continued at Saint Mary's, at least for a time, but he no doubt regretted being a burden to his mother, and perhaps he often climbed the hill behind his grandfather's house, stared across the Kaskaskia and beyond the Mississippi, and dreamed of the day when he could heed the call to go west.

2

Apprenticeship in the West

WHATEVER Kaskaskia lacked in excitement or prosperity could be found in abundance in Saint Louis, then burgeoning into one of the most important cities in the West. By the early 1840s, hundreds of steamboats and other vessels tied up at the docks which stretched for more than a mile along the Mississippi to unload manufactured goods from Cincinnati, Pittsburgh, or New Orleans. Stevadores, many of them black, loaded the agricultural products from rich farms in Missouri, Illinois, or neighboring states on board outbound ships headed for the East Coast or Europe. Behind the dozens of limestone warehouses facing the river rose the city's flourishing business district: "a dense mass of buildings," one visitor portrayed it, "seemingly mingling with the horizon in the distance, with here and there a church tower, a belfry, or a steeple looming to the skies . . . ."[1]

Above all, Saint Louis became the gateway to the West. From here travelers departed up the Missouri River, across the plains to Oregon, along the Santa Fe Trail to Mexico, and into the fur-laden Rocky Mountains and beyond. Everyone stopped to buy supplies and bid farewell to civilization. Many stores catered to the western trade. Nine hotels served visitors, and a fine new one, the Planters, was under construction in the early 1840s. "It requires no gift of prophecy," concluded a foreign visitor who exaggerated only slightly, to predict that Saint Louis "will ultimately become the largest city in the western world."[2]

The bustle of commercial activity which usually characterized Saint Louis was accelerated during May, 1842, because of the presence in the city of a young lieutenant in the United States Corps of Topographical Engineers, John C. Frémont. Born in Savannah, Georgia, twenty-nine years before, pursued throughout his life by the stain of illigitimacy, Frémont nonetheless possessed native abilities that had brought him to the attention of South Carolina politician Joel R. Poinsett, who had secured for him a teaching position aboard a Navy sloop. By 1835 he was teaching mathematics at West Point, and three years later the distinguished French scientist Joseph Nicollet hired Frémont to assist in exploring the upper Missouri and Mississippi rivers.[3] The two got along famously. Frémont learned to keep careful scientific records, collect botanical and geological specimens, prepare accurate maps based on astronomical observations, and write factual but readable reports.[4] By 1842 he had become, in the words of his best-known biographer, "the first distinctively scientific explorer produced by the United States."[5]

Frémont's prestige had been further enhanced by his marriage in October, 1841, to Jessie Benton, the beautiful young daughter of Missouri's powerful Senator Thomas Hart Benton, a leading proponent of United States expansion toward the Pacific.[6] Together, Benton and Frémont had planned a comprehensive government expedition to map the trail to Oregon as far west as the continental divide. Not only would such a project mark a route that overland emigrants could follow west, but also it would demonstrate the government's support of frontier settlement. Not surprisingly, Frémont was named to head the expedition, and in May, 1842, he arrived in Saint Louis to prepare for departure.[7]

Frémont had worked with the Chouteaus before, and he relied on their firm to provide most of the food, supplies, and livestock he needed. Scientific instruments shipped by boat from New York had to be unpacked, assembled, and checked. A Saint Louis pharmacist provided quick-

By 1842 Saint Louis had become a thriving center of western commerce

silver and nitric acid for experiments, laudanum, arrow-root, purgative pills, and emetics for the first aid kit.[8] Frémont delegated minor responsibilities to others in order to reserve his time for interviewing the "valuable and experienced men" needed to accompany him. Charles Preuss, a German, had signed on in Washington as topographer and artist. Randolph Brant, with whose parents Frémont lodged in Saint Louis, worked as a general aide. Most others were Frenchmen, voyageurs with names like Tessier, Clément, Benoist, and Badeau, experienced as trappers and traders in the West. Auguste Janisse was black. Most received a dollar a day for their services. Clément Lambert, the camp conductor, received $1.85¾ a day. The young man hired as chief hunter, paid $1.66½ a day, was Lucien B. Maxwell, formerly of Kaskaskia.[9]

What Lucien had been doing since the death of his father eight years before, is largely conjectural. He had matured and gained considerable physical strength, for

22

and industry. Courtesy Missouri Historical Society.

Frémont estimated that he was four years older than he actually was, describing him as "about five feet ten inches in
height, and strongly built." He had traded with the western Indians, to whom he was "personally known," according to Frémont, was "accustomed to life on the prairies,"
and had become a "resolute man and good hunter."[10] Little
more can be known with certainty. Maxwell shared none
of Frémont's preoccupation with writing and seldom reported his activities to his own family; only a handful of
letters in his hand exist for the entire span of his lifetime.

A plausible but largely undocumented scenario has
Lucien departing Kaskaskia about 1835 or 1836, when he
was seventeen or eighteen, soon after leaving school at
Saint Mary's. He must have traveled to Saint Louis, where
he no doubt knew, or carried letters of reference to, his
grandfather's business acquaintances or his step-grand-
mother's relatives, the Chouteaus. In all likelihood their
connections in the West helped him locate employment

John C. Frémont, whom Maxwell accompanied on several western expeditions. Courtesy of the Library of Congress.

with trappers or traders, more likely the latter, perhaps with the American Fur Company.[11] As a young man, new to the frontier, Lucien must have served what amounted to an apprenticeship, accompanying older, veteran traders on expeditions up the Missouri or the Platte, into the Rockies, perhaps even to the distant towns of northern Mexico.[12]

He learned to accept and even relish the hardships of western life. Hot, scorching days, sudden midnight thunderstorms, piercing cold wind, and heavy blizzards often brought physical discomfort, and not a few of those who ventured into the plains died of thirst or froze to death during a storm. Even when food and water were available, the usual fare, according to Maxwell's friend Kit Carson, consisted entirely of what could be obtained with a rifle. Only rarely were such "luxuries" as bread, coffee, or sugar available.[13] At times Lucien, like other mountaineers, went to bed hungry or had to make do with a few dried beans, a hard piece of jerky, or a cactus fruit. He may have had to drink blood or slurp the fluids from a buffalo stomach to keep alive.[14] Superior muscle power was imperative under such conditions, and by the time Lucien reached his majority, his physique was compared to that of a Greek wrestler. Another writer characterized him as a "dark and stocky young man, of withdrawn and almost sullen disposition."[15] Early exposure to Indian life at Kaskaskia must have served him well, too, for he learned to trade with the great mounted tribes of the plains, especially the Arapahos. His knowledge of English, French, and probably Spanish was supplemented by a newfound ability to communicate with a number of different Indian tribes.[16]

Not for long could Lucien have lived in the West without learning how competitive the fur trade had become on the high plains. The senior firm operating along the edge of the Rockies was the American Fur Company, founded by New York millionaire John Jacob Astor and controlled after 1834 by Saint Louis businessmen led by Pierre Chouteau, Jr. Each year the company sent out expe-

Jean Pierre Chouteau, the Missouri fur trader who probably introduced Maxwell to the fur trade in the West. Courtesy Missouri Historical Society.

ditions carrying goods to be exchanged for the furs collected by the Indians. Andrew Drips, who was recommended to Frémont as the best guide on the frontier, headed these parties after 1836, and Lucien Maxwell may well have accompanied him one or more times. In addition, the company supported trapping expeditions commanded by legendary mountain men such as William Sublette and Jim Bridger—whom Maxwell must have known—and established trading posts at strategic locations in the Indian country, the largest being Fort John, on the Laramie.[17]

Challenging the supremacy of the Chouteaus was the newer firm of Bent, St. Vrain, and Company. Charles and William Bent were Missourians who had gone to New Mexico as traders in 1829. Céran St. Vrain, the son of a Saint Louis brewer whose sister had married a Menard, had gone west even earlier. The firm was organized in 1830 to trade furs with independent American, French Canadian, and Mexican trappers, or with the Indians of the Southwest.[18] Their headquarters in New Mexico was at the northern town of Taos until late 1832 or early 1833, when they began construction of a massive adobe trading post, Bent's Fort, alongside the Santa Fe Trail on the north (United States) bank of the Arkansas River.

Bent's Fort soon dominated the fur trade in the Southwest. Fourteen-foot-high walls nearly three feet thick created an almost impregnable fortress. Round towers on two corners provided a vantage point from which attacking Indians or arriving wagon trains could be identified. The walls formed a huge trapezoid, 137 by 178 feet, inside of which were living quarters, storerooms, and workshops for nearly a hundred employees. Usually supervised by William Bent, the fort became the hub of the company's high plains trading activities. Employees fanned out in all directions to obtain pelts, traveling far into the Rockies, north to Wyoming and beyond, and northeast as far as Nebraska and the Dakotas. Each year hundreds of bundles of buffalo robes and beaver pelts were shipped to Saint Louis.[19]

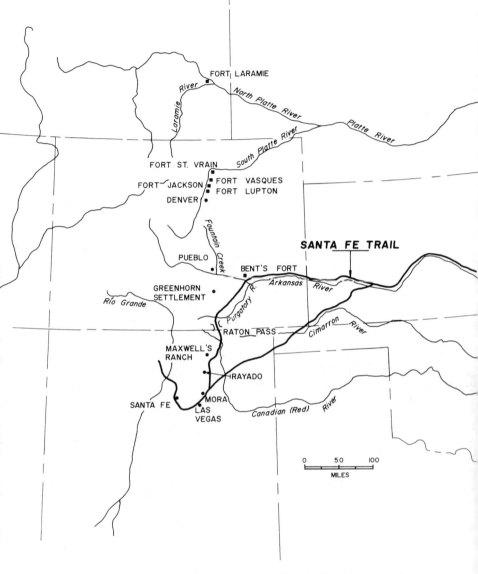

The Rocky Mountain West in the 1840s.
Map drawn by Kevin E. Coveart
© *1983 by the University of Oklahoma Press*

As word spread of Bent, St. Vrain and Company's aggressive expansion, Pierre Chouteau's American Fur Company feared the loss of their own dominance of the northern trade. For a time the two companies competed directly, seeking to outmaneuver one another to win the friendship of the Indians and sending expeditions into each other's country. To counter the construction of Bent's Fort, Chouteau encouraged Bill Sublette and Robert Campbell to erect a log trading post, Fort Laramie, near the intersection of the Laramie and North Platte rivers in southeastern Wyoming. The Bents responded by establishing Fort St. Vrain on the South Platte. In 1838, however, the two giants of the western fur trade negotiated an agreement which partitioned the trade between them. The Bents and St. Vrain monopolized activities south of the North Platte, leaving the American Fur Company everything north of the river. Thereafter the Chouteaus, Bents, and St. Vrain became close friends, and they often conducted business with each other.[20]

Whatever Lucien Maxwell's direct role in this struggle may have been before, in 1839 he, a relative of the Chouteaus, began working for Bent, St. Vrain and Company. For years afterward he remained a good friend of the company and its proprietors. He may have been stationed at the main fort for a time, supervising livestock, overseeing the Mexican laborers, and having "general charge" of the place.[21] He also spent time at Fort St. Vrain on the South Platte. A log enclosure 100 by 125 feet, with walls 14 feet high, it was designed to help the company compete against numerous small traders, many with their own private forts, operating in the area.[22] The man in charge of the post was Marcellin St. Vrain, the younger brother of Céran St. Vrain. He had a reputation as a ladies' man and a sportsman, who enjoyed hunting, riding, and horse racing more than managing his brother's business. He was especially famous for standing on his head and waving his legs to attract antelopes. In 1840, probably while Maxwell was stationed there, Marcellin married thir-

Céran St. Vrain, the Missouri native who, with Charles and William Bent, operated the largest fur trading company in the Southwest. Collection of the author.

teen-year-old Royal, or Rel, a Sioux girl reported to have been a sister of Chief Red Cloud.[23]

Another person with whom Maxwell no doubt worked at Fort St. Vrain was Jim Beckwourth, the tall, mulatto mountain man whose violent temper and preference for the company of Indians rather than whites were notorious. Beckwourth had worked for the American Fur Company for a time and in the summer of 1840 transferred to Bent, St. Vrain and Company, who assigned him to trade out of Fort St. Vrain. Few details of Beckwourth's relationship with Maxwell are known. On one occasion, however, Indians attacked the post because Beckwourth refused to sell them whiskey on credit. According to his story, which may be apocryphal, Lucien repelled the Indians and saved the day.[24]

One independent trader who refused to honor the Bent monopoly was Lancaster Lupton, a former army lieutenant who had built his own fort on the South Platte. Competition for Indian favors could be keen, even cutthroat, and few mountaineers were above using alcohol to win the allegiance of a powerful tribe or marriage to a chief's daughter to assure preferred treatment. Maxwell undoubtedly participated in the trade war between Lupton and Bent, St. Vrain which continued until 1840 or 1841, when Lupton succumbed and came to an agreement with the larger, better-financed company.[25] According to one probably spurious account, the Bents, Lupton, Maxwell, and Taos merchant Charles Beaubien established a settlement on Adobe Creek, near present Pueblo, Colorado. Presumably Lupton agreed to move off the South Platte in exchange for help in building a new post elsewhere.[26]

Sooner or later every fur man got to Taos, the northern New Mexico town where the fur trade in the Southwest had its headquarters. Taos has a unique ambience which has appealed to visitors and residents for hundreds of years. Taos Pueblo was old when the first Spanish explorers arrived, and settlement on the site of the present

Marcellin St. Vrain, the colorful trader and trapper with whom Maxwell worked. Courtesy Colorado Historical Society.

town of Taos began in the seventeenth century. It continues to draw artists, retirees, and tourists to the present day. Part of its attraction to nineteenth-century frontiersmen was its location: set at the foot of Taos Mountain, it looked westward across the flat, barren plains toward the Río Grande gorge. Expeditions into the Salt River country of Arizona or even to California found it a convenient departure point. Northward in the Colorado Rockies were many of the richest beaver streams in the West, and it was an easy trek up Taos Canyon and across the mesas of the Sangre de Cristos to the Santa Fe Trail. Taos was far enough from the capital of New Mexico at Santa Fe that Mexican officials seldom imposed too many restrictions or collected taxes too regularly from its residents. As a result it became a haven for foreigners, especially French Canadians and Americans, and the "commercial capital of the trappers' and traders' world in the West."[27]

Taos also offered attractive amenities to men weary of hardship and deprivation. As George Ruxton, a chronicler of life in the mountains, observed, Taos abounded in "civilized relaxation coveted by mountaineers." There were clean beds, good food, and pleasant companionship. Many a trapper or trader found a wife in Taos, and most grew fond of the potent "Taos Lightning" whiskey. Taos residents became accustomed, Ruxton recalled, to "dashing white hunters" swaggering through town "in all the pride of fringe and leather."[28]

When Lucien Maxwell first went to Taos is uncertain, but he was there the winter of 1841–42, and it was his principal residence in several subsequent seasons. People he met there influenced the rest of his life. The most important of his new acquaintances was Charles Beaubien, who, with the Bents and St. Vrain, led the town's powerful foreign community. A French Canadian born not far from the original home of the Menards, Beaubien had emigrated to New Mexico in the 1820s, settled in Taos, married the daughter of a prominent local family, and taken out Mexican citizenship. He may have trapped or

Taos, the northern New Mexico town where Maxwell frequently spent the winter, became friends with Kit Carson, and found his wife. From W. W. H. Davis, El Gringo: or, New Mexico and Her People.

traded for a few years, but by the 1840s he had settled down to become one of the most important Taos merchants. He also dabbled in local politics and was in the process of accumulating large landholdings.[29]

In January, 1841, the year before Lucien is known to have arrived in Taos, Beaubien and Santa Fean Guadalupe Miranda had petitioned New Mexico's Governor Manuel Armijo for a grant of land east of Taos along the Santa Fe Trail. The two contended that, in spite of abundant water, plentiful timber, fertile soil, and rich mineral deposits, New Mexico was one of the least-developed areas of the Mexican Republic. What was needed, they argued, were enterprising individuals who could utilize the unproductive labor in the province to develop idle land. "This is the age of progress and the march of intellect," the two continued, "and they are so rapid that we may expect at a day not far distant, they will reach even us." The boundaries of the tract they requested were so vaguely stated that it would be generations before anyone knew for certain what land was to be included. The ranch would stretch along the front range of the Sangre de Cristos, astride the Santa Fe Trail, commencing at the junction of the Rayado and Colorado (Canadian) rivers; proceed north to the Uña de Gato Creek; continue east to the summit of the mountains (which mountains was unclear); and return south to the first corner.[30] In part because he wanted to encourage the development of frontier areas as a buffer against United States encroachment, and also to reward Miranda, Armijo scrawled his approval on the margin of the petition only three days after it was submitted. With that signature, Beaubien and Miranda received authorization to "make the proper use" of their grant "which the law allows."[31]

Lucien Maxwell certainly discussed the land grant with Beaubien and perhaps described the trouble his great-uncle, Father James Maxwell, had had in obtaining, and receiving American confirmation of, his Spanish land grant in Missouri. Beaubien also had a good deal in common with Lucien's grandfather Menard, with whom he had done business and whom he may even have visited in Kaskaskia. Perhaps the two men previously had met there.[32] The two also discussed the difficulties of securing a good education for a boy born and reared in New Mexico. About 1841, probably on Maxwell's recommendation, Beaubien sent his eldest son to Saint Mary's, which by then had moved its preparatory department to Cape Girardeau.[33] Maxwell's French surely came in handy during these conversations, and the manners taught by his mother and the fathers at school must have helped make a favorable impression. The social graces were not unimportant, for there was more than polite conversation behind Lucien's visits to the Beaubien home. There he met and fell in love with the family's eldest daughter, Luz, who became Mrs. Lucien Maxwell in Taos, May 27, 1842.[34]

Charles Beaubien, Lucien's father-in-law, the co-owner of one of the largest land grants in New Mexico. Collection of the author.

There was another man in Taos that winter who played an important role in Lucien's later life and in large measure propelled his name into the national limelight. Christopher Carson, nine years Maxwell's senior, was born in Kentucky. His father moved to Missouri when Kit, as he was already known, was very young. After a year of unhappy apprenticeship, Carson ran off with a Santa Fe caravan to New Mexico. He ended up in Taos, where he trapped, first with a family friend named Kincaid, later with such famous mountaineers as Ewing Young, Tom "Broken Hand" Fitzpatrick, Jim Bridger, and Milton Sublette. He sought furs throughout the Rockies, traveled as far west as California, and treated with Indians in the plains and mountains.[35] Later, given national publicity by Frémont, Kit Carson became one of the most famous men on the American frontier. But in the early 1840s he was just another independent fur man, "just a free trapper," as his latest biographer explains, "who managed to scrape up a living for himself and his squaw and two children."[36] Carson had a winning personality, however, that won him a great many admirers, not the least of whom was Lucien Maxwell, who became his boon companion, closest friend, and frequent business partner.

Exactly how and when the two met is, like so many aspects of Maxwell's early life, uncertain. Carson took a job as a hunter for Bent, St. Vrain, and Company out of Bent's Fort for a dollar a day in the fall of 1841. Maxwell later claimed experience as a hunter and received a recommendation from Carson, suggesting that the two may have worked together. Carson also spent at least part of the winter of 1841–42 in Taos, where he was baptized into the Catholic church January 28, 1842. Surely the two saw a great deal of one another in the small foreign community, and they may even have shared accommodations.[37]

Carson and Maxwell traveled together to Saint Louis during the spring of 1842. Kit had not returned home since his departure years earlier, but now he had a four-year-old daughter, Adeline, whose Indian mother had died, probably the preceding winter. He planned to take the girl to Missouri to be raised by relatives. Lucien, too, was eager to visit Kaskaskia, since he had presumably been away for several years. Perhaps he hoped to see his grandfather, who was in failing health. Late in March or early in April, 1842, only days after Lucien's marriage, the two men left Taos with Charles Bent, traveled up Taos Canyon, crossed the mesa tops to the Santa Fe Trail, and continued through Raton Pass to Bent's Fort. There they joined a large Bent, St. Vrain and Company caravan transporting the year's catch of beaver pelts and buffalo robes east. By May 19, the *St. Louis Republican* reported their arrival in Missouri.[38]

According to family tradition, Lucien hurried to Kaskaskia where he recounted his adventures in the West to his relatives, reported on his recent matrimony, and announced that he would remain permanently in the Southwest, making Taos his home.[39] The luxury of a few days at his old home must have been inviting, but there was scant time either to enjoy his mother's cooking or discuss Amer-

Kit Carson was a young, little-known, free trapper when Lucien Maxwell first met him. Collection of the author.

ica's westward expansion with his grandfather Menard. By early June, Lucien had to be back in Saint Louis, where he joined Frémont's exploring party.

Both Kit Carson and Lucien Maxwell accompanied John C. Frémont on his first major expedition into the Trans-Mississippi West. Frémont later reported that he had signed a number of voyageurs in Saint Louis. No one was chosen as guide, and Frémont was on board a steamboat headed for Cyprian Chouteau's trading post at the confluence of the Kansas and Missouri rivers when he met Carson. "I was pleased with him and his manner and address at the first meeting," Frémont reported, describing Carson as "of medium height, broad shouldered, and deep-chested, with a clear steady blue eye and frank speech and address; quiet and unassuming." Frémont recalled that he was so impressed with Carson that he immediately offered him the position as guide at a salary of three dollars a day, three times what he had received the previous year from Bent, St. Vrain.[40] Carson's version of the incident differs. "I spoke to Colonel Fremont," Kit reported in his autobiography dictated many years later, "informed him that I had been some time in the mountains and thought I could guide him to any point he would wish to go." Frémont responded that he would "make inquiries" regarding Carson's credentials; only after that had been done, presumably aboard the steamboat, was the job offered.[41] Whether Carson was hired and then recommended his friend Maxwell or Maxwell recommended Carson to Frémont is impossible to discern. But there is no doubt that the two men worked together, that their friendship grew stronger during the expedition, and that both established their reputations as a result of the favorable comments about them included in Frémont's widely circulated report of the expedition.[42]

During several days at Chouteau's trading post, Frémont and his men put everything in order, checked and rechecked the supplies, and worked out a system of duties and responsibilities. Their departure was postponed until the sky cleared sufficiently for Frémont to take his initial astronomical observations. The expedition finally left on June 10. Ahead, according to Frémont, was "an ocean of prairie, which . . . stretched without interruption almost to the base of the Rocky Mountains."[43]

The trip started off badly. No sooner had the men established their routine than a heavy midnight storm drenched them. "We were all soaked," reported Frémont, "and glad when morning came." The storm turned the Kansas River into a raging torrent two hundred yards wide, making it extremely difficult to get the expedition across. The livestock had to be driven in and forced to swim to the opposite bank. The mules and horses herded easily, but the oxen kept returning to the near side. It was the next morning before the last animal was safely across. Frémont had brought an India rubber boat into which the dismantled carts and the luggage were loaded. Basil Lajeunesse, the strongest swimmer in the group, swam ahead with a rope between his teeth so that he could tug the boat from the west side. When the vessel capsized, sending everything into the water, everyone jumped to the rescue. Both Carson and Maxwell were "much in the water," proving their value, but both became ill as a result. Maxwell, the younger and more resilient of the two, quickly recovered, but Kit's continued indisposition forced the expedition to remain the next day in camp.[44]

Although Maxwell had been hired as hunter and Carson as guide, the two worked as a team in providing food for the expedition. June 20, for example, as the explorers moved across Kansas, Carson brought in a "fine deer" for supper. Several days later, they entered the buffalo country, spotting at first a few scattered animals. Soon vast herds were "swarming in immense numbers over the plains." "In sight of such a mass of life," Frémont recalled, "the traveller feels a strange emotion of grandeur. We had heard from a distance a dull and confused murmuring, and, when we came in view of their dark masses, there was not one among us who did not feel his heart beat quicker." Maxwell and Carson rode off together in pursuit. Kit had already shot one cow and was chasing a second when his horse stumbled and fell. He was "considerably hurt" but suffered no broken bones. Maxwell chased Kit's horse, which sprang up after the fall and ran on with the buffalo. He was willing to shoot the mount if necessary to save the Spanish silver bridle it wore, but fine riding skills and a fleet horse enabled him to catch the animal, winning him Carson's thanks, much credit among the men, and a favorable paragraph in Frémont's book about the expedition.[45]

The next day, no doubt recalling their previous success, Frémont asked Carson and Maxwell to accompany him on a buffalo hunt. The trio approached to within three hundred yards of the herd before they were discovered, whereupon the buffalo thundered off. "We started together at a hard gallop, riding steadily abreast of each other," wrote Frémont, "and here the interest of the chase became so engrossingly intense that we were sensible to nothing else." Every few seconds one of the bulls bringing up the rear turned around to look at his pursuers, then dashed on after the herd. At thirty yards the three men shouted loudly and broke into the herd. Frémont, his horse's "eyes flashing and foam flying from his mouth," went after a cow "like a tiger," rode alongside, rose up in his stirrups, and fired a single fatal bullet into the heart. Carson got his cow and quickly tied his horse to its horns as he prepared to begin butchering. "Among the scattered bands," reported Frémont, "at some distance below, I caught a glimpse of Maxwell; and while I was looking, a little wreath of white smoke curled away from his gun, from which I was too far to hear the report." Frémont renewed the chase, riding into the dust raised by the buffalo, before he ended the hunt and returned with Carson and Maxwell to the caravan several miles away.[46]

The excitement of a buffalo chase soon gave way to the more serious work for which the expedition was responsible. Frémont's announced objective was to follow

During a buffalo hunt early in the Frémont expedition, Maxwell and Carson proved their skill and demonstrated their daring. This illustration from Frémont's Memoirs of My Life probably was drawn from a description of the hunt by Frémont.

the North Platte as far west as the continental divide. He also hoped to reconnoiter along the South Platte to make astronomical observations and map its tributaries as far south as Fort Saint Vrain. Moreover, he was to recommend locations for military installations. On July 4, in order to accomplish these tasks more efficiently, he split the expedition in two. The majority of the group, headed by Lambert and including Carson, continued along the North Platte, caching as many supplies as possible, and waited at the American Fur Company's Fort Laramie. A smaller party, headed by Frémont and including Preuss, Maxwell, Basil Lajeunesse, two other voyageurs, and several Cheyenne Indians, proceeded along the South Platte. Only one extra horse and a mule were available to carry provisions, so the party traveled light. The cook provided them with flour, coffee, and sugar; the men's rifles were to procure the rest of their food supply. Each man was limited to his saddle, a saddle blanket, one change of clothing, and one blanket. To ward off possible attack, everyone carried rifles or double-barreled shotguns. Maxwell and Frémont had "excellent pistols."

Obtaining food turned out to be troublesome. Antelope were plentiful but so shy and difficult to approach that hunting them was tedious and time-consuming. Large gray rabbits populated the plains in great numbers, but Frémont deemed them "hardly worth the delay of stopping to shoot." Late one afternoon the expedition sighted a couple of old buffalo bulls so engaged in fighting that they seemed oblivious to the approach of humans. The one the party killed for dinner was so tough that Preuss found it inedible and made do with a piece of bread; besides, he complained, the cook had forgotten to send salt or pepper. The hardships of the expedition proved too much for Preuss, who returned to the main party after a couple of days, leaving Maxwell, Frémont, and the others to continue without his complaints.[47]

Two days after Preuss departed, Frémont and his men came to a place along the trail where the tracks of Indian horses entirely covered the ground. Buffalo, previously numerous, disappeared. Everyone watched carefully for signs of the horsemen they knew were near, but none could be seen; the "dark-looking objects" among the hills on the left were presumed to be buffalo coming toward the Platte for water. Suddenly Maxwell turned to see the Cheyennes accompanying the party "whipping up furiously." Another glance at the dark objects showed them to be Indians "coming up at speed."

There was no time for quiet consultation or deliberate decision-making. It was impossible to rejoin the main expedition, so Frémont hurried his men toward a clump of timber several miles distant. Tired horses and heavy scientific instruments slowed the pace to a canter, and the Indians quickly caught up. "Group after group darted into view at the top of the hills, until all the little eminences seemed in motion, and, in a few minutes from the time they were first discovered, two or three hundred naked to the breech cloth, were speeding across the prairie." When Frémont realized that the trees toward which he was headed were across a river, doom seemed inevitable. "Men in such circumstances generally act from instinct," Frémont recalled later in a more philosophical tone, "and a charge from three hundred naked savages is a circumstance not well calculated to promote a cool exercise of judgement."

Maxwell came to the rescue. Just as he was about to fire on the lead Indian, Lucien recognized him as someone with whom he had traded. "You're a fool, God damn you, don't you know me?" Lucien screamed in the language of the Indians. Hearing his own language from a white man, the warrior swerved his horse and passed the Americans "like an arrow." The tenor of the encounter reversed instantly, as the horseman turned about, offered his hand to Frémont, struck his chest, and identified himself as "Arapaho!" The near-battle became a reunion — the pursuers turned out to be from a village where Maxwell had lived as a trader a year or two before. "We were soon in the midst of the band," wrote Frémont, "answering

44

as well as we could a multitude of questions." The women arrived, riding side-saddle, naked to the waist, to help cut up the buffalo that had been killed. That evening the expedition visited a village of 125 Cheyenne and Arapaho lodges "disposed in a scattering manner on both sides of a broad irregular street" along the Platte. Frémont was surprised at how "scrupulously clean" everything was; it reminded him of scenes of feudal chivalry. One of the chiefs invited the lieutenant to a buffalo feast during which a peace pipe was passed. Another gave Maxwell a bundle of dried meat, which the Americans took with them when they left at dusk.[48]

Two days later the men reached Fort St. Vrain. Since Maxwell had spent several years between there and Taos, he knew everyone and was "at home, and among his friends." Marcellin St. Vrain, the post commander, sold Frémont two horses and three badly needed mules. Unfortunately, the fort's supplies had not yet arrived from Taos, so only a few pounds of coffee could be spared.[49]

The route from the South to the North fork of the Platte became more and more desolate. There was no wood, so the cooks built evening fires with buffalo chips. Cactus plants blanketed one wide plain they crossed; most streambeds were dry. "We had suffered much to-day, both men and horses, for want of water," Frémont chronicled after a particularly bad day, adding that a diet of dried meat heightened the men's thirst. They camped beside a stream that night, but the next day brought them to the most "barren and arid country" Frémont had ever seen. The flatlands looked as if they "had been swept by fires," and the stunted pines on the hills wore "the same ashen hue of desolation." In mid-July the expedition finally reached their destination on the North Platte, the American Fur Company's Fort Laramie, an imposing structure with high whitewashed, picketed walls and large corner towers. Sioux Indians had pitched their lodges beneath the walls. Not far away Frémont found the rest of his expedition awaiting him.[50]

After nearly a week's rest, during which Frémont tried

to demonstrate to the Indians how powerful his government was, the explorers pointed west. Frémont had been
warned that a band of young Indians angered by an attack
on their people planned to assault his train. Undaunted
by advice not to go on, he took the precaution of leaving
the two youngest members of the party behind with the
heaviest baggage and abandoned his heavy tents in favor
of a huge Sioux tipi. A couple of days out, the scouts
reported Indians approaching. Frémont lined up the wagons to form a barricade, ordered the horses hobbled, and
had his men fire warning shots into the air. An Indian
who accompanied the party persuaded the approaching
horsemen not to attack and escorted two braves into camp.
Some Americans, believing that the natives had recently
besieged and killed several settlers, favored executing
them on the spot. Frémont said no, however, and the
Indians soon headed off toward Fort Laramie.[51]

As game became scarcer, the importance of Maxwell
and the other hunters increased. Whenever a herd of buffalo was spotted, Frémont halted the expedition and ordered a chase. One day the marksmen brought back three
fat cows. "We live in luxury and have our swill," rejoiced
the usually grumpy Preuss. Next day, with five or six
more cows having been slaughtered, the cooks erected
low wooden scaffolds on which the thinly sliced strips of
meat dried above a slow fire. "Our people have recovered
their gayety" [sic] wrote Frémont, "and the busy figures
around the blazing fires give a picturesque air to the
camp."[52]

Such optimism proved short-lived. Frémont soon met
some Indians who told him that because of an unusually
severe drought and a plague of grasshoppers, the country
ahead was barren of grass and game. The natives had survived only by abandoning their lodges and eating their
horses. Joseph Bissonette, an experienced frontiersman,
recommended turning back. Not Frémont. Assembling his
men, he explained the perilous situation and expressed his
own "fixed determination" to continue. Everyone agreed

to go, with Basil Lajeunesse stoically proclaiming: "We'll eat the mules." To accelerate progress, the carts were emptied and hidden in the willows, and all but the most vital supplies were cached. Ahead they found sparse vegetation, few buffalo, and rocky terrain. Fortunately, timely summer thunderstorms relieved the drought, and the fresh grass that shot up provided needed fodder for the livestock.

On August 7 the expedition reached its official destination, South Pass. Frémont had anticipated a rugged alpine gap and found the wide, gently sloping plain disappointing. The ascent was so gradual and the scenery so ordinary that only Carson could determine the exact spot at which the continent divided. "I should compare the elevation which we surmounted immediately at the Pass," Frémont reported, "to the ascent of Capitol hill from the avenue at Washington." Hardly a major accomplishment!

Ignoring orders to explore only as far as South Pass, Frémont had hoped to conduct a detailed reconnaissance of the mountains beyond. Now that plan seemed impossible, because many of the men were exhausted from the hardships they had suffered, and morale was low. There had been no bread for weeks, only a few pounds of coffee remained, and even the macaroni sacks were almost empty. Dried buffalo meat fried in butter was never tasty, and much of it had spoiled because of poor preservation. The remainder was as hard as wood and as succulent as tree bark.[53]

Still, frustrated by the absence of a spectacular mountain ascent at South Pass, Frémont was determined to find and conquer a real mountain. He picked his fifteen strongest men and set out to climb the highest peak in sight, which he erroneously claimed to be the highest in the Rockies. Preuss went along, as did Maxwell, Carson, and such trusted lieutenants as Clément Lambert and Basil Lajeunesse. A single pack mule carried the provisions, including a coffee pot, a kettle, and several drinking cups.

Each man tied his blanket to his saddle; they took turns toting the scientific gear.

For the first time the expedition encountered truly spectacular scenery. "It seems as if from the vast expanse of uninteresting prairie we had passed over," Frémont wrote, "Nature had collected all her beauties together in one place." They passed emerald green mountain lakes set in deep green valleys, inhaled the fragrant odor of pines, and reveled at the sparkling colors of wild flowers in brilliant summer bloom. A roaring waterfall interrupted the quiet stillness of the woods. "I realized this delightful morning the pleasure of breathing that mountain air which makes a constant theme of the hunter's praise," declared Frémont, "and which now makes us feel as if we had all been drinking some exhilarating gas."

Mountain climbing could be dangerous as well as exhilarating, however. When the trail grew steeper and the rocks more treacherous, Frémont left the animals behind. His men carried only their guns and the scientific equipment; some of them foolishly left their coats behind. Once, while crossing a dangerous rock slide, Maxwell slipped and fell toward a steep cliff. Only by throwing himself on the ground and clutching at the loose rock was he able to save himself from what surely would have been a fatal plunge. That night the adventurers camped beside a high mountain lake, with nothing to eat. Frémont developed severe headaches from the altitude, and the campfire provided but little relief from the piercing night wind.

The next day was even worse. Frémont angrily criticized Carson, who was leading the climb, for moving too fast and replaced him with another guide. Lambert and one of the voyageurs became so ill that they had to be left behind; Frémont's headaches returned, he felt giddy and started vomiting. Preuss, like Maxwell, slipped on a rock slide and tumbled head over heels some hundred feet down the mountain, fortunately suffering only minor bruises. Carson found what he thought was a route to the top, but Frémont was so ill that he ordered Basil Lajeunesse and four others back for supplies while he, Maxwell, and Ayot huddled on an exposed ledge. After more than an hour of shivering in the cold wind, they retreated toward the previous night's campsite, where Basil brought blankets, dried meat, coffee, and five of the mules. The night was spent rolled up beside a fire, with no more progress having been made toward the objective.

The next day Carson, Maxwell, and most of the party went back to bring up the rest of the mules and scientific instruments. Preuss, Lajeunesse, Lambert, and two voyageurs stayed with Frémont, and, soon after breakfast, began a final assault on the peak. With relatively little trouble they reached a ridge which ran along the top; and, high above the timberline, they peered warily into the valleys on both sides, gasping at the spectacular beauty of the tiny mountain lakes below and speculating about the origins of the many springs that flowed from the rocky ground. The men left their mules in a grassy meadow and ascended through snowdrifts and across perilous rocky spines to the crest. "I sprang upon the summit," announced Frémont, "and another step would have precipitated me into an immense snow field five hundred feet below." The peak was so quiet that even a bumble bee disturbed the serenity. The men fired their pistols and unfurled a flag Frémont had brought along; their "hurrahs" echoed across the surrounding peaks. "We had accomplished an object of laudable ambition and beyond the strict order of our instructions," boasted Frémont. "We had climbed the loftiest peak of the Rocky mountains and looked down upon the snow a thousand feet below, and standing where never human foot had stood before, felt the enthusiasm of first explorers."[54]

Frémont's men followed the snowbanks down to the meadow where their mules had been staked, then headed into the rock fields below. Basil Lajeunesse, who took the lead, lost his way several times, forcing them to dismount and shove their mules through the rocks. At the camp where they expected to find Carson, Maxwell, and the rest of the group—and breakfast—a note reported that the main party had moved on. Frémont lost his temper again, raved at Carson for disobeying orders, and threatened to dismiss everybody and go home. Pushing rapidly on, they rejoined the main party that evening, and by that time Frémont had calmed down enough that he scolded Carson less harshly than Preuss had feared he might.[55]

The major goals of the expedition having been accomplished, Frémont pushed his men rapidly eastward across the plains. Except for an ill-conceived and almost catastrophic attempt to float down the Platte on a raft, the trip proved uneventful. Carson left the expedition at Fort Laramie, either to return to Taos or to join Bent, St. Vrain and Company, leaving Maxwell as the principal hunter. Not everyone trusted Lucien's ability. Charles Preuss feared that with Kit gone the quantity and quality of his food would decline. He explained in his diary that "Mac," as he called Lucien, was "only half dependable" and could not be counted on to bring in the fat deer or buffalo cows like Carson had. The only compensating factor, which reveals something about the reputation which Maxwell had already established, was that Lucien was "ambitious enough to do his best." A couple of weeks later Preuss noted that, as expected, there was "quite a difference" between Carson's cows" and Maxwell's. The problem stemmed from the fact that the fattest animals ran in the front of the herd and were, therefore, the most difficult to kill. "Kit did not shirk the effort," the German wrote, "but now often only the stragglers are shot. One notices this when one sits down to dinner."[56]

On they hurried, reaching Cyprian Chouteau's trading post on October 10 and Saint Louis by October 17. By month's end, Frémont was in Washington preparing the report that would win him and many of those who accompanied him, especially Carson, considerable fame. Lucien's salary for the expedition totaled $234.75. In addition, he sold four mules to Frémont through P. M. Chouteau, and he received another $160.00, presumably for two more mules and a horse that had died en route. The total, nearly $500.00, was a considerable amount for a young man just completing his apprenticeship on the frontier.[57]

Maxwell's return to Saint Louis in the fall of 1842 marked an important milestone in his life. He had gone west and proven his natural abilities as a frontiersman. He was tough, strong, and determined. Friends such as Carson and Beaubien and Frémont had taught him added skills and helped him win new positions. He had gained the respect and admiration of many persons who called the west their home. He had tasted life on the frontier and liked it. Now that his apprenticeship had ended, Lucien Maxwell was ready to participate in America's headlong rush toward the Pacific and to begin building his own empire in the Southwest.

3
The Courses of Empire

LUCIEN MAXWELL's interest in the Far West predated by a decade that of most of his countrymen. Some hardy Americans had gone west ever since the famed Pacific trek of Lewis and Clark and later government-sponsored expeditions. Free and company trappers, Santa Fe traders, missionaries, and farmers had ventured into such faraway realms as Oregon, California, New Mexico, and Texas, but their numbers had been small. Other interests had occupied the minds of most easterners, and only a few dreamed that one day the United States would expand to the Pacific.

By the mid-1840s the nation had caught up. Almost everyone looked anxiously westward, and expansion became a national obsession. Politicians debated not if but when, how, and how much of the trans-Mississippi region would be annexed. Texas, having won its independence from Mexico, cried for entry into the Union; presidential candidates threatened war unless Britain relinquished its claim to the Oregon country; no one doubted that the United States would eventually annex New Mexico and California. Many factors united to produce this rising interest, but of no small importance were the brilliant reports John Charles Frémont prepared to describe his first western expedition, in which Lucien Maxwell had participated. "They were adventure books," chronicler Bernard De Voto has explained, "they were charters of Manifest Destiny, they were texts of navigation for the uncharted sea so many dreamed of crossing."[1]

Neither Frémont nor Maxwell had yet left the stage of American history. The Pathfinder's two subsequent expeditions, in both of which Maxwell participated, contributed significantly to the acquisition of California. When war with Mexico finally broke out, Maxwell witnessed some of the most critical and fascinating events in the history of the West. Meanwhile, Maxwell began to build his own empire on the New Mexican frontier. Having secured the rights to a vast land grant, his father-in-law, Charles Beaubien, began to establish colonies in the wilderness. At first Beaubien turned primarily to Charles Bent to superintend the new settlements and anticipated the time when his eldest son could inherit them. But the death of both Bent and young Narciso Beaubien in a bloody night of terror would leave Lucien Maxwell as Beaubien's principal heir and successor.

Not untypically, what Lucien did immediately after reaching Saint Louis in the fall of 1842 is uncertain. He made a short visit home, perhaps, followed by a hurried trip across the plains to see Luz before bad weather made travel impossible. Or he may have spent the winter in Kaskaskia, visiting with his family, helping his mother and elder brother on their farm. Still another possibility is that Lucien returned to the Indian trade, perhaps in the employ of Bent, St. Vrain and Company, accompanying Kit Carson.[2]

The most important events of the winter, whether Lucien was present to witness them or not, occurred in Taos. In February, Kit Carson took a new wife, Josefa Jaramillo, the teenaged daughter of a well-known Mexican family.[3] At the Beaubien household, key events concerned the land grant Charles and Guadalupe Miranda had acquired. Because of anti-foreign sentiments following an 1841 invasion of the territory by Texans, it was February of 1843 before the grantees asked Taos Justice of the Peace Cornelio Vigil to perform the rites required to put them in formal possession of the land. Although some historians have questioned that the required ceremonies occurred, official documents reported that before month's end the co-owners accompanied the judge and several witnesses across the Sangre de Cristos. They erected seven mounds outlining the boundaries. "I took them by the hand," Vigil attested, "walked with them, caused them to throw earth, pull up weeds, and show other evidences of possession." The ceremony bestowed "perfect and personal" possession of the grant on Beaubien and Miranda, their children and successors.[4]

Despite the alleged performance of these rituals, Beaubien and Miranda realized that changes in the political climate or their failure to develop the land as promised could result in its forfeiture. In New Mexico, the support of Governor Manuel Armijo was imperative.[5] What better way to motivate his assistance and alleviate his fears of a foreign intrigue, thus assuring continued support where it was needed, than to make him a partner in the venture? And so, not surprisingly—perhaps even as an unwritten condition for receiving the grant—on March 2, 1843, Beaubien and Miranda deeded a one-fourth interest in the land to the governor.[6] Thereafter, he consistently defended the grantees' rights, and late in 1843 he approved another grant to Beaubien's son Narciso, who was away at school, and Stephen Louis Lee, a Taos trapper and storekeeper.[7]

Beaubien also needed to begin developing the land as his original petition had promised. Both he and Miranda were too old and too heavily burdened by other responsibilities to take on such a task. What was needed was someone experienced in establishing frontier settlements who could recruit settlers, select sites, procure supplies, and superintend the initial phases of construction. Charles Bent, Beaubien's close friend and frequent business associate, was an ideal candidate. No one had been more successful than he in founding trading posts and farms on the high plains bordering New Mexico. His friendship with the Indians would be valuable in protecting new settlements, and he had dozens of employees and acquaintances who could be induced to help organize towns. Thus

*Charles Bent, fur trader,
governor of New Mexico, and
friend of Maxwell's, who died
in the Taos uprising.
Collection of the author.*

the same day that Armijo received his interest in the grant,
Charles Bent obtained a one-quarter share in exchange for
instigating and supervising the establishment of colonies.[8]

Meanwhile, more immediate events were unfolding
in the east. By late May, 1843, Maxwell was at Cyprian
Chouteau's trading post on the Kansas River. His destination was Taos. Traveling alone or with only a few companions was too dangerous, so when he heard that Lieutenant Frémont was about to depart on a second major expedition into the West, Maxwell asked for and was granted
permission to accompany him part of the way.[9]

Differences between Frémont's first and second expeditions reflected the changes in American attitudes toward
the West. Frémont's earlier venture had been limited to
exploring United States territory. This time no one cared
whether or not he crossed international boundaries. He
was to survey a route to Oregon, under joint occupation
by the United States and Britain, and conduct a reconnaissance of California, still the property of Mexico. Before,

the wagons had been loaded with foodstuffs and scientific instruments; now Frémont took along a twelve-pound howitzer. So many men wanted to accompany the famed explorer that his recruiting meetings in Saint Louis caused a near riot.[10] In place of Carson, who was still in New Mexico, Frémont hired Tom ("Broken Hand") Fitzpatrick. Preuss was there again, along with other regulars such as Basil Lajeunesse and Alexis Ayot.[11]

Frémont hurried out onto the plains before month's end.[12] A week later, after an uneventful journey over the same route followed earlier, Maxwell came dashing into camp during a stream crossing to report that a war party of Osage Indians, dressed in "gay red blankets, and heads shaved to the scalp lock," were close on his heels. Lucien reported that he had returned alone to the site of the previous night's camp in an attempt to find a runaway horse, saddle, bridle, and holster pistols. The Indians had chased him six miles, probably unaware of the size of the party with which he was traveling. The Osages soon withdrew, after running off several horses, which were recaptured after a "hard chase."[13]

Nothing of importance occurred before the expedition reached Fort St. Vrain, whence Maxwell planned to depart for Taos. Frémont badly needed more mules and supplies. Learning that mules from California could be bought in Taos and that Charles Beaubien could sell him provisions, Frémont asked Lucien to obtain ten or twelve mules, pack them with "provisions and other necessaries," and bring them to him at the confluence of Fountain Creek and the Arkansas River, near the future site of Pueblo, Colorado. A week later, when Frémont reached the rendezvous point, he learned that Maxwell had passed through en route to Taos on July 9.

Exactly what happened to Maxwell is not known. Ute Indians were on the rampage, and Frémont concluded that Maxwell's chances for survival were slight. Moreover, Frémont learned that an expedition of Texans led by Jacob Snively had invaded New Mexico and was preying on

Santa Fe caravans. Another band of Texans, commanded by Charles A. Warfield, had attacked Mora, a frontier village southeast of Taos. Local reaction to these events had been swift and predictable. In Taos the homes of many foreigners, including Charles Beaubien, had been plundered, and their families had been mistreated. Even if Maxwell had made it to Taos, the chances of his being able to buy mules and supplies were remote. When Lucien still had not reached Pueblo by July 16, Frémont left a note instructing him to meet the expedition at Bent's Fort if he could.[14] Maxwell never appeared, but his reasons must have been sufficient to satisfy Frémont, who did not hold the incident against him. Frémont continued west on a route that took him through South Pass, along the Snake River to Oregon, and through the Central Valley of California. Kit Carson, who joined the explorer several days after Lucien's departure, served as guide and hunter.[15]

Meanwhile, Maxwell turned his attention to the concerns of his wife's family. One of the most vocal and influential New Mexicans was Taos priest José Antonio Martínez, a brilliant man whose accomplishments included establishing the first newspaper in the Southwest and opening a respected church school. Martínez took upon himself the protection of ordinary Mexicans and Indians against the intrigues of foreigners. He objected, for example, to granting a huge tract of potentially valuable land to Beaubien and Miranda, not only because the grant encompassed grazing lands traditionally utilized by the Indians of Taos Pueblo, but also because, as everyone knew, Charles Bent was deeply involved in the scheme. Martínez demanded that the grant be suspended until his charges could be investigated. For once the pendulum of New Mexico politics had swung in the priest's direction. Armijo was out of office; the new governor detested foreigners; Miranda had lost his influence; and the anti-Texas rage had spread to include all Anglos. As a result, on February 27, 1844, the government in Santa Fe suspended the grant.[16]

The rejoinder the grantees submitted contained ob-

José Antonio Martínez, the Taos priest who inspired Mexican and Indian opposition to the American takeover of New Mexico. Courtesy Museum of New Mexico.

vious lies and assertions that caused the grant owners trouble for years to come. They denied that Bent owned any part of the land and claimed that the grant contained only fifteen to eighteen leagues, just over 100,000 acres. The truth was that an interest had been transferred to Bent more than a year before, and later owners claimed that the Beaubien and Miranda grant included nearly 2 million acres. It was also untrue, Beaubien continued more honestly, that the Taos Indians hunted in the area, or that buffalo on which they depended for food would be exterminated by the settlers. It was vital, he insisted, that the settlers who were ready to move into the area be allowed to establish towns and ranches. Progress would be impeded unless the priest's objections were overruled and the grant owners' rights restored. The Departmental Assembly considered the matter at their spring meeting, and in mid-April they declared the Martínez objections invalid and restored the land to the claimants.[17]

The land that Beaubien and Miranda received, the future site of Lucien Maxwell's empire, included some of the most scenic and potentially valuable country in New Mexico. Stretching along the front range of the Sangre de Cristo Mountains, it was intersected by a series of mountain streams that watered a narrow strip of fertile valley land. In the south, where the trail from Taos met the Santa Fe Trail, the Rayado poured out of a rugged canyon en route to the Canadian. The next stream to the north was the tiny Uracca, which flowed off lava-topped mesas, followed by the Cimarroncito, born in high peaks visible from far out on the plains. The most important stream crossing the grant was the Cimarron River, which flowed out of the Moreno Valley, a broad, flat, nearly barren gap between the Cimarron range and the Taos Mountains beyond. It meandered for miles through a scenic canyon before reaching the flats. Farther north, the Ponil and Vermejo rivers flowed more lazily between high sandstone walls on their way to the plains.

The territory offered everything a frontier settler

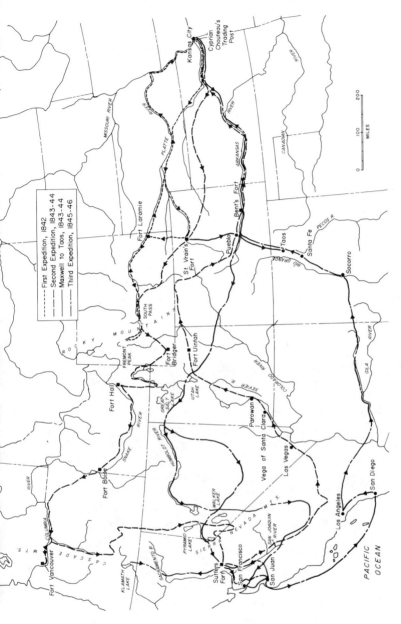

Maxwell and Frémont Explore the West, 1842–46.
Map drawn by Kevin E. Coveart
© 1983 by the University of Oklahoma Press

First Expedition, 1842
Second Expedition, 1843–44
Maxwell to Taos, 1843–44
Third Expedition, 1845–46

could want. The high mountains contained virgin timber and green, grassy meadows promising adequate wood supplies and plenty of summer grazing. Intermediate woodlands were covered with handsome Ponderosa forests, fragrant piñons, and junipers. The best sites for settlements lay at the foot of the mountains, where low hills provided protection against winter blizzards and Indian attack, and well-watered, fertile soil abounded. Toward the east stretched plains where one day millions of cattle would graze on tall prairie grasses.[18]

Plans to colonize the region were already well under way by late 1843. During the fall, Lucien Maxwell had traveled to Fort Platte to purchase livestock—presumably for the new ranches on the Beaubien and Miranda grant—from owners John Sibille and David Adams. Fifty head of cattle cost him $15 each, payment to be made in blankets valued at $7.50 apiece. He also bought a few mules and other livestock.[19] The next spring, settlers, mostly Mexicans from Taos, began packing their goods, loading possessions onto carts, and hauling them to the eastern side of the mountains. Beaubien and Charles Bent began a settlement at what they called El Ponil, near where Ponil Creek left the mountains. Cornelio Vigil, the Taos justice of the peace, established a colony along the Cimarron River, near the place where Lucien Maxwell would establish his ranch at the present-day town of Cimarron.[20]

Government opposition to the presence of foreigners so near the border between Mexico and the United States led to the abandonment of the new settlements once the crops had been harvested in the fall, but the next spring the colonists returned.[21] Kit Carson, back from having traveled with Frémont to the Pacific Coast, arrived with a friend, Dick Owens, who had been living with an Indian woman at the Greenhorn trading post in southern Colorado. The two, as Carson recalled in his memoirs, "concluded that, as we had rambled enough, that it would be advisable for us to go and settle on some good stream and make us a farm." Not far away, on the Ponil, two other mountaineers, Tom Boggs and John Hatcher, also commenced farming that year.[22]

What Lucien Maxwell was doing is not known. According to one report he tried farming along the Rayado, the southernmost stream on the grant.[23] During the fall of 1844, James J. Webb, a Santa Fe trader and diarist, met Maxwell and Carson along the Culebra River in the San Luis Valley of southern Colorado. Accompanied by mountaineer Timothy Goodale, the pair rode into Webb's camp one afternoon, leading their spare mounts. They quickly unbridled and started a fire to begin making coffee. Soon a prairie dog was roasting over the coals. The visitors had little time to chat, since they had left Pueblo that morning and said they hoped to be in Taos by nightfall. As soon as their dinner was down, they saddled their mounts, caught their extra horses, and rode off. "Look out for your har, boys!" Carson shouted as they left, "the Utes are plenty about here."[24] Maxwell was back in Pueblo in December, when he tried unsuccessfully to buy a mule for bankrupt trader Lancaster Lupton.[25]

Further evidence that Maxwell was not yet ready to settle down came the following spring, when he bade farewell to his friends and family in Taos. By May he was back in Saint Louis, ready to join Frémont on yet another major western exploring expedition. The pathfinder welcomed him, making no mention of his previous failings, and included him among the "old men" joining the party.[26]

Historians have vigorously debated the purpose of Frémont's third western expedition. Several clues suggest that it was far more than a scientific activity. American relations with Mexico had deteriorated rapidly, and keen observers guessed, especially after the United States annexed Texas early in 1845, that war was inevitable. Moreover, acquisition of California had become a major objective of the new President, James K. Polk. Frémont's expedition was discussed at a cabinet meeting in the context of a possible American takeover of the area. The expedition was larger and better supplied than its two predecessors. The sixty men carried the finest rifles that could be bought.[27]

Frémont seemed eager to get across the plains and into the far west as quickly as possible. Instead of his usual vivid descriptions of Indian attacks and buffalo hunts, he noted only that "the usual prairie incidents of Indians and large game" furnished "wholesome excitement." Tom Fitzpatrick, whom Frémont had hired as guide, left the expedition at Bent's Fort, along with John Hatcher, the Ponil settler who had accompanied them part way. Frémont sent a message to Carson, who was farming on the Cimarron, to ask him to assume the important post vacated by Fitzpatrick. "He had promised that he would come in the event I would need him," Frémont recalled, "and I knew that he would not fail me." The unnamed messenger, perhaps Maxwell, found Kit busy "starting the convivial work of making up a stock ranch." Without hesitation, Carson sold his farm and cattle for, as he recalled, "about half [what] it was worth," and he and Owens joined the expedition. "This was like Carson," Frémont noted in his memoirs, "prompt, self-sacrificing and true. I received them both with great satisfaction."[28]

Together, Maxwell and Carson once again contributed their skills to aid in assuring success for the expedition. From Bent's Fort they moved up the Arkansas and through the Rockies into Utah, where they explored both Utah Lake and the Great Salt Lake. Ahead stretched a desert so inhospitable that no white man had ever crossed it. Even the local Indians found it fearsome. Spotting a distant peak from which signals could be sent, Frémont ordered Carson to lead a small reconnaissance party consisting of Maxwell and Auguste Archambeau across the desert at night. They took only one pack mule loaded with water and provisions. Whenever they found grass and water, they were to send smoke signals telling Frémont to come ahead with the rest of the group. The country proved to be as wretched as expected—sixty miles without a "particle of vegetation," Carson said, the ground as "level as a barn floor." On the other side, where grass and water were plentiful, Carson lit a fire to summon Frémont. Two days later the entire expedition had crossed the salt flats.[29]

After a day of much needed rest, Frémont pushed on, dividing the men in two in order to cover as much of the desolate Great Basin as possible. The party reunited briefly at Walker Lake, on the western edge of the Humboldt Sink, before Frémont took off with a lead contingent including Carson, Maxwell, Owens, and several Delaware Indians serving as scouts. They hurried in order to avoid the winter snows that would soon close the Sierra passes, and by December 3 had reached the massive adobe post, New Helvetia, erected by Swiss-born rancher John A. Sutter near the juncture of the American and Sacramento rivers.[30]

Frémont's true interests became more evident after they left Sutter's Fort. These were Americans traveling without invitation or permission in what was unquestionably Mexico. Frémont, however, acted as though his government already controlled California. For example, the expedition came upon so many horse tracks that Frémont thought "Horse Thief" Indians must have recently raided nearby ranches and took it upon himself to punish them. He ordered Maxwell, Dick Owens, and two Delawares to find the thieves. Frémont and the remainder who trailed behind had found a camping spot for the night when they heard rifle fire and barking dogs in the distance. Off they rode. Maxwell and his companions had been discovered by Indians, who were yelling at them in Spanish. Howling Indian women and children sought shelter, while the men tried to surround the small hill on which the two Americans and their Indian scouts were hiding. At one point Owens killed the lead Indian, forcing the remainder to withdraw. Frémont's men soon rescued their colleagues, and the entire party withdrew from the Indian village.

Next day the Americans hurried on. Rather than ride through the oak-covered foothills, the expedition dropped down into the open flatlands of the San Joaquin Valley. Maxwell, who rode ahead to scout for Indians, spotted a well-mounted native and rode off in swift pursuit. With the help of his fast horse, Lucien soon caught up. "It was open ground over rolling hills, and we were all in sight of each other," Frémont recalled. By the time he, Alexis Godey, and two Delawares rode up, Lucien and the Indian were dueling, "both on foot, Maxwell with pistols, the Indian with arrows." Only ten or twelve feet separated them. Frémont would have preferred to take the man prisoner, but before he could do so, Lucien shot the Indian dead.[31]

Meanwhile, Mexican officials who learned of Frémont's presence grew increasingly nervous. When the Americans camped near San Juan, erected a quasi-military log fort, and raised an American flag, the Mexicans could no longer tolerate the situation. March 8, 1846, the commander of Mexican troops in Upper California denounced the "band of robbers" that had "daringly intruded themselves into the country" and called on his people to rally and expel them before "our liberties and independence" were destroyed.[32] Fighting seemed unavoidable until Frémont, recognizing the immense odds against him, withdrew from his camp and pointed his men toward Oregon. Little did he know that soon General Zachary Taylor would lead troops into contested land along the Río Grande, precipitating a Mexican attack against the American soldiers April 25 and a United States declaration of war May 11.[33]

Frémont, as though biding his time until this news reached him, led his troops along the streams and through the fertile valleys of northern California and southern Oregon. They encountered more hostility from the Klamath Indians. One night just after Frémont had gone to sleep, Carson called to Basil Lajeunesse, who was resting nearby: "What's the matter over there?" Hearing no reply, Kit, soon joined by Maxwell, Owens, Frémont, and several Delawares, jumped from his bed. The noise Kit had heard was the dull thud of an ax driven through the skull of Lajeunesse, one of Frémont's most trusted comrades. The camp came alive. Shooting erupted as the Americans sought vengeance; Indians fled for their lives. Maxwell fired on one of the attackers, a Klamath chief, whom he hit in the leg. A follow-up bullet in the back from Joseph Stepp's rifle killed the intruder. Next day Carson took revenge for Basil's death by using the dead man's own ax to knock his skull to pieces. The Delawares collected his scalp.[34]

The desire for revenge persisted. Shortly afterward, Maxwell and Archambeau were riding ahead of the main party when they encountered an Indian carrying a bunch of crows. According to Carson, the two had no wish to hurt the native and only wanted to talk, but the Indian proved hostile. He put his birds down, took up his bow, and loosed an attack on the pair. The firing kept up as he came nearer. Lucien jumped off his mount just in time to escape an arrow that barely missed the seat of his saddle. Maxwell commenced firing, and, after an exchange of shots, the Indian fell dead. Lucien and his companion pulled the dead man's scalp, attached it to an arrow, and stood it in the middle of the trail as a warning. "We were getting roughened into Indian customs," noted Frémont, observing that the natives deserved "respect for their daring, but their bravery is improvident and uncalculating. Like tigers, their first spring is the dangerous one."[35]

During the months that followed, Lucien Maxwell was more an observer than a participant. He had a rare opportunity to witness firsthand a dramatic episode in his country's history. The English-speaking residents of California were preparing to follow the example set a decade before in Texas and declare independence from Mexico. June 10, 1846, soon after Frémont returned from Oregon, the leader of the revolutionaries, William Ide, visited his camp. Several men, including Carson, asked for discharges in order to participate in the revolt. Frémont said no. At least one historian has included Lucien Maxwell among those who captured a herd of Mexican horses and surrounded the Sonoma house of General Mariano Vallejo four days later. The next day they called their Republic of California into existence by hoisting a flag showing a grizzly bear and a single star.[36]

Edward Kern's painting of Frémont's men fighting the Klamath Indians. Courtesy of the Bancroft Library.

Frémont's neutrality was short-lived. Soon he joined the Bear Flaggers in resisting Mexican efforts to put down the revolt. Initial successes in driving the Mexican troops out of San Francisco and a gala Fourth of July celebration encouraged Frémont to organize the California Battalion, 224 men strong, to conquer California for the United States. Events moved quickly. United States naval forces off the coast received permission to assault the capital of Monterey. Commodore Robert F. Stockton led a combined land and sea operation, in which many of Frémont's men — perhaps including Maxwell — participated, that captured the last stronghold at Los Angeles in mid-August. In less than three months California had been added to the American empire.[37]

Because it was necessary for news of the conquest of California to reach Washington as quickly as possible,

Frémont asked Carson to choose fifteen men to carry dispatches east. Maxwell was one of those selected and seems to have acted as Carson's chief lieutenant and advisor. Kit led his men out of Los Angeles September 5. The couriers proceeded up the Gila Trail, encountering no trouble until they got within ten miles of the Santa Rita copper mines. There, in the middle of their trail, sat a village of warlike Apaches. "I knew that by staying where we were," Carson recalled, "we would be seen, and if we endeavored to pass them, they would also see us." After seeking Maxwell's counsel, Carson decided to try sneaking past under cover of the nearby timber. The ploy failed; no more than a hundred yards separated the Americans from the Apaches when they were discovered. Fortunately the Indians proved friendly and soon commenced trading with the whites. Carson was even able to buy badly needed replacement mounts before continuing east toward the Río Grande.[38]

October 6, 1846, as they moved up the Río Grande toward Santa Fe, Carson and his men noticed a large dust cloud in the distance. More Indians? No, as they came closer the group appeared to be soldiers, American troops, five companies of them. When Carson met their commander, General Stephen Watts Kearny, he learned that this was the Army of the West. Kit blurted out the news that soldiers led by Frémont and Stockton had already captured California.[39] What Carson, Maxwell, and the others learned affected their homes, families, and futures in New Mexico.

No sooner had the United States declared war on Mexico the preceding May, they were told, than President Polk had ordered Kearny to lead his dragoons and Missouri volunteers into the Southwest. Four companies of Mormons later joined the expedition, and its mission was extended to include the capture of California. Nearly twenty-five hundred Americans departed for the West late in June, carrying sixteen howitzers, more than fifteen hundred wagons, thirty-five hundred draft mules, and nearly fifteen thousand cattle and oxen. They followed the Santa Fe Trail route that was familiar to Carson and Maxwell from the Missouri River to Bent's Fort, which they reached by the end of July.

August saw the invaders worming their way along the Arkansas River, through Raton Pass, and into New Mexico. Preparations for battle intensified when Governor Armijo issued a call to arms and mustered four thousand soldiers to challenge Kearny. The army entered the Mexican town of Las Vegas without opposition, however, and as it pressed toward the capital Armijo and his army melted away. August 18, 1846, Kearny's men rolled into Santa Fe, where ceremonies transferring control over New Mexico to the United States were held that day and the next.

Kearny had spent the next month receiving the surrender of Mexican officials throughout the region, establishing a system of taxation, and promulgating a code of laws under which the territory could be governed. Lucien's old friend Charles Bent received appointment as the first governor; his father-in-law, Charles Beaubien, was named a circuit judge. By September 25, his work transferring New Mexico to American authority complete, Kearny sent part of his troops south toward Chihuahua, ordered the Mormon Battalion through southern New Mexico and Arizona, and led the rest down the Río Grande and west toward California. Ten days later he met Carson.[40]

Kearny ordered Carson to abandon his messenger's assignment, initiating bad feelings between himself and Frémont that subsequently grew into a major controversy. Loyalty to Frémont tempted Carson to refuse the order and "escape" during the night, but "a good friend," Maxwell, persuaded him that he should obey. "With sullen resignation," as Tom Fitzpatrick, who assumed responsibility for the letters, remembered, Carson "turned again to the west."[41] Lucien and the rest of the fifteen continued east. Whether or not they stopped in Taos is uncertain, but they left Santa Fe October 14 and arrived in Saint Louis a month later.[42]

Lucien must have gone no farther, for late in January, 1847, he was at Bent's Fort awaiting a wagon train with which he could travel home. The morning of January 28 an old mountaineer, Louis Simonds, brought news of a bloody massacre in Taos ten days before. "Well, you see the Purblos [*sic*]," he explained in broken English to Lucien, writer Lewis H. Garrard, and others present, "was mity mad fur the 'Mericans to come in thar diggings an' take everything so easy like." They had sworn to "count coups when they could." An opportunity arose January 18, when Governor Bent, ignoring warnings of possible trouble, traveled to Taos with several other prominent Americans. That night attackers broke down the governor's door and shot and scalped him. Who else had died? the anxious men asked. Another victim was Narciso Beaubien, Lucien's brother-in-law, who had just completed school in Missouri. No one knew how many more were dead or whether the rebellion might have spread to Santa Fe. "The news had quite a depressing effect upon us," recalled Garrard, who feared that, with raids having already occured as near as the Ponil, a Mexican expedition might soon be on its way to Bent's Fort.[43]

The next afternoon twenty-three men, many aching for revenge, left the fort. Most of them worked for Bent, St. Vrain and Company. Garrard joined them, as did several Taoseños who were eager to learn the fates of their families, and Maxwell. Most were "cast down" from worry that their relatives might be "subject to the lawlessness of the infuriated populace." Long after everyone else had gone to bed, Maxwell and several other men were still awake, "too uneasy to sleep for thought of their homes." Guards were added after they crossed the Raton Mountains, and Maxwell went ahead to scout for trouble. An Indian they met reported that Colonel Sterling Price, who took command of United States troops in New Mexico when Kearny left, had come to Taos with a contingent of soldiers to put down the revolt. His troops had attacked Taos Pueblo, where the insurgents took refuge, killing two hundred

Mexicans and Indians. When they heard that Céran St. Vrain had led one victorious company, the travelers burst forth with "cheers of exultation." Maxwell and two others could stand the suspense no longer and hurried on toward Taos from the Vermejo, leaving Garrard and the rest to follow at a more leisurely pace.[44]

What Lucien learned at home confirmed much of what he already knew. Bent had been killed, along with District Attorney J. W. Leal, Justice of the Peace Cornelio Vigil, and Narciso Beaubien. Young Beaubien, he learned, had hidden under straw and refuse (some reports said in a privy) with a friend or Indian slave. A family servant had summoned the raiders, admonishing them to "kill the young ones, and they will never be men to trouble us." The pair were discovered, cruelly butchered, and scalped. Stephen Louis Lee, Narciso's partner in the Sangre de Cristo grant, had also been killed.[45] Fortunately, Judge Beaubien was away holding court in Tierra Amarilla. According to family tradition, Lucien's wife, Luz, was trying to escape when she met a man taking his wagon to get firewood. He allowed her to hide in his house while he finished his chores and sheltered her until the danger had passed.[46]

Many of those who led the uprising died during the military attack on Taos Pueblo. The ringleader, Tomás Ortiz, escaped to Mexico. Father Martínez, popularly believed to have inspired, if not organized, the revolt, never came to trial. According to Beaubien family descendants, Mrs. Beaubien burned a book listing all the participants in order to avoid further bloodshed.[47] Those brought to trial appeared before what one historian has characterized as a "Traders and Trappers' court" that met for two weeks during April, 1847. Charles Beaubien sat as judge. The juries included such prominent mountaineers as Charles Town, Baptiste Charlefou, Charles Ortebus, Louis Simonds, and John Hatcher. Lucien Maxwell, only a few weeks after returning home, was called for jury duty and served during four of the trials.[48]

The first case that Lucien heard, the earliest to come to trial, concerned José Manuel García, indicted for murder. Lewis H. Garrard, who attended sessions in the small, oblong courtroom, remembered that it was "dimly lighted by two narrow windows; a thin railing kept the bystanders from contact with the functionaries." Charles Bent's widow sometimes attended court, as did Kit Carson's young wife. The attorneys were youthful volunteer soldiers whose presentations focused more on the bravery of American soldiers than on the facts of the case. García, like all the accused, pleaded innocent. His counsel was unprepared for trial, so the proceedings were postponed—from the morning to the afternoon of April 6. The case moved swiftly. Witnesses, touching their lips to a Bible before testifying, seemed terrified of the Anglos, "as much frightened," Garrard recalled, "as the prisoners at the bar." The afternoon was still young when Lucien and the others found García guilty as charged. The next day Beaubien sentenced him to die. "When the concluding words 'muerto, muerto, muerto'—'dead, dead, dead'—were pronounced by Judge Beaubien in his solemn and impressive manner," Garrard reported, "the painful stillness that reigned in the courtroom and the subdued grief manifested by a few bystanders were noticed not without an inward sympathy."[49]

Friday, April 9, García and five others convicted of murder or treason moved to gallows near the jail on the northern edge of town. Women and children, Luz and her sisters undoubtedly among them, crowded the surrounding roofs. The military commander, Lieutenant Colonel Willock, paraded his men past as the six were herded onto a government wagon, where ropes were placed around their necks. Garrard stood with a crowd of mountaineers, surely including Lucien. In their final utterances, most of the condemned admitted guilt; one convicted of treason defiantly denounced his trial and those who had condemned him. Then the wagon moved away, and the men were soon hanging free, their bodies jerking and convulsing toward death.[50]

Many people, including Garrard, questioned the fairness of the trials. The men seemed to have died for "defend[ing] to the last their country and their homes," while those who ran the court and judged their guilt were often close friends or relatives of the dead.[51] The court's reputation is somewhat exonerated by the fact that not everyone was found guilty. In the next trial in which Maxwell participated, for example, an Indian named Ascencio was judged to be innocent and ordered freed. Another jury on which he sat found Jesús Silva, who had been accused of larceny, innocent as well. However, Silva was returned to jail, and a second jury found him guilty of similar charges the next day. Beaubien sentenced him to receive twenty-five lashes. A final case against Mariano Martínez, accused of having received stolen goods, was dropped at the request of the prosecuting attorney after the evidence had been heard.[52]

Once the trials ended, Taos residents began rebuilding their lives. Certainly New Mexico and California would remain part of the United States, even though fighting continued in Mexico until the fall of the capital in September, and the Treaty of Guadalupe Hidalgo, formally transferring control, would not be signed until February, 1848. Charles Beaubien's plans had been thoroughly disrupted by the uprising. Those who had previously helped him — Charles Bent, Stephen Louis Lee, and Cornelio Vigil — were dead, and so was his eldest son and heir apparent. His partner, Guadalupe Miranda, had fled to Mexico and could not take an active role in developing the land grant.

For a time Beaubien, perhaps out of desperation or depression, considered selling the grant to a company of American soldiers, but the deal fell through.[53] Eventually he turned to his son-in-law Lucien Maxwell, who, once he returned from the third Frémont expedition, seemed ready to settle down. He and his wife, Luz, must have talked of raising a family, a more serious discussion after she announced her pregnancy during the fall of 1847. Their first child, Peter Menard Maxwell, was born in Taos April 27,

1848. A daughter, Virginia, arrived December 12, 1850.[54] Now, as his family responsibilities increased, was the time for Lucien to begin the work of a lifetime. He and Beaubien must have talked seriously during the summer and fall following the Taos trials, and the next spring Maxwell was ready to begin building an empire across the mountains along the Rayado River.

4

Rayado

Lucien Maxwell had passed through Rayado dozens, perhaps hundreds, of times. Nearly every wagon train that followed the Santa Fe Trail stopped there either for the night or for a refreshing break from hot, dusty travel.[1] Most travelers from Taos to Bent's Fort or Missouri headed up Taos Canyon, twisting and turning as the valley climbed toward the summit, then turned south, avoiding the Moreno Valley route used by modern highways, before ascending onto high, grass-carpeted mesas. From the top of LaGrulla Mesa the plains stretched toward the horizon, the many lakes and ponds sparkling like tiny mirrors. A steep descent brought travelers to the Santa Fe Trail. After 1848, a turn northward for a few miles would have brought the traveler to Lucien Maxwell's settlement along the first stream—the beginnings of his empire in the Southwest.

In Spanish, Rayado meant "streaked," referring to lines drawn across a surface. How the word came to be applied to this area is difficult to determine. Perhaps the original "streaks" were faults or strata marks on the cliffs that lined the stream. Plains Indians called "Rayados" by the Spaniards because of painted or tatooed lines on their faces may have lent their names to the region.[2] Other accounts mention a famous Comanche chief named Rayado.[3] Still another possibility, raised recently, is that the word originally applied to the crest of the mountains between the plains and Taos. First the trail leading to the top of the mountains was called Rayado, and both "the Rayado

River and the settlement of Rayado . . . got their names because of their association with the trail."[4]

Maxwell established the first lasting settlement on the eastern side of the Sangre de Cristos in northeastern New Mexico near the place where the Rayado River emerged from the mountains and entered the Great Plains. The stream was born a dozen miles west and thousands of feet higher in the mountains. On the way downhill, its waters cascaded through deep channels carved between rock walls. "If a man wanted to get himself really lost, really isolated in the most uncharted and unreachable depths of the . . . wilds," a modern outdoorsman has written, "he could not have chosen a more likely area than the upper reaches of Rayado Canyon."[5] Downstream the river flowed more quietly and its pace slowed as it moved toward the flats. Grassy meadows provided excellent grazing, low hills protected the area from the worst winter storms and surprise Indian attacks, and the slow-moving water could be ditched onto parched fields. Farther east stretched the plains, their flatness broken occasionally by the protrusion of a few lofty mesas.[6]

Dr. Peters, Kit Carson's earliest biographer, argued that the scenery at Rayado was "[un]surpassed by anything of the kind in America." Stand on a foothill, he recommended, "and look down and out on the prairies, and nothing can be more enchanting than the view that is thus presented." Enveloping the valley were "lofty hills, which, when green with grass and foliage add a magic beauty to the scene."[7] Here seemed an ideal place to plant a new town. Fertile land along the valley floor could produce food for several hundred families; the mountains provided timber for construction and firewood for cooking and heating. The climate was milder, reportedly, than it was in Santa Fe and most other sections of New Mexico, and summer rainstorms alleviated any oppressive heat.[8]

One reason the Rayado country had not been settled earlier was the presence of Indians opposed to the establishment of ranches or towns in their traditional homelands. Because the Indians created a buffer between New Mexico and the United States, the Mexican government had given little encouragement to expanding settlements and sent no troops to defend ranches against attack. The perspective changed dramatically after the United States took over the region. The Santa Fe Trail, a vital artery between Missouri and the Southwest, had to be kept open. Establishing a string of settlements along the trail and protecting them with soldiers was one good way of accomplishing this objective. The same troops that had captured the territory from New Mexico and put down the Taos rebels could be expected to pursue any hostile Indians.[9]

Of all the Indians whom Lucien Maxwell encountered at Rayado and later at Cimarron, those with the strongest claim to the area were Jicarilla Apaches, whose name was derived from the Spanish word for a round pot or basket for carrying chocolate.[10] The Jicarillas were living along the edge of the Sangre de Cristos in the early eighteenth century when Spanish explorers first traversed the country, known as "La Jicarilla," the land of the Jicarillas.[11] In the mid-nineteenth century, they occupied villages along many of the streams north and south of Rayado, and the fact that none lived along the Rayado itself may have encouraged Maxwell to settle there.[12]

The economy of the Jicarillas was fragile. Men spent their time hunting deer, elk, antelope, buffalo, and other game that inhabited the region. Women's duties included gathering wild fruit, nuts, greens, and roots. Long before any American plow pierced the soil of this area, the Apaches began small-scale farming. According to one Indian, nearly three-fourths of the tribesmen living along the Cimarron had farms. "In my boyhood," a tribal elder explained, "the people depended quite a bit on agriculture. The wild foods were not certain. You might go several years without having a good crop of berries. Those who were not lazy," he continued, "and took care of their fields ate every day and had plenty." Their principal crop was corn, although they also raised beans, pumpkins, tobacco, and melons.[13]

Invaders posed the greatest danger to the Jicarillas. From the northeast their homeland was threatened by the Moache Utes, who pushed southward out of Utah and Colorado in the late seventeenth and early eighteenth centuries. At first the Utes fought the Apaches, but by the end of the eighteenth century the two tribes had allied, sometimes intermarrying and often sharing campgrounds.[14] What brought these two peoples together was, in part, increased danger from the plains. Few North American Indians were better warriors than the Comanches. "War," the leading chroniclers of the tribe have concluded, "became the pattern of life; the military cult became the ideal of the aspiring young man."[15] Comanche incursions seldom reached as far west as the front range of the Sangre de Cristos until the early nineteenth century, when the settlement of tribes from the southeastern United States in the Indian Territory and the expansion of Texas settlements into the plains region pushed the Comanches farther west. Raids into eastern New Mexico and even to the homeland of the Jicarillas became common.[16] Beginning about 1820, Cheyennes, Arapahos, and Kiowas from the north also began raids against the Jicarillas and Utes, whose buffalo hunts onto the plains became increasingly dangerous.[17]

The precarious existence of the Jicarillas and Moaches had become critical by the time Lucien Maxwell moved into their homeland at mid-century. "These Indians were scarey," a tribal spokesman recalled years later. "At the first sound, even a shout, they all made for the brush. When they went out on the plains, they saw many good spots, level places with streams flowing and good soil. But they were afraid to stay there and farm."[18] As raids by the Plains Indians and the increased presence of Mexicans and Americans in the area reduced their food supply, the Utes and Apaches turned to robbing settlers. Between 1846 and 1850, unprecedented raids reflected their growing desperation: the Apaches alone stole an estimated 450,000 sheep from ranchers in eastern New Mexico.[19] It was apparent that the fierce and proud Indian inhabitants of the Rayado country would not allow Lucien Maxwell and his associates to establish a new settlement on their land without considerable resistance.

The first settlers started for Rayado in March, 1848. It is not clear why they moved so early in the year, but the weather in northern New Mexico can be mild in spring when there is little precipitation and plentiful sunshine. Perhaps Maxwell hoped to take advantage of an early spring to get the first crops planted and the houses under construction before the summer rains began. Maybe, too, he hoped to earn money by selling supplies and livestock to William Gilpin, whom he had met on the Frémont expedition. Gilpin was camped on the Mora that winter, preparing for a campaign against the Comanches, and he obtained horses from Maxwell, who brought them from the Arkansas.[20] Whatever the reasons, Lucien's calculations proved wrong. A snowfall in the mountains between Taos and Rayado caught several pioneer settlers, delayed their crossing, and led to the death of a mule.[21]

Exactly who financed the founding of Rayado is unknown. Charles Beaubien owned a one-quarter interest in the land grant on which Rayado was clearly located. Other shares belonged to Miranda, who fled to Mexico after the American invasion; to the estate of the dead Charles Bent; and to Manuel Armijo, who had also left New Mexico. None but Beaubien could take an active role in managing the property. Moreover, Beaubien was one of the few men in the territory who were sufficiently wealthy to buy supplies and otherwise bankroll such an ambitious undertaking. It is likely that Maxwell and Beaubien entered into an agreement, probably oral, creating some kind of a partnership. Cattle stolen from the Ponil late in 1847, for example, were described as "Beaubien's and Maxwell's." Other possibilities result from the fact that the previous year Maxwell had formed a partnership with Taos merchant James H. Quinn, a Maryland native about Lucien's age, who had lived for a time in Kaskaskia. At least in part, the Rayado venture may have represented a company endeavor.[22]

Knowledge of Lucien's financial position is complicated by the fact that he never explained his business arrangements, and he seems to have allowed, even encouraged, visitors to assume that he owned something whether he did or not. Most observers estimated his wealth to be higher than it was. Maxwell's descendants have claimed that he founded Rayado "without the aid or assistance from Beaubien and Miranda" and that "they never exercised possession or control over Lucien's ranch."[23] In view of Maxwell's early poverty and his lack of any legal right to the Rayado ranch except through Beaubien, this statement is impossible to accept.

Although Maxwell superintended the establishment of the Rayado settlement and was often identified as its owner, others were responsible for much of the actual work. Four farmers arrived the first year; the next season fifteen families plus several single men immigrated from Taos. Many were Mexican Americans from Taos, perhaps some of the same individuals who had previously begun farming along the Ponil and the Cimarron. They generally worked on shares, receiving a portion of the profits from their farms in exchange for their labor. Some of them probably left their families in Taos and returned there during the off season. Maxwell's wife, Luz, remained in Taos for the birth of their daughter Virginia late in 1850; but by the time another child, Emilia, was born in 1852, she had joined Lucien at Rayado.[24]

Other Rayado pioneers were former mountaineers who were growing old and sought new sources of income once trapping and trading opportunities had diminished. Not a few had lived at one of the trading posts, towns, or ranches along the Arkansas River in southern Colorado. Manuel LaFavre (sometimes spelled La Fevre or Lefaivre) had accompanied Lucien on the sad, anxious trip from Bent's Fort to Taos the previous year; now he moved with Maxwell to the Rayado. Tim Goodale, an Illinois native, had trapped, traded, and lived with a succession of Indian

wives during years along the Greenhorn River before settling down at Rayado. Calvin Jones, a Kentuckian four
years Lucien's junior, had been associated with mountain
man Bill Williams. Early in 1848 he and Goodale herded
cattle from Bent's Fort to Rayado. They stayed on for
several years, working for Maxwell part of the time and
trapping or farming for themselves the remainder.[25]

One of the busiest men at Rayado the first season must
have been James White, a carpenter charged with erecting
houses, barns, and other buildings. At first the accommodations were necessarily crude—probably simple lean-tos
such as those often observed elsewhere in the area.[26] But
Lucien Maxwell had visions of a better life, and soon he
had crews of men busy cutting timber to erect larger, more
luxurious structures. By the time Calvin Jones arrived
with the cattle, enough lumber had already been downed,
trimmed, cut into boards, and hauled in to build three or
four rooms.[27]

Construction was still in its initial stages when Maxwell departed northward. The exact purpose of the trip is
unknown. Perhaps he dashed across the plains to Kansas
or Missouri to buy supplies needed at Rayado, but probably, he went no farther than Bent's Fort or the other
trading posts on the Arkansas. He met Archibald Metcalf,
who worked for him and Quinn, suggesting that he may
have been on business connected with their partnership.
William Gilpin, who bought horses from Lucien earlier
in the spring, was at Fort Mann, where the Santa Fe Trail
crossed the Arkansas, and Maxwell may have gone there
to reclaim stock.[28] Whatever the exact motive for the trip,
Lucien returned with Santa Fe trader Preston Beck, mountaineer Tom Boggs, and storekeeper John Brown, who
was accompanied by his wife and baby son. Metcalf came
with six hundred deerskins that belonged to Maxwell and
Quinn; the party was joined by Indian George, a former
servant of Charles Bent, who apparently worked for Maxwell, and trader Charles Town.[29]

The entire party pointed south from the Greenhorn

the first week in June, a dozen or so people with a hundred horses and mules, some loaded with deerskins. On June 12, Jicarilla Apaches attacked them along Apache Creek and drove off their horses. Mrs. Brown, pursued by the Indians, clutched her baby to her side, spurred her mount across a deep ravine, and sped back toward the settlements. Meanwhile, Lucien and the other men found cover and began to return the fire. Three Indians were killed before the Americans retreated toward the Greenhorn. Later a company of Missouri volunteers stationed in Taos pursued the hostile natives and recaptured some of the stolen horses. They failed to follow up on the campaign, however, and probably only antagonized the already jittery Indians.[30]

Maxwell waited a week before again attempting to return home. This time he was accompanied by Town, merchant Peter Joseph, Elliott Lee (brother of the murdered Stephen Louis Lee), Indian George, and several other Indian and Mexican laborers. Fearing another Indian attack if they followed the usual route through the Raton Mountains, they herded their horses and mules east toward Manco Burro Pass. What followed has been characterized as "one of the bloodiest battles with these Indians that any of the mountain men ever had."[31] Lucien Maxwell came the closest he ever would to being killed in a battle, one that demonstrated his own courage and that of his associates.

It was June 19, 1848. The party had camped in a pleasant valley atop Manco Burro Pass to eat dinner when suddenly they heard the screams of Indians driving off their livestock. Shots fired at the circling natives had only a momentary impact, for twenty minutes later the Jicarillas were setting grass fires in an effort to drive the traders away from their baggage. In the four-hour battle that followed, five of the Americans were wounded and one killed. Elliott Lee was shot in the hand and thigh. When a bullet crushed one of Charles Town's legs, he had to be left behind "to the mercy of the Indians." The Apaches captured two small children, later ransomed. Maxwell fainted after receiving a bullet in the neck. His servant Indian George crossed dangerous, open ground to get Maxwell to water and hauled him on his back as they fled. Later Maxwell cared for George when he was wounded.

Under the cover of nightfall, the survivors struggled out of the mountains. The first night they pushed on until they found water, then huddled together and tried to sleep. "Having lost everything save what we had on our backs," Lee recalled, "we suffered much from cold and could not sleep." They hid the next day, afraid of being found by their attackers, and at dusk proceeded toward Taos. Lee was unable to keep up with the others and had to be abandoned. After a week of wandering alone through the wilderness, he was rescued by a wagon train.[32] Meanwhile, friendly Arapahos told army officials in Taos about the attack. Forty soldiers, guided by R. L. ("Uncle Dick") Wootton, the trapper who subsequently operated a toll gate atop Raton Pass, found the bedraggled expedition in "pitiable condition." They had lost most of their clothing from crawling through the brush. Maxwell himself had nothing left but an old flannel shirt and a pair of torn pants. Days without food had weakened everyone until they had difficulty standing, and their open wounds had in some cases become badly infected.[33]

The attack seriously limited Lucien's ability to direct the new Rayado settlement. Apparently for the first time in his life, he had been seriously injured. The bullet lodged deep in his neck caused him extreme pain, and as soon as possible he sought medical aid in Santa Fe, where a doctor performed the "extremely difficult" operation necessary to remove the lead ball. It would be a long time before he was back to full strength, and rather than return to Rayado, he apparently went to Taos to recover.[34]

One of Maxwell's principal concerns in Taos was recovering some of the money lost the previous season. The Manco Burro Pass tragedy had cost him and partner James H. Quinn $7,200 worth of mules, horses, and deerskins. Probably unaware that the national government had a

Uncle Dick Wootton, who helped rescue Maxwell after the Manco Burro Pass massacre. Later both he and Maxwell drove sheep to California. From Inman, The Old Santa Fé Trail.

program compensating citizens for losses to Indians, the pair failed to file their claim until 1854, by which time the deadline had passed. No compensation was ever received.[35] That money was badly needed to pay expenses at Rayado. Maxwell reportedly borrowed $1,000 from Carson to tide him over, and he was no doubt more dependent than ever on Beaubien. Throughout the winter he worked at his father-in-law's Taos store, where he was, according to one report, "doing a very prosperous business as a merchant and contractor for the troops."[36]

Maxwell was in the Beaubien store with his friends Dick Owens and Kit Carson one evening late in January when two bearded strangers entered. No sign of recognition crossed Owens's face, but Maxwell knew immediately who they were. "Why don't you recognize the Captain?" he asked. Everyone soon realized that it was their old commander, John C. Frémont, accompanied by mountaineer Alexis Godey. Both had suffered terribly from cold and hunger. After a brief reception Frémont was helped to Carson's house, where he remained to recuperate. Next day Godey returned to rescue the remainder of the expedition.[37]

Over the next few days, as his strength returned, Frémont told Carson, Maxwell, and other Taos acquaintances of the series of events that had befallen him since their last meeting. Trouble had begun not long after Carson and Maxwell left California with news of the conquest. Both General Stephen Watts Kearny, whose Army of the West Maxwell and Carson had met in southern New Mexico, and Commodore Robert F. Stockton, commander of the Pacific Fleet, had claimed to be in charge of United States forces in California; Frémont was caught in between. He refused to obey Kearny's orders, whereupon the general had him arrested on charges of mutiny, disobedience, and "conduct to the prejudice of good order and military discipline." A court-martial convened at Fort Monroe, Virginia, lasted from November, 1847, through January, 1848. Many of Frémont's witnesses were disallowed, and, despite support from Stockton and Senator Benton, the court ruled him guilty, recommending "lenient consideration" to President Polk. The President reversed the guilty verdict on the mutiny charge, and, because of the "peculiar circumstances" of the case and Frémont's "previous meritorious and valuable service," ordered him reinstated to duty.[38]

Despite the President's action, Frémont was in disgrace and foresaw no opportunity to lead another government expedition. Senator Benton, however, arranged for him to lead a privately-sponsored reconnaissance aimed at identifying railroad routes to California. Frémont and about thirty seasoned explorers pushed toward the Rockies in the fall of 1848. After they left Bent's Fort in late November, everything went wrong. It snowed incessantly, building up six-foot drifts in the mountains; temperatures fell far below freezing; pack animals dropped dead from lack of food; nearly everyone suffered frostbite. In desperation, Frémont sent four men toward Taos for help. Meanwhile, the terrible cold began to take its human toll, as one man after another collapsed by the wayside. Many who lost the will to live, froze to death. When the rescue team failed to return by January 11, Frémont took the strongest survivors and led them toward Taos for help. Ten days of hard travel through the San Luis Valley, guided part of the way by a friendly Ute, brought them to Taos, whence Godey led a relief party back to where the remainder of the expedition had camped. Ten men died; many others suffered severe frostbite and malnutrition. "There has never," one participant concluded, "been a more total defeat of any party in these mountains."[39]

Frémont's arrival in Taos precipitated a momentous decision for Carson. His old commander needed his aid, and when Frémont asked if Kit would accompany him to California, Carson seemed inclined to accept. On the other hand, there were family considerations—perhaps the time had come to abandon the "roving life" and settle down. Carson finally refused the Pathfinder's request, arguing that he could not "break off from Maxwell and family connections" and announced his intention to move to Rayado. "Now was the time, if ever," Carson recalled in his memoirs, "to make a home for ourselves and our children. We were getting old and could not expect to remain any length of time able to gain a livelihood as we had been [for] such a number of years." Carson and Frémont stood together for a final photograph before bidding farewell. The Pathfinder left Taos February 13, bound for California with most of his surviving men. In April, Carson and Maxwell crossed the mountains to Rayado to begin "building . . . , making improvements, and . . . becoming prosperous."[40]

Carson's move to Rayado contributed significantly to the growth of the settlement and the ultimate development of Lucien Maxwell's empire in the Southwest. The place became famous largely because of Kit's presence. Moreover, his experience as a mountaineer, hunter, and Indian scout proved valuable in warding off Indian attack and negotiating with the tribes that frequented the front range of the Rockies. Maxwell had a reputation, probably deserved, for being obstinate and unwilling to accept the advice of others. Be that as it may, one man he respected, his mentor in the ways of the frontier, was Kit Carson. Lucien undoubtedly learned a great deal from the older man during their association. Important, too, were Kit's connections with the army. If help from soldiers was needed to protect the settlement, he had the prestige and influence needed to persuade the troops to come.

Carson was only one of a number of new settlers who immigrated to Rayado in the spring of 1849. By mid-summer, visitor Charles E. Pancoast reported the presence of more than a dozen Mexicans and Americans, twenty Indian men, and several Indian women. All ate together at a single table, which, the Pennsylvania visitor observed after noticing how much was wasted around the place, was "of no mean order." The new settlers brought in cattle, sheep, horses, and mules, all of which grew fat from the lush grass in the region. Four farmers who arrived that spring began tilling the soil and digging ditches to bring water to their fields. The buildings could not, according to Pancoast, "be said to be stylish." Inside high adobe walls built for protection against the Indians were a two-storied log house and several adobe buildings. Outside were several more huts, a corral, stables, and a slaughter-house.[41]

Indians posed serious threats to the frontier settlement. At almost the same time Pancoast was visiting Rayado, Lieutenant John Whittlesey reported from Taos that the Apaches were "robbing everywhere throughout the mountains." In order to prevent anyone in the area from being massacred, he ordered Sergeant Williams, fifteen dragoons, and thirty volunteers to Rayado.[42] Their presence did not eliminate attacks. In October, 1849, James M. White, a prominent trader, left New Mexico en route to Missouri with thirteen loaded wagons and a party that included his wife, small daughter, and a number of other employees and travelers. Apaches attacked them sometime the twenty-fourth or twenty-fifth, while White was camped along the Cimarron branch of the Santa Fe Trail, forty-five miles east of Rayado. The next train that passed found the dead bodies of White and other men. Mrs. White, her daughter, and a black woman slave were missing, presumably kidnapped by the Indians.[43]

New Mexican governor James S. Calhoun moved swiftly to rally whatever forces he could to save the women. Major William N. Grier led an army expedition to Rayado, where they met Carson. Kit reached the scene of the attack first. The trunks had been broken open, the harnesses cut, and "everything destroyed that the Indians could not carry with them." For ten or twelve days they pursued the Apaches, but the Jicarillas split into groups of two or three, making pursuit very difficult. When they finally caught sight of the Indians, Major Grier and his men waited to parley. The Apaches seemed to be packing up when suddenly, without warning, a shot rang out. Grier was hit. Fortunately the ball struck his pocket, inside of which were his heavy riding gloves. The shot imbedded itself in the leather, causing Grier no more serious injury than a sick stomach. Grier quickly recovered his wits and ordered an attack. Too late. Only one Indian remained in camp, and nearby lay the warm body of Mrs. White, dead less than five minutes. Carson was horrified and angry at what he considered to be a poor decision on Grier's part, even though in the pursuit that followed one Indian was killed and two or three more taken prisoner. The ultimate irony came when Carson found a popular dime novel among the Whites' baggage which extolled Carson's heroism as an Indian fighter. "I have often thought that as Mrs. White would read the same," Carson recalled bitterly, "and knowing that I lived near, she would pray for my appearance and that she would be saved."[44]

Publicity given the White massacre convinced the army of the need to station soldiers in the area. Only by locating men along the Santa Fe Trail, ready to take the offense whenever necessary, they believed, could the Indians be pacified. The presence of troops at or near Rayado would deter Indians from attacking. Other advantages soon became apparent: there were few potential purchasers for the fodder, livestock, garden produce, and other items grown at a settlement like Rayado. The army provided an excellent market and source of income, as Maxwell and Beaubien had already discovered in Taos. Elsewhere, ambitious entrepreneurs exaggerated the Indian menace in order to obtain lucrative contracts from army posts near their ranches, and the possibility of such a situation at Rayado cannot be entirely ignored.[45] Grier ordered a Sergeant Holbrook, whom Carson characterized as a "gallant and brave soldier," and ten dragoons to spend the winter at Rayado on temporary reassignment from Taos.[46]

The Jicarillas soon provided additional evidence to justify the permanent assignment of soldiers in the region. Two miles from Rayado, probably along the river west of the houses, Maxwell had set up a small "rancho" presided over by two men, where gentle riding stock grazed. In March, 1850, the Indians swept down on the pair, severely wounding both. One summoned help from Rayado, and the next morning Carson, Sergeant Holbrook, his men, and three civilian volunteers rode off in pursuit. Twenty-five miles out they charged the Indians, killing five, and recaptured all but four of the stolen horses. It was time for vengeance: the victors peeled off five bloody Indian scalps, which they carried back to Rayado in triumph. "I regard the affair as a very handsome one," reported Captain Grier, apparently unashamed of such brutality, and "very creditable to the sergeant and his men."[47]

Not long after this successful foray, one of Maxwell's oldest friends died at Rayado. Bill New, like Lucien an Illinois native, had worked for Bent, St. Vrain and Company at the same time as Maxwell and later raised stock in southern Colorado. In 1850, New moved to Rayado, where he had built a cabin for his wife and three children. In March he accompanied Carson on the triumphant expedition to recover the stolen horses. Later that spring, New was plowing his fields near Rayado when a band of Jicarilla Apaches surprised him. He managed to grab a gun and put up what has been characterized as a "desperate fight for his life by clubbing his enemies" with his rifle. All efforts were insufficient, however, and he was killed — the end, lamented Carson, of a "brave and experienced trapper."[48]

The murders of Mrs. White and Bill New plus constant attacks on livestock persuaded the army to establish a permanent military station at Rayado. The required orders were issued May 24, 1850, creating what was called "Post at Rayado." The initial complement consisted of forty-three men from Companies G and I of the First Dragoons. Each had a horse and a carbine. A six-pound cannon and a mountain howitzer added to the firepower of the tiny post. The presence of the army added to Maxwell's growing prosperity. The soldiers moved into the building where Lucien and his family had resided; a new house was constructed for the officers. Sheds twelve feet wide around the inside of an adobe corral provided protection for the dragoons' horses. All these facilities Lucien rented to the government for $200 a month.[49]

The presence of the soldiers provided Maxwell with advantages over other settlements. The only other troops in the entire region were at Taos and Las Vegas. Major George A. McCall, who inspected the post in September, 1850, found it an ideal place from which to defend the area. "It is," he explained, "near the range of the Comanches and

and other wild tribes of the prairie, and, at the same time covers better than any other point the line of highly fertile yet unsettled lands that stretch along the base of the mountains and border the numerous streams which gush from their sides." From Rayado it was possible to strike at the Apaches' winter camps along the Canadian River; Indian traffic between Taos and the plains could be intercepted. It appeared to be, he summarized, "in every respect, a most eligible site for a frontier post."[50]

Maxwell earned his first substantial income from the army. Besides the $2,400 annually paid him for quarters, which increased in 1851 to $3,400, Maxwell negotiated with Lieutenant Whittlesey to sell "fair quality" native hay cut four miles from the settlement for $20 per ton. He delivered a total of nearly thirty thousand pounds during the last quarter of 1851 alone. Moreover, Lucien sold supplies and food to individual soldiers, and the army provided employment for three civilian herders and two teamsters at Rayado. An army inspector, after reviewing the costs of the post, admitted that it was "somewhat expensive" to maintain.[51] There may have been other profits, too. According to one story, perhaps apocryphal, Lieutenant Whittlesey felt sorry for Maxwell because of his losses in the Manco Burro Pass massacre and offered him a "lift." Jesse Nelson, who accompanied Carson back to Rayado from Missouri in 1851, recalled that he had been employed by Lucien to buy up forage from farmers in the Rayado area. They sold it to Fort Union for $48 a ton, twice what they had paid for it and much more than the army paid at Rayado. And they were not even big tons, Nelson added.[52]

The establishment of the Post at Rayado and the income it provided to Maxwell encouraged the commencement of a major building project at the new settlement. With soldiers occupying his original home, Lucien began construction of an immense house, consisting eventually of sixteen to twenty rooms facing onto a square that contained nearly an acre of land. Even though the structures were flat-roofed and built of adobe, many of their archi-

Maxwell's Rayado home, which has been preserved by the Philmont Scout Ranch with very few changes. The original roof was flat.

tectural features were reminiscent of the Menard mansion and other fine buildings in Kaskaskia and Sainte Genevieve. Maxwell's house had dormered windows, for example, and wide porches facing the front and the court. Maxwell installed wooden floors, heavy doors, and planed sashes. "They were," observed Calvin Jones, "the best houses there were in that country at that time."[53]

Despite the advantages of their presence, the soldiers failed to halt Indian attacks. During the summer of 1850, soon after the troops reached Rayado, Utes or Apaches (no

Courtesy Seton Museum, Cimarron, New Mexico.

one was certain which) drove off a herd of livestock almost within sight of the town. Maxwell lost four mules, six horses, and 175 head of cattle valued at over $5,000. The Indians killed an army bugler walking alone in the nearby countryside and one of the farmers living at Rayado.[54] Taos citizens including Maxwell, Beaubien, and Carson petitioned Governor John Monroe for an expedition against the marauders. By late July, 1850, more than 150 men led by Grier, who was now breveted to the rank of major, left Rayado in pursuit. They caught up with the Jicarillas in the mountains west of modern-day Raton, but before an attack could be launched the Indians fled into the timber. Several Apaches were killed, and much of the livestock stolen from Maxwell was recovered. In November the Apaches again drove off several hundred cattle from Rayado. This time Carson led soldiers onto the plains, where they recovered the stolen animals, killed seven Indians, and captured a child.[55]

Although the troops provided protection for Rayado, government officials questioned whether or not they should remain. Some authorities wondered whether Rayado was the best location for a post. In March, 1851, Lieutenant John G. Parke concluded that trees, brush, and low hills surrounding the settlement provided such excellent cover for Indians that it was impossible to detect a surprise attack. Parke suggested a site ten miles north, between the Cimarron and Ponil creeks. Other military officials debated the broader question of whether it was advisable to station small contingents of soldiers at a number of remote locations such as Rayado or to establish a few large forts manned by enough soldiers to conduct major campaigns against the Indians. E. V. Sumner, who took command of the Ninth Military Department in 1851, favored the latter policy, and in mid-May he initiated construction of a massive post, Fort Union, along the Moro River south of Rayado. On July 25, therefore, he ordered the post at Rayado broken up.[56]

Lucien Maxwell protested. In leaving his and other settlements without protection, he argued, the government was inviting the massacre of dozens of innocent settlers. Maxwell must have been sufficiently persuasive or influential that Sumner agreed that a guard composed of one noncommissioned officer and fourteen privates could remain at Rayado for another three months. He required that Lucien provide free quarters and stabling, however, and that he escort Captain John Pope on an expedition to explore a possible wagon route between Rayado and Fort Leavenworth.[57]

Maxwell's activities were not limited to Rayado and its growing pains. He and Carson spent part of the summer of 1851 with eighteen others who were trapping in Colorado and Wyoming. It was a sentimental return to country they had once known well—along the South Platte through Old and New Park, down the Arkansas to the plains, and south to Rayado. "This was more of a pleasure trip," Kit's most recent biographer concluded, "organized as a final farewell to the old life that Carson loved so well . . . ." The expedition proved profitable, too, for the party brought back a successful catch of furs.[58] During the fall of 1851 Maxwell accompanied Pope on an exploration of the plains east of Rayado.[59]

Other trips were more extensive. Ever since the discovery of gold at John Sutter's mill in 1848, the attention of America had focused on California. As thousands of gold seekers trekked across the continent, food supplies on the Pacific coast became increasingly scarce and expensive. In 1852 "Uncle Dick" Wootton, the mountaineer who had helped rescue Lucien after the Manco Burro Pass massacre, bought 9,000 New Mexico sheep and drove them overland to the gold country. They brought ten times what he had paid for them, earning Wootton more than $40,000.[60] Others soon took advantage of what appeared to be a lucrative opportunity. John Hatcher, who had settled on the Ponil several years earlier, departed for California in late January, 1853; the next month Kit Carson acquired 6,500 head of sheep in southern New Mexico and headed them to Rayado, where he joined Henry Mercure, John Bernavette, and others for the trip west.

Maxwell set out a month later with still a third herd. The trip north to Wyoming and then west along what was now a well-traveled route followed by thousands of prospectors and their families was uneventful. Maxwell sold his sheep in Sacramento, then joined Carson for the return trip. Lucien traveled by steamer down the coast to Los Angeles, arriving fifteen days before Kit, who rode a mule in order to avoid the seasickness he had suffered during a similar voyage with Frémont. The two returned to New Mexico along the Gila River route pioneered by F. X. Aubrey, and by Christmas, 1853, they were back in Taos.[61] The trip proved extremely profitable. Estimates of Lucien's income range from $20,000 to $50,000. John Boggs recalled that when Kit and Lucien returned to Taos, "they had so much money they didn't know what to do with it."[62]

Several reports describe other trips taken by Maxwell and Carson to California, but none is based on substantial documentary evidence, and all probably represent embellishments of the 1853 visit. William L. Ryus, who came to Cimarron in the 1860s, described a journey to California during which Carson and Maxwell earned nearly $100,000. On the way home along the Oregon Trail they lost all the proceeds to bandits. According to Ryus, they quickly got together two more herds of sheep, drove them to California, and returned safely.[63] Antoine Leroux, a veteran mountaineer and acquaintance of Maxwell, recalled that on another occasion Maxwell set off for California with four or five thousand sheep, but he went only as far as the Great Salt Lake, where the animals were sold to Mormons.[64]

The money Lucien made selling sheep to the miners helped him support a growing family. The increased safety at Rayado must have persuaded Lucien to bring his family across the mountains from Taos sometime in the early 1850s, and daughter Emilia was born at Rayado in 1852. Sofia was born there in 1854, as was Maria Eleanore, two years later.[65] Maxwell's older children were baptized in Taos, probably by Father Antonio José Martínez, but the names of the last two girls do not appear in the Taos Parish records, suggesting either that the journey across the mountains was too arduous or that the family worshipped elsewhere, perhaps in Mora. There is also evidence that Lucien himself lacked serious religious interests, although Mrs. Maxwell probably was more devout.[66]

Growing prosperity also made it possible for Lucien to provide his family with comfortable accommodations. Dr. Dewitt C. Peters, a Taos army doctor who wrote the first biography of Kit Carson, described Lucien's mansion, which he probably had visited, as "an ornament to any country." Its "lofty ceilings, large and airy rooms, and its fine yard in the center of the square" presented "a picture of sumptuous living rarely seen within the pale of civilization." The neighboring countryside along the Rayado contained the houses of others who worked at the settlement and all the needed outbuildings. Maxwell had devoted a great deal of time and money to developing the property, Dr. Peters reported, and he showed "honest pride" in "being master of a model farm."[67]

No matter what Maxwell did, however, only the pacification of the Indians could ultimately bring prosperity to the eastern side of the Sangre de Cristos. Just how serious the situation had become was demonstrated by Indian attacks which continued until the mid-1850s. In 1852 a band including Jicarillas, Utes, and Navajos raided the Greenhorn settlement in southern Colorado, where many Rayado farmers had lived. Soon afterward they ambushed a detachment of soldiers, perhaps part of the Rayado guard, in Ute Park along the Cimarron River. In a third incident, Indians stole cattle from Samuel B. Watrous, a rancher south of Rayado. They were pursued onto the plains by United States troops, and during a brief skirmish an important Jicarilla chief named Lobo was killed, along with several other Indians and soldiers. Apparently in retaliation, in March, 1854, Apaches attacked, perhaps from ambush, sixty soldiers led by Lieutenant John W. Davidson along Cieneguilla Creek between Rayado and Taos. Many of the troops died, including Sergeant Holbrook, who had commanded the Rayado contingent.[68]

April 8, 1854, the *Santa Fe Weekly Gazette* announced a "terrible slaughter by Indians" at Rayado. According to reports the paper had received, Indians had attacked the Maxwell ranch several days earlier and "killed every body living in it, in all, eight women, and ten men, and two or three children." According to the paper, the Apaches had crossed the mountains soon after the Battle of Cieneguilla, found Rayado "comparatively defenseless," and obliterated it. The *Gazette* used the story to challenge the government's existing Indian policy. "This is," the editor angrily proclaimed, "but *another* outrage to add to their catalogue of crimes yet, we hope, to be dearly atoned for, *another* of the many acts of violence and blood which follow their trail, and with which the history of this Territory abounds." "Is it not time," he asked, "for the government to change its existing Indian policy?"[69]

The report of the Rayado attack, even though entirely inaccurate, helped bring about the changes which the Santa Fe editor and many others urged. In 1854, Kit Carson was appointed Indian agent for northern New Mexico. He had seen at first hand the death and destruction wrought by the Indians, and he argued that if only the power of the government were made known to the natives, they would abandon their attacks, cease being so arrogant, and settle down on a reservation.[70] Encouraged by Carson, the army initiated a series of important campaigns to chastise the Utes and Apaches. During the early summer of 1854, Colonel Philip St. George Cooke led a hundred regular troops and forty volunteer "spies" commanded by Maxwell's business associate James H. Quinn against the Jicarillas. They located and attacked an Apache camp atop a mesa near Raton Pass. Most of the Indians escaped, but nearly all their supplies and camp gear were destroyed.[71] The next year Colonel Thomas Fauntleroy organized an even larger expedition that included regular dragoons, an artillery company, and volunteers. More than five hundred men left Fort Massachusetts March 14. Attacks on Ute camps during the spring inflicted several "stinging defeats." They also pursued the Jicarillas throughout the mountains of southern Colorado and northern New Mexico. Although no decisive engagement was fought, the Indians were sufficiently weakened by the unremitting pursuit that they were ready for peace.[72]

By September, 1855, the Utes and Apaches were willing to conclude a formal treaty with the Americans. The five hundred Indians who met New Mexico's Governor David Meriwether at Abiquiu "expressed themselves tired of war, and desirous to live upon friendly terms with the whites." In the treaty they negotiated, the Indians agreed to move west to a new reservation beyond the Río Grande.[73] Taos residents, led by Judge Beaubien and Father Martínez, objected to the treaty because it located the Indians too near their settlements, and ultimately the federal government refused to ratify it. The Indians were left without a designated reservation and became dependent on agent Carson for handouts of food, blankets, and clothing.[74] Never again did they pose a serious threat to the inhabitants of the northeastern frontier of New Mexico.

Not so the Comanches, Kiowas, and Arapahos. After the defeat of their traditional mountain enemies, the Plains Indians made still more frequent visits to Rayado and other settlements to demand food and steal whatever they could. Once a German boy who was getting water from the Rayado found himself confronted by a party of Plains Indians. They soon congregated outside the main gate of the Maxwell compound to demand food. Mountaineer Tom Boggs, a longtime employee of Maxwell, recommended that the settlers offer a feast while someone rode to Fort Union to get help from the soldiers. The women spent the day preparing food and serving it to the chiefs. Fortunately, just as the Indians' impatience was growing to the point where an attack seemed imminent, Carson and a company of troops rode in from Fort Union, and the warriors left.[75]

This incident is indicative of Maxwell's pragmatic approach to dealing with Indians. For years the Plains tribes had paid what one author terms "dinner stops" to ranches along the frontier. Lucien recognized that he was helpless to prevent them from coming to Rayado and accepted their visits gracefully. Indians could expect to receive food, clothing, and other supplies from Lucien, who sometimes traded horses with them. On occasion he provided the Comanches with "good conduct" certificates. On the other hand, Maxwell had learned that federal compensation was available for losses to hostile Indians, so whenever something was stolen, he complained to the government, called on the army to pacify the natives, and filed for compensation. In July, 1855, for example, Maxwell reported that Comanches had killed two hundred of his sheep, stolen a mule, and taken off whatever "loose property" they could carry. Governor Meriwether found Maxwell's seemingly contradictory behavior puzzling, but to Lucien it represented an ingenious way of dealing with a difficult situation.[76]

Despite the continuing menace of the Plains tribes, the land along the eastern edge of the Rockies in northeastern New Mexico had been substantially pacified by the mid-1850s. Whereas a decade earlier only the bravest settlers dared inhabit the area, and even the most venturesome left their families in Taos, the number of farmers and towns was now increasing rapidly. Livestock grazed on the rich grasses in relative security, and it was seldom necessary to summon troops. The Utes and Jicarillas had been driven near submission, and a kind of rapprochement had been established with the Plains tribes. During the years he had lived at Rayado, Lucien Maxwell had accumulated substantial wealth—enough to free himself from dependence on his friends and relatives. The time had come, Lucien concluded by about 1857, to leave Rayado and found a new settlement that could be entirely his own.

5

Maxwell's Ranch

CHANGES in New Mexico by the late 1850s offered exceptional opportunities to an ambitious young man like Lucien Maxwell. The military occupation largely ended as the army began to defend rather than oppress the area's Mexican-American residents. As the northern frontier became increasingly safe after the defeat of the Utes and Jicarillas, farmers and ranchers pushed onto new lands, built homes, guided plows across virgin fields, and began to reap the products of their labor. Settlers came to New Mexico hoping to get ahead in a hurry, make themselves wealthy, and assume positions of social, political, and economic influence far beyond their own backgrounds or proven abilities. Some migrated to Santa Fe, where they served in the territorial government, established stores, ran hotels, opened law offices, bought up land, sold supplies to the army, or simply encouraged more easterners to come west. Others, like Maxwell, chose to make their fortunes at a distance from the capital, in the parts of New Mexico where there were still frontiers to be conquered.

One way by which men like Maxwell amassed wealth and power was by taking over Mexican land grants. In the 1848 Treaty of Guadalupe Hidalgo a provision designed to protect Mexicans in the ownership of their land assured that land titles that had been valid according to Mexican law remained intact under the United States.[1] It was 1854, however, before the United States Congress established procedures for verifying titles and appointed William G.

Pelham as surveyor general for New Mexico. Soon after his arrival in Santa Fe, Pelham advertised in the *Weekly Gazette* that anyone claiming land by virtue of a Mexican grant should present documentary evidence to his office for consideration.[2] Lucien's father-in-law, Charles Beaubien, like other claimants, began compiling information. Perhaps to avoid many arduous trips from Taos to Santa Fe, Beaubien paid the prominent Santa Fe law firm of Houghton, Wheaton, and Smith $490 to investigate the legality of the grant obtained by him and Guadalupe Miranda. The petition that the attorneys filed with Pelham February 23, 1857, pointed out that part of the land had been "cultivated and improved" for twelve years, and had, as a result, "become of great value." Since the tract had never been surveyed, the attorneys explained that no "certain estimate of its contents" was possible. Only a "small portion," was fit for cultivation; "the balance owing to its mountainous character and scarcity of water" could be used only for pasturing livestock. Since no one else claimed the same tract or planned to contest the claimant's rights, the petitioners prayed that the grant be "confirmed to them under the laws of the United States."[3]

The process of confirmation continued during the spring and summer of 1857. Once he had received the necessary papers, Pelham scheduled a public hearing for the third Thursday in March. In inviting public comment he identified the Beaubien and Miranda property as the "Rayado grant," suggesting that Lucien Maxwell's settlement there had become the principal identifying landmark in the region.[4] No hearing was held until July 28, when several long-term residents, including Kit Carson, testified that the required legal ceremonies had been conducted and that farms and ranches had indeed been established.[5] Pelham seemed satisfied, despite the obvious questions as to the extent of the claim, and on September 17, 1857, reported to the General Land Office in Washington that the Beaubien and Miranda claim was "a good and valid grant according to the laws and customs of the Republic of Mexico and the decisions of the Supreme Court of the United States."[6]

These activities occurred without the participation of Miranda. After the American takeover of New Mexico, the former Mexican official had fled the territory, and in February, 1858, he was living in El Paso del Norte (later renamed Ciudad Juarez), Chihuahua, Mexico. He apparently crossed the border to the Texas town of Franklin February 24, 1858, to write to Beaubien describing the lamentable state into which he had fallen. "Thrust out from my own country, a portion of my property abandoned, the rest for a year and months at the mercy of my enemies," he explained, his resources had been so reduced that he found it difficult to support his family. His sole remaining asset was the property he and Beaubien owned jointly. Once before, Charles Bent had proposed purchasing the grant, he continued, but the offer had been rejected because Miranda wished to reserve it for his "sons as New Mexicans." Now he had no choice. Already several offers had been received, but Miranda was reluctant to conclude a sale without consulting his partner, to whom he now gave the first option to buy. "So if you do not wish to purchase my part," Miranda finished, "then I will sell it to another of those who seek to purchase." Miranda himself was unable or unwilling to return to New Mexico, but he promised to send his son Pablo with power to act in his place.[7]

Beaubien had no interest in purchasing Miranda's share, but he introduced Pablo Miranda to his son-in-law, Lucien Maxwell. On April 7, 1858, Maxwell signed papers by which he acquired Miranda's share. He paid $1,000 down and promised a second $1,000 installment on July 1, 1858, and $500 when Congress confirmed the grant. In addition, Maxwell paid Beaubien $245 for half the expenses incurred in having the legality of the grant investigated.[8] With the conveyance of deeds, for a total payment of only $2,745, Lucien Maxwell took a gigantic step toward establishing himself as a major figure in the history of New Mexico.

The acquisition of Miranda's share of the grant coincided with another strategic move on Maxwell's part. For close to two decades he had served apprenticeships on the frontier, gaining important knowledge and skills from the likes of Frémont, Carson, and Beaubien. He had been an able student, acquiring abilities needed to operate successfully in the Southwest. He had come a poor man, had adroitly accumulated the profits of several successful business ventures, and had ended up with enough money to make more extensive plans. Rayado, Lucien realized, was no place to build his empire. He knew, even if his visitors often thought otherwise, that the settlement had been founded and to some extent remained under Beaubien's auspices. Whoever lived there would inevitably fall under Beaubien's shadow. Moreover, once the danger of Indian attack subsided, wagon trains more often cut directly across the plains, east of what became known as Kit Carson Mesa, missing Rayado entirely.[9] The old trail across the mountains to Taos fell into disuse as other, more direct routes developed. And perhaps then, as occasionally is still the case, a drought revealed to Maxwell how fickle a stream the Rayado could be. Without water crops died and livestock had to be sold.

The banks of the Cimarron River, ten miles to the north, offered better possibilities. The word "cimarron" had originally described a fugitive West Indian slave but came to be used more broadly to refer to people or animals that were wild or unruly. In New Mexico wild bighorn sheep were called *cimarrones;* some have argued that the Cimarron River and the region through which it flows were named because of the presence of these magnificent animals in the area.[10] Others have generalized more broadly that the river, the whole country, or the people who inhabited it were wild. "The Spanish word *cimarron* means wild, untamed, unbroken," wrote Agnes Morley Cleveland, and its history could be perceived as a series of largely unsuccessful attempts to tame the Cimarron country. "All the wildness of this wild land," she concluded, "was rounded up and left to bellow in the tiny New Mexican town which Lucien B. Maxwell founded . . . ."[11]

The Cimarron had many advantages over the Rayado. It was a larger, stronger stream, better fed and more reliable. As it poured out of the mountains through a narrow, picturesque canyon today followed by U.S. 64, it flowed onto a broad, fertile plain, protected from winter storms by low, surrounding hills and mesas. Here was ample room for thousands of sheep and cattle to graze and for vast fields of corn, wheat, and fodder. Most of the Jicarilla Apaches who had once camped along its banks were gone, and, as Surveyor John G. Parke had noted in recommending alternative military sites to Rayado, the area had many strategic advantages in case of attack by the Plains Indians.[12] Stages running between the eastern settlements and Santa Fe often camped there for the night, and the Cimarron River had cut a fairly direct, although as yet largely undeveloped, route toward Taos. With sufficient energy and capital, the area could be developed into an important crossroads in northern New Mexico.

Exactly when Lucien moved his headquarters to the Cimarron is not known. Farmers had lived there at least seasonally since the mid-1840s, and at first the Cimarron may have been one of several locations where herders watched over Maxwell's cattle and sheep. Probably by the mid-1850s, Mexican-Americans who had farmed at Rayado moved there and began work on a substantial residence and other buildings for Maxwell. According to family tradition, Lucien talked about his plans during an 1858 visit to Kaskaskia, during which daughter Marie Elenore died before her second birthday. Lucien reportedly encouraged his elderly mother to accompany him back to New Mexico, but she declined, because of her advanced age.[13] One of his objectives in making the long trip may well have been to purchase furniture and other goods for the new house, and probably by 1858 or early 1859 the Maxwell family had established itself on the Cimarron at what soon became known as "Maxwell's Ranche [sic]."

Before the move could be completed, Lucien had to dispose of his Rayado interests. Whatever informal agreements may have existed between him and Beaubien, no deed had ever formally transferred possession of the Rayado tract, perhaps partly because such legal formalities were not customary on the New Mexican frontier. This potentially troublesome situation was cleared up in September, 1858, perhaps while Maxwell was still in Kaskaskia, when Beaubien and his wife signed a quitclaim deed transferring to Lucien title in the Rayado Ranch stretching two and a half miles in every direction from what was termed "Maxwell's Plaza." The price, recognizing contributions Maxwell had made to the development of the property over the preceding ten years, was only $500. Almost immediately Maxwell sold the property to Spaniard José Pley, a resident of Mora who had married the sister of Stephen Louis Lee, the partner of Beaubien's son Narciso, killed in the Taos uprising. The couple soon divorced, and Pley shortly sold the tract to Jesús Abreú, the husband of Beaubien's daughter Petra, who farmed it for many years.[14]

Not everyone was pleased at the property transfers occurring along the Sangre de Cristos. In March, 1843, in exchange for his supervision of the colonization of their grant, Beaubien and Miranda had given Charles Bent a one-fourth interest in the property.[15] Bent, of course, died in the Taos uprising before he could contribute significantly to the settlement of the region, whereupon Beaubien and Miranda either forgot their agreement or assumed that with Bent dead the deal was cancelled. In September, 1859, however, the Bent heirs—a son, two daughters, and their husbands—sued Miranda, Beaubien, Pley, and Maxwell in New Mexico district court, claiming a one-third (later modified to one-fourth) interest in the grant.[16] The case was complicated and dragged on for many years before it was settled.

Meanwhile, the house which Lucien had built on the Cimarron became one of the best-known landmarks in northern New Mexico. One visitor characterized it as "a

Jesús G. Abreú, Maxwell's brother-in-law and successor at Rayado. Courtesy Seton Museum, Cimarron, New Mexico.

palace when compared to the prevailing style of architecture of that country."[17] "Palacial for that region," said another, while a third visitor termed it "exceedingly comfortable."[18] The main building, like nearly all houses in New Mexico, was built of adobe bricks, which were easily manufactured and provided excellent insulation against chilling winter wind and dry summer heat. The general design of the house was reminiscent of the styles prevalent at Kaskaskia when Lucien grew up there. Comparisons with Grandfather Menard's mansion overlooking the Mississippi are unavoidable: a wide porch across the front, dormer windows on the second floor, and massive brick chimneys rising above the peaked roof could well have been copied from the famed Illinois mansion where Lucien had spent much of his youth.[19] "It was large and roomy," recalled Colonel Henry Inman, a frequent visitor to the Cimarron, "purely American in its construction." "The rooms were large," remembered Irving Howbert, "having high ceilings finished with moulding."[20]

The main dining room, where Maxwell entertained

his male visitors, was "an extended rectangular affair," which, in Inman's opinion, "might properly have been termed the Baronial Hall . . . . There," he continued, "Maxwell received his friends, transacted business with his vassals, and held high carnival at times." A separate dining room and parlor were provided for the women in accordance with local custom. And there were numerous sleeping rooms for family members, guests, and servants.[21]

Some rooms were elaborately decorated, with "deep-piled carpets, heavy velvet draperies, gold framed paintings." The furniture, much of it hauled across the Santa Fe Trail, was "of the most massive Victorian sort." Even to this day, no antique is more prized by old families in northeastern New Mexican than one reputed to have come from the Maxwell mansion. Reportedly, Lucien purchased and brought from the states four pianos, two for the first floor of the house and two more for the second. "It still seems to me," a writer who had visited the house as a child recalled after many years, "a little overdone, even now."[22]

Not all the rooms, at least in the early days, were so lavish. "The room we slept in," Howbert recalled, "was carpeted but had not even a chair. However, in one corner there was a pile of wool mattresses and bedding from which the servants made beds for us on the floor at night. So far as we saw," he went on, "there was only one room in the house that had a bedstead, and that was the one occupied by Maxwell and his wife."[23] "I have slept on its hardwood floor," Henry Inman pridefully reminisced, "rolled up in my blanket." "I have sat there in the long winter evenings, when the great room was lighted only by the cheerful blaze of the crackling logs roaring up the huge throats of its two fireplaces, built diagonally across opposite corners, watching Maxwell, Kit Carson, and half a dozen chiefs . . . until the glimmer of Aurora announced the advent of another day."[24]

The house was only one of several structures Maxwell had built on the south bank of the Cimarron. A large wooden barn reminded one visitor of many he had ob-

Maxwell's house on the Cimarron. From Inman, The Old Santa
Fé Trail.

served in Pennsylvania.[25] The structure may not have been
entirely suited to New Mexico, for one of the Indian agents
assigned to Cimarron complained of having to store his
annuity goods there, mixed up with Lucien's "produce
and dye stuffs," because they were subject to the destructive powers of "hundreds of industrious mice."[26] In another, smaller building two Navajo women spent their days
weaving rugs on Indian looms. Nearby was a general store,
"well filled with everything necessary for a frontier man's
life," supplying goods to local residents and serving as a
wholesaler to a number of little outlying stores in the
region. This business must have been one of Lucien's
more profitable activities, for, as William Hoehne, who
traded there for many years, reported, a 300 to 500 percent
markup on merchandise was common.[27] Later Lucien acquired a second store in Taos, purchased from a Jewish
merchant named Soloman Beuthner and run by Henry
Stillman; he also bought a store in Elizabethtown from

Santa Fe businessman V. S. Shelby, and opened one on
Ute Creek for miners living there.[28]

Maxwell's most ambitious building project was a massive stone mill for grinding corn and wheat into flour.
Alone among his major buildings, it has survived well
over a hundred years and serves today as a museum preserving historic relics from the area. By 1860, to supervise
its construction, Maxwell had already hired a Boston-born
engineer, B. M. Blackmore; millwright Emory Williams,
a New Yorker; and a Vermont-born mason, James Truax.
Building costs reportedly totaled $48,000.[29] The work went
slowly, for in mid-summer, 1864, the Santa Fe *New Mexican*
reported that Maxwell, "one of our most prominent and
successful stockmen," was building a "grist mill capable of
turning out three hundred barrels of flour per day." The
editor added that "we welcome all such enterprises as indi-
cations of the onward progress of our territory."[30] Two
years later, a visitor found the "lately finished" mill to be
"well and complete[ly] constructed, and the machinery
perfect." The excellence of the flour that he saw attested
to the general success of the undertaking.[31]

The mill, too, turned a handsome profit for Maxwell.
It was capable of grinding fifteen thousand pounds of wheat
a day, producing forty-four barrels of flour. Local residents
consumed some of the produce, and more was sold in the
growing towns of New Mexico and Colorado. The location
of an Indian agency at Cimarron after 1861, the arrival of
many new settlers and gold miners in the area, and shortages caused by the Civil War contributed to increasing
Maxwell's profits. As a result, John D. Lee reported that
once the mill was complete it kept grinding "most all the
time" just to keep up with the increasing demand. By
1869 miller Isaah Rinehart estimated annual profits from
the grist mill at $26,440.[32]

Besides Maxwell and his family, a substantial community grew up along the Cimarron. Except for Jesús
Abreú and a man named Valdez who lived on the Rayado,
all residents, recalled Albert W. Archibald, were "in some

manner the tenants of Maxwell."[33] Many resided in the
Maxwell mansion itself. Rancher A. J. Calhoun recalled
that whenever he was working for Lucien or during frequent visits he "lived in the house as one of the family."
William R. Walker characterized the Maxwell residence as
"the resort of old-timers," recalling that people came there
from far and near—army officers, retired mountain men,
and aging pioneers.[34] Most area residents came originally
from Rayado. Calvin Jones, who had known Maxwell since
the 1840s, reported that when Lucien left the Rayado, he
took "the whole outfit with him." Others came from Mora,
Taos, or other towns in the area. The majority were Mexican-Americans—Sandovals and Vigils, Montoyas, Garcías,
and Lobatos, the ancestors of families whose names still
fill the telephone books and adorn the rural mailboxes of
northeastern New Mexico.[35]

Irving Howbert wrote that when he visited Maxwell's,
"a considerable part" of the land in the area was being
worked by "tenants or peons belonging to Maxwell" and
estimated their total number at a thousand.[36] John D. Lee
recalled that when he first went to the Cimarron in the
mid-1860s, men working under Maxwell were cultivating
land along the Cimarron from the mouth of Cimarron
Canyon to the river's intersection with the Ponil, seven
or eight miles, and along the Ponil from the mouth of its
canyon to the Cimarron, another five or six miles.[37] An
abundance of land and shortages of water limited cultivation to a small proportion of the irrigable property, which
John Howell, who served as general superintendent of
Maxwell's farms for ten years, estimated could be increased
to 400,000 acres or more by sinking artesian wells or building ditches.[38] Henry Inman guessed the number of farmers
at five hundred, adding that even though most were peons,
Maxwell was "not a hard governor, and his people really
loved him, as he was ever their friend and adviser."[39] Benjamin H. Eaton, who later became governor of the state of
Colorado, exaggerated in describing himself as "one of
Maxwell's peons," and many others—Anglos as well as

Mexican Americans—who began farming on Maxwell's land later became well known and successful farmers, businessmen, or professionals.[40] In some cases Maxwell leased land on a sharecropping basis; he provided the seed and farm equipment, the farmers furnished the labor, and the profits were divided equally. Howell estimated in 1870 that even though some farmers had abandoned their farms to take up mining, Maxwell collected 100,000 bushels of wheat, corn, and oats as rent.[41]

At the bottom of the social ladder was a class of Indian slaves, nearly always women and children. During the 1850s and 1860s, Mexican-American soldiers were frequently encouraged to go to war with the Navajo Indians with promises that they could retain as personal slaves or booty any Indian they captured. Maxwell, like many New Mexicans at the time, purchased Indians, who were forced to carry out the most burdensome and disagreeable tasks with little hope of freedom. In Lucien's house, for example, the government census taker found in 1850, and again a decade later, and still in 1870, Indian servants, children aged seven or nine or thirteen, whose birthplace could be given with no more certainty than "Navajo Indian country."[42] Many took the Maxwell name, and one, Deluvina Maxwell, became famous as a friend of bandit Billy the Kid.[43]

The importance of the Maxwell ranch received official recognition in 1861 when the United States government established a post office at the place henceforth to be known as Cimarron. The first postmaster, not surprisingly, was Lucien Maxwell.[44] The same year, Maxwell's became a stop on the newly established Missouri Stage Company line linking Kansas City with Sante Fe,[45] and in 1868 the opening of a telegraph office at Lucien's connected Cimarron directly with the East.[46]

The empire that Lucien Maxwell established during the 1850s and early 1860s was based primarily on agriculture. "The sources of his wealth," concluded Colonel Inman, "were his cattle, sheep, and the products of his area of cultivated acres—barley, oats, and corn principally . . . ."[47] In 1864, the *Santa Fe New Mexican* reported that the grain raised at Lucien's ranch was "immense in quantity," and that he owned hundreds of cattle, mostly cows, "of improved breeds from the States." Even earlier, Lucien had shown Albert W. Archibald a thoroughbred bull that he had imported at a cost of between $1,500 and $2,000.[48] By 1866, Lucien had become interested in sheep raising. One visitor was impressed that he had bought a Spanish Merino from Vermont for the princely sum of $2,000. That might seem expensive, the writer explained, "but he is more than worth it to a man who has between twenty-five and thirty thousand head in his flocks."[49] William A. Bell concluded that Maxwell's introduction of high-quality sheep had "conferred a great benefit on the country." Lucien even imported cashmere goats, which were reported to "thrive well in this district." Maxwell's horses, his dogs, even his chickens, were reportedly "of the same style—the best that can be had."[50]

As his wealth increased, Maxwell became interested in fine race horses. Irving Howbert, during his 1865 visit to the ranch, found "many fine blooded horses, several of which were noted race animals." Near the house Lucien built a racetrack where people from all over New Mexico witnessed matches.[51] Another frequent visitor, Colonel Inman, reported that Lucien's "stud" included "some of the fleetest animals in the Territory," adding that "had he lived in England, he might have ruled the turf." In May of 1865, Maxwell's interest in racing led him to employ Squire T. Hart to take charge of the horses. For the next six years Hart raced Maxwell's horses against some of the best in the southwest. "He run [*sic*] a race every week or two," Hart recalled in old age, "and sometimes every day."[52] Upcoming races were frequently announced in the Pueblo and Santa Fe papers, often with predictions that high stakes would be bet on the outcomes.[53]

As the Cimarron ranch became better established, visitors commonly stopped there for the night on their way between the States and Santa Fe. Some were unable to proceed because of high water, severe storms, or the fall of darkness; others deliberately took advantage of an opportunity to spend an evening with a man whose fame was rapidly spreading. "A man is always welcome to Maxwell," reported one visitor, while another noted that Lucien was "one of the kindest, most generous and charitable men that lives."[54] One of Lucien's granddaughters, Adelina Welborn, recalled years later how much Maxwell enjoyed having guests and how the housekeepers knew to keep the massive dining room table set for "dozens of people at each meal." "Seldom," she went on, "was there a vacant place."[55] William Walker recalled having seen as many as fifty people sitting down to a meal at Maxwell's. There were so many guests to feed that Maxwell had a beef killed every day or two and ten or twelve sheep daily.[56] Those who partook of Maxwell's hospitality never forgot the occasion. William H. Ryus, an 1864 visitor to the ranch, recalled — as did many others — that the tables were thick with solid silver serving dishes and cutlery. The tablecloths were made of the finest woven floss. Huge platters of excellent, although presumably simple, fare flowed from a kitchen "presided over by dark faced maidens bossed by experienced old cronies [sic]."[57]

Even unexpected visitors were treated well. William Walker recalled that once he was conducting business at Fort Union when the doctor asked him to take some medicine to Maxwell. "I got to his house about 10 o'clock at night," Walker recalled years later. Maxwell was still up, and the two men went to the barn, put up the horses, and returned to the house. Even though it was late at night, Lucien called an Indian woman to prepare supper, and after eating, the two retired to Maxwell's room where they talked until midnight.[58]

On at least one occasion, however, Maxwell's hospitality failed to live up to its usual standard. It was near midnight when the coach carrying the first Sisters of Charity to come to New Mexico arrived in Cimarron. "The people were all asleep," recalled Sister Mallon, and there were "Indians lying about." The male passengers and the driver quickly disappeared, but the nuns, not knowing whether the Indians were "savage or civilized," spent the night huddled together in the coach. The next morning, when "the people found where we were," she continued, "they invited us into breakfast which invitation was gladly accepted." "Mrs. Maxwell treated us very kindly." The meal included hot green chili, and it was the first time the sisters had encountered this New Mexico specialty. "Each one kept quiet about the hot dish until all got well burned." Then, Sister Mallon confessed with embarrassment years later, came the exclamations, "Oh, I am burning up."[59]

There was never a charge for eating or sleeping at Maxwell's. Frequently, jockey Squire Hart recalled, when a man asked Maxwell for his bill after an overnight stay, Lucien answered, "What in hell have I sold you?" "Why I have stayed all night with you, sir," came the reply. "Why I don't keep a hotel," rebutted Maxwell, ending the conversation.[60] According to another widely repeated tale, one morning after he had enjoyed food and lodging from Lucien, a well-to-do Easterner approached his host to ask how much he owed. This time Maxwell was angered at the suggestion that he would take money for his hospitality and retorted that the charge would be twenty dollars. The astonished man had no choice but to pay and handed over a crisp federal greenback. With all the arrogance he could muster up, Maxwell rolled up the bill, ignited it at the fireplace, and used it to light his cigar.[61]

Such displays led many of Maxwell's visitors to assess his character and demeanor. "Maxwell is a well-built man with a fine face," reported one observer, "in which one sees the determination and self-reliance which had made him what he is, one of the most prominent men in New Mexico." Judge Kirby Benedict, writing in the *New Mexican*, added that he was "one of the most marked men, in the qualities of his character, to be found in any territory. . . . Nothing about him is narrow or diminutive. He is beloved and esteemed by his neighbors and dependents. He is a man of no personal parade. He is severely plain and unostentacious [sic]." His character was such that he would "face a regiment of tortures sooner than indulge for a moment the consciousness of mean action. . . . Such is Lucien B. Maxwell—he is an eminent illustration of what great energy and integrity can accomplish in this land."[62]

William R. Walker, a soldier at Fort Union during the 1860s and a frequent visitor to Maxwell's, estimated that Lucien's influence extended "all over New Mexico, more or less, at least 100 miles around him." "What was it," a questioner probed, "that enabled him to wield such power and influence?" "His generosity, hospitality, and disposition to do what was right by everybody and to treat everybody right, and his known bravery and manly way of dealing with everybody," Walker answered, won him "respect and confidence." But there was more: Maxwell's "firmness of will." "Where his mind was set on accomplishing an object," Walker continued, "there was nothing to prevent him from attempting to carry it out regardless of danger or cost or anything that stood in his way."[63] Another observer, while certain that he would have been a leader "if he had not had an acre of land," reported that "the people looked up to Maxwell as a kind of prince because he owned his grant property. . . . They generally sought his advice."[64]

Other stories recounted Lucien's generosity. Maurice LeDuc, an aging fur trapper, was living at the Cimarron in 1866 or 1867, when he became ill. Hopeful that the waters at Las Vegas Hot Springs would cure him, he helped himself to one of Maxwell's strongest burros, packed his few possessions aboard, and without asking permission or saying a word to Maxwell headed south to Las Vegas, where he found a room and began daily visits to the springs. Eventually he heard that Lucien was staying at one of the town's hotels. According to the report of the man with whom LeDuc was staying, he "buckled on an old single-barrelled pistol that he had, put a knife in his belt and went over to the hotel." Approaching Maxwell from the back, his right hand crossed to his pistol, he "struck an attitude, and shouted 'Hulloa, Maxwell.'" Lucien turned, recognized LeDuc, and laughed. "'Maybe you think I stole your burro,'" said Maurice, adding that Maxwell was welcome to take the animal back. "'You keep the burro, Maurice, he's yours,'" came the response. "'I'll give him to you, and if there's anything else you want, just let me know.'" Anytime he got tired of Las Vegas, Maxwell encouraged LeDuc to come back to his house to stay. "'Just make yourself at home, and stay there as long as you want to.'"[65]

Such generosity reflected only one side of Maxwell's personality, for, probably unsuspected by most of those who knew him only on the basis of brief and infrequent visits to the Cimarron mansion, Lucien also could be extremely brutal. Inman recorded a revealing story about Maxwell's handling of money. Despite the fact that he often kept large accumulations of gold, silver, greenbacks, and government securities in his house, Maxwell refused to acquire a safe and kept all his cash in the bottom drawer of a dresser. When Inman questioned the safety of such an insecure arrangement, Maxwell "only smiled, while a strange, resolute look flashed from his dark eyes, as he said: 'God help the man who attempted to rob me and I knew him!'"[66]

Others perceived the same determination. "He was a man that nothing in the world would prevent him from accomplishing what he undertook to do," testified William R. Walker, "in fact no one ever dared to . . . stand in the way of anything that he started to accomplish." Squire Hart, another Maxwell confidant, reckoned that it was "not safe for a man to oppose him." "I mean," he explained, "I think he would be a dangerous man to oppose . . . ."[67] William Hoehne, a Trinidad businessman, had heard similar reports. "His reputation was when he undertook anything he would carry it out, whether right or wrong." "I never saw the man in all my life," concluded pioneer Jacob Beard, who knew Maxwell for years, "that wielded as much influence over the community, people of all classes and kinds, ages and sexes, as he."[68]

Moreover, Maxwell carried out such threats often enough to be taken seriously. Calvin Jones recalled that "his power was just as if he owned the whole outfit, the same as a man who owned slaves in the south before the war." To illustrate his point, Jones recalled a typical incident.

If a Mexican servant didn't suit him or did anything against his orders, he took a board or a plank or anything he could get hold of, and whipped him with it. I knew him to tie up one man, a Mexican, and shave off the side of his head close to the skin with a butcher knife, then he struck him fifteen or twenty lashes with a cowhide, and told him if he ever caught him on the place again, he would kill him. Some twelve or fifteen years later, he came back with a bunch of stolen horses, and Maxwell did kill him.[69]

Moreover, Maxwell saw himself as the arbiter of what he defined as justice. He once told Squire Hart that when two Mexicans sued one another, "he made both tell their stories, and then he would settle it right there, and make them stand for it."[70] Another time two men broke into Maxwell's store and stole several hundred dollars worth of goods, together with a prized horse. A private posse sent after the bandits caught one trying to sell the loot near Rayado and returned him to Cimarron. Lucien reportedly locked a forty-pound log chain around the unfortunate man's neck and locked him in a cellar. Two days later, during which the man had been allowed neither food nor water, Maxwell exclaimed, "I forgot my prisoner," and called one of his employees to produce the accused. Maxwell ordered the culprit stripped naked, tied to a post, and given twenty-five lashes with a cowhide whip. Lucien became irritated because the hide had not been laid on with sufficient vigor, and ordered that the prisoner be released and the whipper stripped and tied. "I will show you how to whip a thief," he lectured, striking the man fourteen or fifteen times, until the victim fainted. "Now when I put you to whip a man," he admonished after the employee had revived, "I want you to do it as I whipped you."[71]

Nor did Maxwell tolerate interference from law enforcement agencies. An Indian servant who had belonged to the Bents—probably the same Indian George who had saved Maxwell during the Manco Burro Pass massacre—lived at Maxwell's after the death of his master. During a visit to Taos, the man "got in a row" and cut several other persons quite seriously. When a Taos constable appeared at Maxwell's to arrest the Indian, Lucien refused to turn him over, allegedly shooting his pistol "off in the man's face and around his head." He "punched him around with it," an observer reported, "and told him to go back and tell the justice to come after him himself, and not to send a constable, as no man could take a man out of his possession."[72]

Explaining Maxwell's seemingly enigmatic character is difficult until one recalls that accounts praising his generosity and kindness generally came from Anglos whom Lucien was entertaining and upon whom he looked with respect, perhaps even awe, when they visited his home. He was a gracious host who no doubt endeavored mightily to display his generosity and kindness. On the other hand, those who suffered most from his tyranny were Hispanics, usually poor farmers using his land. Maxwell expected those around him to obey his every word, to accept his supremacy without question. "What was Mr. Maxwell's reputation among the Mexicans, generally[,] in northern New Mexico?" an attorney asked Calvin Jones. "They feared him as being a blood-thirsty, overbearing man," came the response.[73] "Did Maxwell intimidate people?" William Hoehne was asked. "He was king of that whole country," Hoehne answered, "and had Indians and Mexicans to do what he bid them to." Just how much influence did he exercise? "He had perfect control," recalled Daniel Taylor.[74]

Even generosity on the part of a Mexican-American could be dangerous. On one occasion Maxwell sent a box containing seven or eight thousand dollars east on the stage. The box somehow fell off and was found by a Mexican who came to Lucien to ask if the money was his. "What box?" asked Maxwell. "Containing money & checks for a large amount; here it is," the man replied. Rather than show gratitude, however, Maxwell pulled twenty-five cents from his pocket and offered it to the man. "Here; go and buy a rope and hang yourself," he reportedly told the man. "If you found a box like that you ought to know enough to keep it."[75]

Despite, or perhaps partly because of, his character, Maxwell managed to become wealthy through his endeavors at the Cimarron. Already in 1860 the census taker estimated his worth at $25,000 in real estate and $39,000 in personal property, making him by far the wealthiest man west of the Sangre de Cristos and one of the richest in New Mexico. Within a few years a writer for the *New Mexican* described him as "rich and powerful," and Colonel Inman reported that during the Civil War, less than a decade after moving to the Cimarron, Maxwell lived "in a sort of barbaric splendour, akin to that of the nobles of England at the time of the Norman conquests."[76]

6

The Cimarron Indian Agency

THE Cimarron country belonged to the Indians long before it became Maxwell's. For generations beyond counting,
Moache Utes and Jicarilla Apaches had pitched tipis in the
verdant meadows, planted corn and beans alongside fertile streams, and pursued deer, antelope, or elk into the
lofty mountains. As white men came into the region, establishing stock ranches, planting crops, and erecting houses,
the Indians found their traditional ways threatened. At
first they fought, but warring against the American army
and frontier settlers proved futile. By the mid-1850s, most
tribesmen in northeastern New Mexico had settled into an
uneasy peace.

They were gone from their traditional homes along
the eastern side of the Sangre de Cristos for half a decade.
No treaty guaranteed their rights or spelled out their obli-
gations, but after 1854 a United States Indian agent safe-
guarded their interests and maintained the peace. The first
was Kit Carson. Because he was also agent for the Pueblos
and had a house in Taos, Carson headquartered there,
where the Indians had to go to conduct business or receive
presents from the government. The arrangement proved
unsatisfactory. Not only was the location inconvenient for
the Indians, but too many tribesmen learned the white men's
vices in Taos. Liquor was particularly devastating, and not
infrequently Indians could be seen stumbling drunkenly
across the town plaza. By 1857 Carson concluded that the
only solution was settling the native peoples as far away

from any town as possible and teaching them to farm. Carson negotiated a treaty that promised the Utes and Apaches a permanent home, only to have it rejected in Washington. No change in the location of the agency occurred until 1861, when Carson resigned his appointment with the Indian service to take up arms in defense of the Union.[1]

Why Lucien Maxwell's Cimarron ranch was selected as the site for the Ute and Jicarilla Apache agency is unclear. Lucien and Kit remained friends. Carson's family had lived at Rayado for several years, and visits between them and the Maxwells occurred frequently. When Kit submitted his bond on being reappointed agent in 1858, for example, Lucien signed as one of the guarantors.[2] Carson's successor as agent explained to New Mexico's superintendent of Indian affairs James L. Collins that "Kit Carson, and a number of wealthy citizens of Taos, also all the prominent citizens on this [the Cimarron] side of the Taos Mountain" suggested the move. Carson denied having made such a recommendation, although he admitted that he might have suggested it as a temporary expedient.[3]

Of greater importance, the Indians trusted Maxwell as much as anyone except Carson. They probably expected that the location of the agency at his ranch would lead to his selection as their agent. Because long trips to Taos would no longer be necessary, the Indians could spend more time tending their fields and hunting deer or buffalo. Moreover, the remoteness of Cimarron was expected to lessen the availability of whiskey.

Few of Maxwell's neighbors shared his enthusiasm at returning the agency to the eastern side of the Sangre de Cristos. The most vigorous complaints came from rancher Samuel B. Watrous, who lived near Fort Union, forty miles south of Cimarron. When he heard of the move, Watrous protested to congressmen H. R. Bennett and E. P. Walton, who passed his letters on to the Indian department. Watrous's principal concern was that location of the agency at Cimarron would draw the Utes and Apaches toward the plains, where they were more likely to attack his livestock. "We deny the right of the gov[ernmen]t to quarter the savages on our flocks and herds, against our will," argued a petition signed by Watrous and other ranchers. What may have been a more important complaint, however, was that only Maxwell would reap the financial benefits of the agency. There was no advantage to Cimarron, the petition continued, "except the convenience of the agent and to subserve the interests of a few who will be benefitted by their trade, or by the disbursement of gov-[ernmen]t funds at that point . . . ."[4] No doubt the location of the agency at Watrous's ranch would have stimulated comparable opposition from Maxwell and his friends.

Just how much influence Maxwell could exert over the agency became apparent soon after the move. The agent appointed to succeed Carson was William F. M. Arny, an Easterner who had never set foot in New Mexico or worked with Indians. A radical Republican, fresh from the abolitionist battlefields of Kansas, Arny, like his successors, fell almost immediately under Maxwell's sway.[5] What other choice did he have? Lucien owned the property where the agency was located, provided temporary rented quarters in which the agent lived, and was the only person who supplied food and other goods to the Indians. More important, fifteen years of intimate association with the Utes and Apaches had given Maxwell more influence over them than any newly-arrived federal agent could hope to muster.

Within a few months after his arrival, Arny developed, no doubt after close consultation with and advice from Maxwell, a plan for an elaborate agency headquarters. Maxwell agreed to lease the government 1,280 acres along Ponil Creek north of his home ranch for a nominal yearly rent of twenty dollars. Construction soon began on buildings to house an Indian school, council chamber, offices, and a residence for the agent and his family. The total cost was $2,000, most of which probably went to Lucien or his employees. Sturdy adobe construction, planed wooden floors, and other expensive additions intimated the permanence

*W. F. M. Arny, the first Indian
agent at Cimarron. Courtesy the
Library of Congress.*

of the location. By April, 1862, the buildings were sufficiently complete that Arny requested leave in order to
bring his family from the States. Not surprisingly, he
assured his Washington bosses that during his absence
interpreter Luke Murray and "Mr. Maxwell" would "attend to the duties of the agency and see that the Indians
are attended to."[6]

Whatever profits accrued directly from the construction of the Ponil agency were minor compared to the
money Lucien made feeding the Indians. Once the Utes
and Apaches had provided for themselves. Now the best
farmland was in the hands of Mexicans or Anglos, and
game was rapidly disappearing from the mountains. As
a result, by the 1860s the government provided almost
constant doles of food to prevent the Indians from stealing. Theoretically, supplies were purchased through a
system of fair, open, competitive bidding. In reality, however, especially at remote locations like Maxwell's, few
bids were received, and obviously Lucien had a compet-

itive edge over anyone located at a distance from the agency. It would not be surprising, although no corroborating documents exist, if Lucien's intimate relationship with the agents enabled him to know what other bids had been submitted before sending in his own. Maxwell became the principal supplier of both beef and grain to the Cimarron agency, earning considerable money thereby. During the second quarter of 1862 alone, Maxwell sold the government $2,827.11 worth of goods, mostly corn and wheat but including some beef, lamb, gunpowder, lead, and caps.[7]

The Civil War drove prices and profits upward. With Santa Fe and most of the Río Grande Valley in Confederate hands after March, 1862, prices for grain, flour, and other goods increased by a third or more. The quartermaster at Fort Union bought everything he could to feed the troops. Corn, which Maxwell had sold the government for $5.00 a fanega just a few weeks before, now brought $7.50. Prices dropped closer to normal by year's end, when the Confederates had been expelled from the territory. Even then, Maxwell, the only bidder to supply grain for the Cimarron agency, earned $5.50 a fanega for shelled corn and $4.50 for clean wheat. Altogether, agency expenses for the first half of 1862 totaled $10,559, most of which went to Lucien Maxwell.[8]

Just how prosperous Lucien became as an immediate result of the location of the Indian agency at Cimarron is evident from a rare personal letter responding to news of the death of his mother in Kaskaskia. Addressing his uncle Edmond Menard in November, 1862, Maxwell noted that he had sent a thousand dollars to his mother the previous month for use in educating his children at school in the East. Moreover, "should my mother when she died have owed or is indebted to any person," he continued, "please advise me of the amount and I will remit it to you on the receipt of your letter." By all means, he admonished Edmond, none of her property should be sold, in accordance with her wish that sister Sofia should have it all.[9]

The letter represented only one connection Lucien had with his family. In August, 1859, his older brother Ferdinand came to New Mexico, and two years later, in July, 1862, he received appointment as a New Mexican Indian agent.[10] Initially he was assigned to the southern Apache agency hundreds of miles from the Cimarron and made his permanent home in Taos, but Ferdinand spent much of his time at Cimarron and worked for a while with the Moache Utes, which may account for the persistent, although incorrect, report that Lucien himself served as an agent to the Indians at his ranch.[11]

While Lucien's initial earnings stemmed largely from the sale of corn and wheat to the government, citizen complaints that Indians were killing their livestock, coupled with Indian protests that there was too little game on which to survive, expanded his potential for profit. During an October, 1862, meeting, leading chiefs from both tribes told Agent Arny that unless provided meat by the government, they would have no alternative but to steal in order to feed their families. With agency expenditures already exceeding appropriations and little hope of supplementary funds as long as the Civil War persisted, Arny turned to the army for help. General James H. Carleton, who recently had come to New Mexico with the famed California Column of Union volunteers, authorized the immediate allocation of sixty head of beef for slaughter at the Cimarron agency.[12] Where the beef was obtained is not known, but it was likely purchased from Maxwell. Lucien's interest in improving and expanding his cattle herds may have stemmed in part from this sudden new market. Thereafter, Maxwell — frequently the only bidder and always the successful contractor — sold beef to the government on a regular and highly profitable basis.

Issue day — when the Indians received their rations — became an important occasion at the Cimarron agency. Colonel Henry Inman, a frequent visitor, watched one such spectacle. Mounted on a magnificent gray horse provided by Lucien, he rode from the ranch house to "an

Ferdinand Maxwell, Lucien's brother who served as an Indian agent in New Mexico. Courtesy of Victor Grant, Taos, New Mexico.

immense enclosed field" where the Indians, "dressed in their best, painted as if for the war-path, gaily bedecked with feathers and armed with rifles and gaudily appointed bows and arrows," awaited the coming of the cows. Nearby sat hundreds of women, their knives ready for the grue-some work ahead. Inman went on:

Suddenly a great cloud of dust rose on the trail from the moun-tains, and on came the maddened animals, fairly shaking the earth with their mighty tread. As soon as the gate was closed behind them, and uttering a characteristic yell that was blood-curdling in its ferocity, the Indians charged upon the now doubly fright-ened herd, and commenced to discharge their rifles, regardless of the presence of any one but themselves.

Inman was unprepared when his horse, at first paralyzed in fright, rushed into the midst of the herd. Indian bullets buzzed past his head. Twenty minutes later the last cow was dead. The warriors departed the field "leaving the squaws to cut up and carry away the meat to their lodges," which, Inman concluded, "they soon accomplished, to the last quivering morsel."[13]

The presence of the agency gave Maxwell immense power over Indian affairs. "It was an Indian country," recalled John D. Lee years later, and Maxwell "was an Indian fighter." He added that Lucien treated the natives with "kindness and gave them anything they might need. . . . I suppose," he went on, "they looked upon him as a man that it wouldn't do to tamper with." Just how much influence did Maxwell have with the Cimarron tribes, a questioner probed. "He could influence them a great deal," Lee replied; "he feared them also."[14]

William A. Bell, who visited Maxwell's in August, 1867, presumed that Lucien was the Indian agent and explained that while the natives had been "most trouble-some . . . . Mr. Maxwell has completely gained their con-fidence and treats them more as children than as depen-dents." Bell found Maxwell seated on the steps of his house

Ute and Jicarilla Apache Indians receiving rations at Maxwell's Cimarron mill. Maxwell's double-winged house is in the background. The stone mill is still standing in Cimarron. Courtesy Museum of New Mexico.

in shirt sleeves, "surrounded by a motley group of squaws, papooses, and warriors, painted up and decorated in their usual style." They had just ridden in from the mountains on a visit, he continued, "They all seemed on the most familiar terms with him—talking and laughing while the children played around."[15]

Despite improved relations, trouble continued to develop whenever the Indians attacked the livestock of farmers living near Maxwell's ranch. The Utes and Apaches argued that the Cimarron country belonged to them as it had to their forefathers. Maxwell had somehow earned sufficient respect that they were willing to allow him to remain, but not the others. Moreover, when an absence of game or the failure of the government to supply adequate food threatened them with starvation, the Indians naturally turned on the settlers' stock. "They were impudent and arrogant in their manner," long-time Cimarron resident Dr. Robert H. Longwell recalled, "and done about as they pleased; they took stock cattle when they wanted it to eat, without paying for it; they often demanded food from the settlers in the outlying settlements, and their demands were complied with when possible."[16]

The only realistic long-term solution was, of course, to move the Indian agency to some still more remote location. Early in 1864 the Indian Department first ordered the removal of the Cimarron agency. The Jicarillas would be sent to the Bosque Redondo, the infamous reservation at Fort Sumner in east central New Mexico, where the Navajos were imprisoned after their defeat by Kit Carson. The Utes were to be relocated to a new reservation along the Conejos River in southcentral Colorado. Agent Arny's successor, Levi J. Keithly, received orders that no presents were to be issued at Cimarron. He was to try to persuade the Apaches to move voluntarily, and Lucien's brother Ferdinand was assigned to move the Utes to Colorado.[17]

The Indians, preferring to remain in Cimarron, ignored these orders, and the government lacked the will or authority to force them to comply. Moreover, government policy lacked conviction. Extreme difficulties, including starvation and vast expenditures at the Bosque Redondo reservation led the government to reconsider its policy. By the end of September, 1864, Ferdinand Maxwell was discharged from the Indian service on grounds that the Southern Apache agency to which he had originally been appointed had been abolished. Lucien's brother complained of mistreatment and endeavored to retain his position. He soon abandoned his work among the Utes and moved to Taos.[18]

Agent Keithly wrote to the New Mexican Indian superintendent early in 1865 to ask for more money with which to buy food and ammunition from Maxwell for the Indians and to inquire if and when they were to be moved from Cimarron. "Our Indian relations have been conducted with so little system," Superintendent Michael Steck confessed with uncommon candor, "that it is impossible to instruct you at this time with reference to the abandonment of your agency." Congress by this time had appointed a special commission to look into Indian policy, and when or if the Cimarron Indians would be moved could only be ascertained after its recommendations had been submitted. In the meantime, Keithly received authorization to buy another $1,500 worth of supplies from Lucien. He hoped they would keep the Utes and Apaches "peace[ful] and quiet" until there was "definite action and established policy."[19]

Such optimism proved unwarranted, for conditions at the Cimarron agency worsened with each passing month. A new agent, Manuel Salazar, reported in February, 1866, that he had received "numerous complaints" from citizens concerning Indian attacks on their sheep and cattle. Salazar pointed out that regular rations of flour, meat, and corn — all bought from Maxwell — had been provided, therefore the Indians had no excuses for robbery. Some of the chiefs denied any blame, arguing that only a few young men over whom they had lost control committed the attacks, but Salazar demanded that the Indians either pay for their

damages or face the prospect of having their food and supplies cut off. The Indians refused, threatening war. "Mr.
Maxwell and myself have fully discussed the subject," Salazar reported, "and he thinks that the remarkable miscon-
duct of these Indians is nigh well beyond endurance."[20]

As if to worsen an already dangerous situation, some
settlers discovered how lucrative the sale of liquor to the
Indians could be. When government inspector J. K. Graves
visited Rayado, he found that liquor was being sold to whites
who passed it on to Indians. Graves warned Salazar that the
practice must be stopped—by seizing the whiskey if necessary. "The losses recently sustained by citizens in this section are no doubt attributable to this practice of supplying
the Indians of your agency with liquor," Graves scolded
Salazar, "which must cease entirely."[21]

When Salazar resigned a few months later, the Utes
and Apaches were left without an agent. Moreover, the
Indians' annual spring buffalo hunt proved disastrous.
Before they even reached the buffalo country, the Cimarron natives were forced back by stronger Plains tribes.
There was so little rain and grass was so scant nearby that
no other game could be found. "They are in a very *desti-
tute* condition, both in food and raiment," reported newly
arrived Indian superintendent A. B. Norton after a visit
to Maxwell's in late June, 1866. "Many of them are almost
naked, some entirely so, having had no goods since last
fall, and for food they are suffering and threatened with
starvation."

The new superintendent, like his predecessors, turned
to Maxwell for advice and assistance. Lucien complained
that the government already owed him seven or eight
thousand dollars for what he had given the natives and
argued that it should not be his responsibility to feed two
thousand Indians to keep them from robbing his neighbors. Norton, who had come from the East only days before, recognized the seriousness of the situation and the
important role Maxwell could play. Lucien gave the Indians two head of beef immediately, and Norton autho-

rized him to continue feeding them "at such times and in such quantities as you may think absolutely necessary to prevent suffering and starvation." Maxwell suggested a price of seven cents a pound for the beef, and Norton accepted without bidding. Expenditures were limited to $500 a month.[22]

No sooner had news of Norton's action reached Washington, than a stinging rebuke was in the mails back to New Mexico. Commissioner of Indian Affairs D. N. Cooley reminded the freshman superintendent that only $50,000 had been appropriated for all of New Mexico's Indians, and more than $30,000 was required to pay for annuity goods. There was no money for lavish expenditures such as had been authorized at Cimarron. Cooley then instructed the novice bureaucrat that feeding Indians prevented them from making a sufficient effort to sustain themselves, especially when they were nomads with unlimited hunting grounds. "The necessities of the Indians may seem to require expenditure exceeding the appropriation," he concluded, "but this is not a question of humanity, but of law."[23]

Norton, naturally disappointed at having his first order disallowed, dutifully informed Lucien that the issues must stop. Maxwell no longer restrained his exasperation with government policy. In an angry letter dated August 7, 1866—one of only a handful of personal letters which survive—he argued that the Indians were starving, and if the "government don't provide for them they will help themselves and take there [*sic*] wants from the people of New Mexico." A Mexican herder had recently been killed by a Ute at Red River, making it difficult to maintain the peace. Now what would happen? "I for my part have always done and do yet all I can," Maxwell promised, "give them from time to time rations on my own account . . . . There is no agent here, and I do all I can to keep them in good humor." He submitted a bill for $716.66 for what he had already provided the Indians and pleaded that the army be persuaded to provide food rather than be forced to fight.[24]

Less than a month later, troubles worse even than

Maxwell had predicted erupted between settlers and Indians. Angry that their food issues had been suspended and failing to understand the complex relationship by which Maxwell had acted for the Office of Indian Affairs, a band of Utes and Apaches surrounded Lucien's Cimarron mansion. Their clamor was so great and their temper so bad that Lucien, fearing for the safety of his family, fled with his household to the huge stone mill nearby. The first official to arrive on the scene was one-time Cimarron agent and now Territorial Secretary and Acting Governor William F. M. Arny. On his own authority Arny ordered Maxwell to renew the distribution of beef and flour, promising payment from the government even if it took a trip to Washington. At the same time, Arny organized two companies of volunteers to keep the peace until permanent protection could be provided by the army.[25]

By August 25, the soldiers had arrived, led by General James H. Carleton, commanding officer of the District of New Mexico. The situation Carleton found was critical. The Indians had no food, there was no game in the mountains, and the Indian Department persisted in its refusal to authorize the issue of rations. What alternative, the general asked, did the Indians have except to steal from the neighboring ranches? "We cannot make war upon people driven to such extremities," he continued,

We have taken possession of their country, their game is all gone, and now to kill them for committing depredations solely to save life cannot be justified. We have but one alternative, we have either to feed the Indians or let them kill the stock of the people at the risk of collision, which will lead to war. This is not only a true story, but the whole story.

Carleton authorized Maxwell to issue half a pound each of meal and meat a day to every Indian. The natives were warned that the issue would stop immediately if any stock was attacked or hostile moves made. "This bounty of the Government," Carleton lectured, "can only be bestowed upon those who behave themselves."[26]

To supervise the issue of food and maintain order at Maxwell's, Carleton ordered Lieutenant George Campbell and a company of mounted troops to remain at Cimarron. Instead of settling the situation, however, the soldiers soon became the center of a new dispute. The first report had the principal chief of the Utes, Kaniatche, visiting the army camp, where he met Lieutenant Campbell, who was reportedly drunk. The officer drew his pistol, held it near the chief's heart, and threatened to kill him. Only last-second intervention by Maxwell prevented a certain calamity.[27] Later accounts, however, claimed that a drunken Indian had entered the army camp and pointed a pistol at one of the soldiers. A sergeant sprang to the man's defense, and drove off the intruder with his gun. Neither Lucien nor Kaniatche participated.[28]

Whatever the truth and whoever the participants, the settlers, the soldiers, and especially the Indians became so suspicious of one another that further trouble seemed unavoidable. It came October 4, 1866, on the Purgatoire River across the Raton Mountains from Maxwell's. When Colonel A. J. Alexander reached Trinidad on October 1, he found that Kaniatche's band was constantly attacking the crops and livestock of the neighborhood farmers. The chief defended his people, arguing that they had to eat or die, and broke off a council convened by Alexander. Two days later the Indians were headed west toward Taos when a farmer named Gutierrez cursed them for stealing his corn, and his son shot and killed one of them. Apparently having heard the shot, Alexander and his men rushed to the scene, where they loosed a flurry of gunfire. Although Alexander initially reported the death of thirteen Indians, it was later learned that the natives had withdrawn before anyone else could be killed.[29]

Everyone agreed that no one but Maxwell could prevent further bloodshed. He and Kit Carson met with the Utes and agreed to protect them from retaliatory action. Meanwhile, Superintendent Norton ordered veteran Indian agent John D. "Jack" Henderson to Cimarron until a permanent agent could take office. He was still forbidden from incurring any expenses, although he could distribute tobacco along with the annual supply of goods as soon as they arrived. The Indians were promised the remainder of their presents if they maintained the peace. The army continued to provide beef and flour purchased from Maxwell. Henderson, Maxwell, Carson, and others interviewed the Indians in order to secure their version of the Campbell and Alexander incidents, and Superintendent Norton invited Maxwell to a high-level meeting at Taos to discuss the future of the agency.[30] "I desire more especially to have your attendance," he wrote Lucien, "as I have great faith in your influence over many of the Indians and would request that you bring the principal chiefs or others whose presence you may consider desirable with you." Maxwell complied, although the superintendent and other dignitaries failed to attend the meeting, which came to nothing.[31]

The collapse of the Taos conference coincided with Norton's development of a plan to solve the dilemma of the Cimarron agency. He argued that the Indians were so attached to the area near Cimarron that they would never leave: "It is useless to talk of removing them elsewhere," he affirmed; "they would resist to the last extremity . . . ." The only real solution was the purchase of Maxwell's "Rayado Grant" as a permanent Indian reservation. Norton had obviously spoken to Maxwell about the possibility, for he reported that the ranch was about forty by sixty miles in size and contained about 1,600,000 acres (the first reference to its size). Already, 3,000 acres were under cultivation, a great many year-around streams provided sufficient water, and improvements included "the best flour mill in the territory," a good sawmill, houses, barns, and corrals. All this, Norton informed Commissioner Cooley, could be purchased for the Indians for $250,000. The Indians would be satisfied, he was certain, and after the first year they would be able to support themselves.[32] Typically, Norton's farsighted recommendation was filed away without serious consideration. The discovery of gold on the grant a few months later led Maxwell not only to enlarge his estimates of the ranch's boundaries but also to abandon any consideration of selling so cheaply.

In the meantime, no permanent agent having yet been appointed to Cimarron, Maxwell took virtual charge of the agency. Since promised annuity goods had not yet arrived by late October, he suggested that Henderson take a stagecoach to Santa Fe in hopes of expediting delivery. Nor was Norton needed to help distribute the goods. Maxwell wrote to the superintendent, saying that he, Carson, and Henderson could "make the issue and see that all is done properly."[33]

The presence of troops at Cimarron July 4, 1867, encouraged Maxwell to plan a celebration. A six-pound howitzer left from the Mexican War was brought near the house. An army officer, perhaps Alexander or Campbell, stood near the muzzle while Maxwell stationed himself at the breech. The weapon was being prepared when it fired prematurely. The soldier lost an arm and an eye; Maxwell's thumb was shattered. A sergeant immediately rushed to Fort Union for medical help. His horse covered the forty-five miles in just over four hours and fell dead in front of the doctor's quarters. The physician, who reached Maxwell's before midnight, succeeded in saving the officer's life and dressed Maxwell's seemingly minor wound.

Several days later, however, Lucien's thumb became "angry-looking." Colonel Henry Inman, who was visiting Cimarron, persuaded Maxwell to go to Fort Union for surgery and invited Carson to come along to "assist in catering to the amusement of my suffering guest." They piled into Maxwell's coach, arriving at the fort in the evening after a "tedious ride." Lucien was tired and feverish. So that he could rest and in order to avoid the heat of the day, the operation was postponed until the following evening.

Lucien, refusing an anesthetic, seated himself in a "common office chair" and held out his infected hand to the doctor. Carson and Inman stood beside him holding kerosene lamps so the surgeon could see as he amputated the thumb. "In a few seconds," Inman recalled,

the operation was concluded, and after the silver-wire ligatures were twisted in their places, I offered Maxwell, who had not permitted a single sigh to escape his lips, a half tumblerful of whiskey, but before I had fairly put it in his mouth, he fell over, having fainted dead away, while great beads of perspiration stood on his forehead, indicative of the pain he had suffered.

After several days of rest at the fort, Maxwell returned home.[34]

Perhaps the frequent presence of Carson at Maxwell's led Indian officials in Washington to conclude that the continuing problems of the Cimarron agency could be alleviated if Kit were reappointed agent. When Henderson, who subsequently became Maxwell's representative in the nearby gold fields, was removed early in May, the commissioner of Indian affairs prepared the necessary papers naming Carson his successor. Kit, probably aware of Ferdinand Maxwell's problems with the government and suffering from declining health, demanded absolute assurance that he would be stationed only at Cimarron. "Arrangements I have already entered into in relation to my family," he explained to the commissioner, "would render my acceptance of the agency at any other place impossible." Besides, he argued, "long continued acquaintance extending to personal knowledge of the Utes" best qualified him to serve at Cimarron. Not till after he returned from Fort Union with Maxwell did Carson learn that the government would make no such iron-clad commitment, even to him, and someone else was appointed to the post.[35]

If Carson could not assist Lucien directly as agent to the Cimarron Indians, he could provide other important service for Maxwell. Poor administration, the loss of documents in the mails, and a rapid turnover of territorial Indian superintendents combined to create long delays in the payment of contractors for foodstuffs and other supplies furnished for the Indians. As one of the largest providers in the Southwest, Maxwell naturally suffered heavily from these problems. When Carson visited Washington late in 1867 with a party of Ute chiefs, he carried with him unpaid vouchers totalling more than $12,000 owed to Maxwell for supplies provided for the Indians during 1865 and 1866. Certificates signed by Colorado's Governor A. C. Hunt, New Mexican attorney John S. Watts, and former Cimarron agent Arny attested that the accounts were valid and had never been paid. Carson had to submit an indemnifying bond for twice the amount due, but before he left the capital in early March it appeared that the money would soon be paid.[36]

Carson's errand in Washington marked the end of the close friendship between him and Maxwell that had lasted more than a quarter-century. Kit was already ailing at the time of his eastern trip, the death of his wife late in April seemed to diminish his will to live, and on May 23, 1868, Carson died apparently without having seen Lucien again. The famed mountain man's will, drafted only a few days before his death, reflected the financial relationship between the two friends. Carson instructed his executor, Thomas O. Boggs, to use the interest from $3,000 owed him by Lucien to pay the burial expenses of himself and his wife. The note itself should either be backed by securities provided by Maxwell or collected and invested at the highest possible interest to support Carson's children.[37]

The new agent at Cimarron, Erasmus B. Denison, found the agency seriously deteriorated. Floods on the Ponil had destroyed buildings erected less than five years before, and once more the agent had no choice but to rely on Maxwell for facilities. In a rare exhibit of independence, Denison protested the servile relationship between himself and Lucien. He disliked having to store his goods in Maxwell's barn. Worse yet, he found himself unable to make independent decisions regarding the Indians. He noted that recently when an army officer charged with issuing supplies to the Utes and Apaches tried to initiate a new distribution system, Maxwell and his cronies raised so much opposition that the modifications had to be dropped. Denison was sure that if he were ever put in charge of the issue, he could not "act and be in harmony with M[axwell] or his surrounding friends." "You understand me," he confided to Superintendent Norton in a tone insinuating that too direct or public a complaint against Maxwell might be imprudent, "comment is unnecessary." Perhaps, he suggested, the agency could be moved to Rayado, where better storage facilities were available and where the agent could conduct his activities "independent of all surroundings."[38]

Nor were relations between Denison and the military officials at Cimarron always cordial. Strains between him and Lieutenant Campbell became evident in mid-June, 1868, when a Pueblo, Colorado, newspaper, the *Colorado Chieftain,* reprinted a telegram attributed to Campbell reporting that the Apaches had raided Maxwell's ranch, stolen twenty-five mules and a valuable horse, beaten a Mexican man to death, and badly injured a boy.[39] Agent Denison defended the Indians, denying the loss of Maxwell's mules, arguing that the horse had been stolen by a Las Vegas thief, and quoting the ill-treated boy as denying that the Indians were from the Cimarron agency.[40]

Evidence suggests that Maxwell exaggerated the Indian danger in order to benefit his own interests, and certainly the presence of the army at Cimarron and the policy of feeding the Indians was profitable to him. Between September, 1866, when the army took charge of issuing rations, and August, 1867, Maxwell's income from selling Indian supplies swelled. He provided more than a hundred tons each of beef and wheat and nearly a ton of salt to an average of more than thirteen hundred Utes and Apaches at a total cost to the government of $33,462.88. Major McLure, the commissary officer who reported the expenses, noted that there had been no additional charges for herding, renting warehouses, or butchering, since Maxwell delivered the cattle on the hoof when they were needed, and the Indians did the slaughtering.[41]

In mid-September, 1868, the *Colorado Chieftain* reprinted the report of a Denver Indian agent that the Cimarron Indians had "been bedeviled by Maxwell and other interests in bringing on a collision, until all hopes of reconciliation seemed lost." Agent Denison, in what may reflect a reversal of his previous antagonism toward Maxwell, defended himself and Lucien. Had the Colorado agent ever visited Cimarron? he asked, and what did he know about activities to "incite the Indians?" The truth, he argued was that for two years the Utes and Apaches had been as "peaceable as any of their neighbors" and steadfastly "loyal to the government." He then launched into a defense of Maxwell. Why would he, as a man "interested pecuniarily to the extent of several hundred thousand dollars, having the safety of a large family at stake, and being, as I believe, of sound mind," ever want to "incite trouble at his very threshold?" he asked, responding that "such a charge is as weak as it is incorrect."[42]

Indeed, Denison seemed more and more willing to defer to Maxwell. Late in 1868, for example, former agent Arny asked Denison to assemble his Indians for a conference at Cimarron on Christmas Day. Denison was in Santa Fe on official business and could not assent, but he suggested that Arny see Maxwell, "who will doubtless give you all assistance to bring together such of the Apaches or Utes who will be in the vicinity." Arny complied and by December 26 could report that "with the assistance of Mr. Lucian [*sic*] B. Maxwell" he had convened a successful conference with the chiefs.[43]

As the decade of the 1860s drew to a close, challenges to Maxwell's dominance increased. The discovery of gold on the slopes of Baldy Mountain brought thousands of prospectors into the region around Cimarron, not only increasing pressure to remove the Indian agency but also introducing into the area a great many individuals who refused to accept Maxwell's will as law. Their presence encouraged the establishment of new ranches that competed for lucrative contracts which had previously been assured to Maxwell. When the army solicited proposals to feed the Cimarron tribes in December, 1868, for example, seven ranchers submitted bids. A year later Lucien offered to feed the natives for seven and a half cents a ration, only to find himself underpriced by F. M. Wilburn and T. L. Stockton, who bid six and forty-three one hundredths cents.[44]

Personnel changes at the agency also undermined Lucien's authority. Dissatisfaction not only with affairs at the Cimarron agency but also with the general direction of Indian relations throughout the West prompted Congress in 1869 to authorize the appointment of army officers on detached service to run the Indian agencies. It was felt that such a change should result in more efficient administration, make it easier to bring troops into action when necessary, and eliminate the excessive power of contractors like Maxwell. The appointee at Cimarron was Lieutenant A. S. B. Keyes.[45]

By the time Keyes arrived at Cimarron late in August, 1869, problems at the agency had worsened. The government's long-standing policy of removing the Utes to Colorado and the Apaches to southern New Mexico was now to be enforced by denying the Indians their annual presents at Cimarron. As soon as Keyes learned of this policy, he conferred with his predecessor Erasmus Denison and with Maxwell, "who are better acquainted with the tribes than myself." Both argued that withholding all or most of the goods would likely result in a war which might involve the Colorado Utes as well as those in New Mexico. Tensions increased in mid-September, when the first signs of winter began to appear in the mountains, and the Indians in Cimarron began asking when their blankets, clothing, and tents would come.[46]

Keyes tried to pacify the natives with promises that their presents would soon arrive. Meanwhile he explained his predicament to his superiors and pleaded for help. More than thirteen hundred Indians needed blankets, yet he had only thirty-nine left from the previous year's presents to distribute. The knives and forks and beaver traps he had were of no value to the Indians. "I would respectfully inquire if there is no possibility of my getting more blankets and of a better quality than those I have?" he asked. "They are really in need of them."[47] Keyes's pleas fell on deaf ears. If the Utes went to their Colorado reservation, the commissioner of Indian affairs responded, they would "find provision made for their care and comfort at that place; and until they do so, it is not the intention of the Department to furnish them with articles of any description."[48]

Once again Lucien's direct involvement became necessary. December 7, 1869, he addressed a long letter to Brigadier General William S. Grier, whom he had known for nearly twenty years, pleading for military protection. The Utes and Apaches, he reported, were "very discontented" at not having received their accustomed supplies, and there was "now imminent danger of a general uprising against the settlements and against the government." He continued:

From my intimate acquaintance with the Indian character, and especially with that of these two tribes arising from an intercourse with them for some quarter of a century, I am enabled to state, most emphatically that, unless prompt measures be taken to anticipate & prevent an outbreak, it will be sure and terrible. Without troops to protect the settlers or to enforce the policy and orders of the government, it will be utterly impossible to preserve peace and avoid bloodshed.

The absence of military forces in the area, he continued, had emboldened the Indians, and any attempt at removal would "result in all the resistance within their power."

Only the immediate stationing of a "military force of cavalry" at Cimarron could prevent war. "Not having been in the habit of calling out 'danger' when none is threatening," Maxwell concluded, "I trust for the sake of humanity that this warning and entreaty shall be heeded, and acted upon, immediately. Trusting that the gravity of the occasion will be considered a sufficient apology for this communication." Maxwell closed by expressing his great respect for Grier.[49]

Maxwell's request received a prompt and positive response. Grier forwarded the letter to his commanding officer, General George W. Getty, who on December 13 ordered no fewer than a hundred cavalry forces to the Cimarron "to be prepared in case the Utes and Apaches should terminate their present attitude by active hostilities." A collision should be avoided if at all possible, but should fighting begin, the troops were to "attack and pursue" the Indians and drive them toward their new reservation.[50] Moreover, the additional blankets which had previously been unavailable suddenly appeared: the Indian agent at Abiquiu received orders to buy an additional 450 and deliver them to Cimarron for distribution as quickly as possible.[51]

Once again Coloradans suspected that a false crisis had been created at Cimarron to benefit Maxwell. Early in February an article in the *Colorado Tribune* reported the views of a "reliable officer of the army" who had passed through Cimarron on January 9:

The rumors of war were started by Maxwell, and he succeeded in getting a troop of Cavalry stationed on his grant, for nothing in God's name but to sell them grain and forage. I also saw Capt. Keyes who claims to be agent for what are known as "Maxwell's Utes" and a few bands of Apaches. He has goods and makes issues to them. He is young and sweet on Maxwell's daughter. The milk in the cocoa nut is satisfactorily accounted for.

When Keyes obtained a copy of the article, he exploded with self-righteous fury. "The Colorado people want to get these Indians of mine to Colorado," he reported in a letter to his mother, "and the papers of that place are always publishing articles to prove that the people of New Mexico want to keep them there, to get the benefit of the contracts." This was untrue, he reported; the Indians simply *"will not go."* He went on to defend

Maxwell as "a man of abundant means, [who] owns a large part of N. Mexico, mines, mill, stock, &c. and would not think twice of the profit of what grain and stuff he could sell the cavalry co. stationed here!" The job of running the Cimarron agency, he concluded, was impossible. "Why don't they send a Quaker here, not a soldier?"[52]

Whatever the truth of these accusations and defenses, at least one element of the Colorado newspaper report was true: Keyes was "sweet on Maxwell's daughter." Virginia Maxwell, Lucien's eldest daughter, described by those who knew her as "beautiful and charming," had only recently returned to New Mexico from the Midwest, where she had attended Catholic schools under the direction of her grandmother and the Menard relatives. She was apparently an independent woman, for she once told a visiting clergyman of her refusal to marry a "wealthy man down the Río Grande" whom her father had in mind. How much courtship went on between Keyes and Miss Maxwell cannot be known with certainty, although Keyes, like his predecessors, probably lived in or very near the Maxwell mansion, frequently visited with the family, and no doubt developed opportunities to be with her.

Once they had decided to marry, the couple began to plan the ceremony. Either Lucien opposed the courtship or they feared that he would object to the marriage, for they decided to keep the arrangements secret. Using the attacks mounted on him in the Colorado press as an excuse, Keyes requested reassignment to his military unit. While he awaited word of the transfer, Virginia approached an itinerant Methodist clergyman, the Reverend Thomas Harwood, who frequently visited Cimarron, to ask if he would perform the ceremony. Harwood saw the request as an opportunity to reveal the repressiveness of the Catholic faith. To him, Virginia's defiance of her father was "one of the noble qualities of Protestantism. It is progress. It is Americanism." He promised to marry the two as soon as he returned from planned visits to the Red River and the Vermejo.

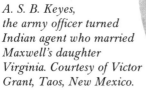

Virginia Maxwell Keyes.
Courtesy of Victor Grant,
Taos, New Mexico.

A. S. B. Keyes,
the army officer turned
Indian agent who married
Maxwell's daughter
Virginia. Courtesy of Victor
Grant, Taos, New Mexico.

Harwood was back in Cimarron March 30, 1870. "No army general could have planned for a battle more wisely than she had planned for this marriage," he recalled years later. It was ration day, and hundreds of Indians were at the mill to receive their meat and flour. Accompanied by the wife of the miller, Mrs. Rinehart, Virginia left home about 4:00 P.M., walked toward the mill, and climbed to the third floor. The room, carpeted with robes, was "a real cozy place for a marriage ceremony." When Keyes and Virginia Maxwell arrived, Harwood united them "in regular Methodist style," with only the Rineharts present. The couple immediately parted, and when Mrs. Maxwell asked her returning daughter where she had been, Virginia reported only having gone down to "see the Indians and got weighed. . . . Guess how much I weigh, mother?" she asked.[53]

Not until early April did Keyes receive the necessary orders relieving him of the Cimarron assignment and ordering him back to his regiment. Harwood reported that the two young people kept their marriage secret until they had left on the northbound stage. Once beyond the grant, near Trinidad, Keyes handed the stage conductor a copy of the marriage certificate for delivery to Maxwell. Harwood also wrote to the Maxwells in order to admit participating in the event "stating at the same time that I felt very sorry for them, but hoped they would take a wise view of the matter and become reconciled." When the messages arrived, Maxwell reportedly first became speechless, then "stormed at a furious rate" before announcing that he would pursue the couple until he caught them. He was dissuaded from a chase, but he ordered that Virginia's name never be mentioned again.[54]

Harwood feared what might happen the next time he encountered Maxwell. Another clergyman warned of a possible attack by Lucien or "some of those who were hanging around him." Indeed, when a man resembling Harwood rode up in front of Lucien's Cimarron store, he was reportedly pulled from his horse and threatened with being dunked or "blacksnake[d]." Others reported that

*The Reverend Thomas
Harwood won Lucien's
animosity by officiating at
the marriage of Maxwell's
daughter Virginia and
A. S. B. Keyes. Courtesy
Museum of New Mexico.*

Maxwell wanted to challenge the clergyman to a duel. "If Mr. Maxwell challenges me to fight a duel with him," Harwood replied, "I shall very respectfully decline. If he calls me a coward, I shall tell him that it is a brave man who can say 'no' against public sentiment." Harwood continued that he had ". . . preached with unusual liberty on wrong-doing in general and lack of moral principle in particular as witnessed in some men who are almost ready to bow down and worship a man if he has money. 'That is idolatry of the meanest kind.'" Nevertheless, the next time Harwood preached at Elizabethtown, he took a roundabout route to avoid going through Cimarron.

According to tradition, Lucien met his daughter only once more, in New York when he was negotiating the sale of the land grant, at which time he gave her a $10,000 gift.[55] This story, however, is untrue. Virginia gave birth to her first child at the Fort Sumner ranch where her father lived in 1871,[56] a circumstance leading to suspicions that the entire chain of events may have been greatly exaggerated by the Reverend Mr. Harwood.

The departure of agent Keyes and, not long afterward, of Lucien Maxwell from Cimarron did nothing to alleviate the problems faced by the Utes and Apaches. Eventually they agreed to leave the region for new reservations in northeastern New Mexico and southern Colorado, although not before more blood had been shed and more suffering had occurred. Ultimately, only Lucien Maxwell benefitted from the location of their agency at his ranch, partly from the sale to the government of supplies for them, but in greater measure because it was they who brought to the attention of the world the existence of valuable mineral resources on the slopes of Baldy Mountain.

7

"The Greatest Gold Producer on the Globe"

Baldy Mountain, its brown, shale-covered peak clearly visible between the deep green forests and the dark blue new Mexican sky, had always been a landmark in the region of the Southwest where Lucien Maxwell lived. From the porches of his Cimarron mansion, Lucien must have gazed toward its lofty peak almost daily, and in speculative moments he might have wondered what was hidden beneath such an austere facade. There was ample reason to speculate, for a decade after James W. Marshall discovered the tiny gold flakes that precipitated the migration of hundreds of thousands of miners to California, prospectors seeking their fortunes in the Rocky Mountains struck riches in Cherry Creek, not three hundred miles north of Lucien's. Dozens of later strikes along the front range and far into the mountains were in places geographically comparable to Maxwell's ranch. By the mid-1860s, Denver had become a major frontier city, and Colorado had earned admission to the Union as a separate territory. In New Mexico, the success of placer mines south of the Cimarron near Santa Fe demonstrated the presence of valuable minerals throughout the Rocky Mountain region.

Evidently these widespread mining activities sparked Maxwell's interest. In 1862, Lucien reportedly told a group of Texans en route home from Colorado that he knew there was gold on his ranch. Presumably because of the Civil War or the lack of adequate transportation, he told them that "the time had not yet come when it could be worked."[1] About the same time, Benjamin Eaton, a former Pikes Peak prospector, sought gold near Cimarron. He found nothing, although he remained optimistic that "the time would come when minerals would be found in paying quantities."[2]

Renewed interest in prospecting Maxwell's mountains coincided with the close of the Civil War. Late in August, 1866, a company of soldiers commanded by Lieutenant George Campbell arrived in Cimarron to protect Maxwell and his family from Indian attack. Most of the soldiers were members of the California Column, which General James H. Carleton had brought to New Mexico during the war, and many had mined in the Mother Lode before coming to the Southwest. According to tradition, the soldiers became interested in pieces of greenish-blue colored rock the Utes and Apaches brought down from Baldy Mountain. One curious soldier climbed high atop Baldy to a place where he found the slopes blanketed with what he knew to be copper float and laid out a claim to what became the Mystic Lode copper mine.[3]

The return of the troops to Fort Union and the discharge of some of the soldiers who had been at Cimarron spurred further activity. Sometime late in 1866 or early in 1867 a party of prospectors was organized and presumably bankrolled by William H. Moore, William Kroenig, and others at Fort Union. The group included Pete Kinsinger, one of Carleton's volunteers who had worked in the California mines, Larry Bronson, and a man named Kelley. They headed back past Maxwell's, continued up the Cimarron River, and turned north into the Moreno Valley on the west side of Baldy. They camped on Willow Creek, one of several streams running off the west side of Baldy, before initiating what was apparently planned as a thorough search for copper mines. According to an often-repeated report, while Bronson and Kinsinger prepared dinner, Kelley washed gravel in a nearby creek. What he found surprised them all—gold! Supper plans abandoned, the cooks picked up tools and set about finding out how extensive the deposits were. Almost every pan they washed during the expedition, which may have lasted several weeks, turned up more gold flakes, convincing the prospectors that they had made an important find.[4]

Maxwell became involved immediately. Together with Kinsinger, Moore, Kroenig, and other Fort Union men, Lucien formed the Copper Mining Company, which filed for claims on Cimarron Creek May 23, 1867. The company tunneled three hundred feet, apparently searching for copper, before they encountered a rich vein of gold ore, the only hard-rock discovery made the first season.[5]

It was June, 1867, before news of the discovery of gold on Baldy Mountain became public. In its issue of June 8, 1867, the *Santa Fe Weekly Gazette* printed a letter dated ten days earlier at La Cueva, near Mora, containing "startling intelligence in regard to the discovery of gold in the northeast part of the territory near Maxwell's ranch." A few men already there were making sixty to eighty dollars a day, the correspondent reported; the excitement at Fort Union was intense, and most men at the fort—presumably the civilian employees or soldiers about to be discharged—planned to leave for the mines within a month. "Rest assured," the correspondent concluded, "that I am not exaggerating anything in particular."[6] The rival *New Mexican,* which claimed initial skepticism about rumored gold discoveries, reported that the Baldy diggings promised to be "as rich as any in California." Three hundred employees of the quartermaster's department at Fort Union had resigned their jobs to take up mining.[7]

The discovery of gold forced Maxwell for the first time to think seriously about the boundaries of the Beaubien and Miranda grant. The lines sketched in the official patent were vague, and the western boundary was described only as following "the top of the mountain which divides the waters of the rivers running toward the west, and thence following the line of said mountains in a southwardly direction until it intersects the first hills south of the Rayado River."[8] But what mountains were being referred to? Those immediately west of Maxwell's mansion? Or father west, including Baldy? Or the larger range that separated the Moreno Valley from the Taos Valley and the Río Grande? Probably Lucien had never seriously pondered these questions himself, for the answer mattered little as long as the land was unoccupied and valueless. But the discovery of gold changed the situation and made the answer critical to control of the mines.

There is evidence that Lucien's interpretation of the western boundary changed as the size and value of the mines grew and, significantly, as he received expert advice from individuals more adept than he at manipulating the law to their own advantage. Years later, Phillip Mould testified that in the summer of 1866, before the Baldy discoveries, he had asked Maxwell "how far the boundaries of his grant extended West." Lucien allegedly replied that they went no "further west than the mouth of the Cimarron Cañon." Mould was concerned that if he prospected Ute Creek, on the east side of Baldy, there would be "trouble with the owners of the grant," but Lucien denied having any "right or title to Ute Creek" and offered to supply provisions to anyone who wished to prospect there.[9] William A. Bell, who visited Maxwell's in August, 1867, reported that when the mines were first discovered Lucien did not ask the prospectors "'what they meant by trespassing on his property;' but he welcomed them as friends—sent them timber from his saw-mill and sheep from his flocks."[10]

As time passed after the discovery of gold, Maxwell's interpretation seems to have changed. He did not yet claim the Moreno Valley, for the earliest reports consistently described the placer discoveries as occurring "near," not "on," Maxwell's ranch; the miners in the Moreno established what they called the Cimarron Mining District and took up claims as though they were on unclaimed federal land. Maxwell made no known protest; in fact, the company in which he participated filed for a claim in exactly the same manner as any other miners. On the other hand, in July, 1867, when a party of miners from the west side of Baldy crossed "over the range," they entered what the author of a contemporary newspaper article described as "what is claimed to be Mr. Maxwell's grant." The miners prospected near Lucien's sawmill in the Cimarron Canyon, found a "very good prospect," and were in the process of digging a ditch to bring water to the site when "Mr. Maxwell ordered them off his land." The prospectors left, although they claimed that their understanding of the "miner's privileges under the United States mining laws" gave them the right to return.[11]

Soon, however, Maxwell's claims became even more expansive. It is impossible to account precisely for the change, but by late summer or early fall, New Mexico's territorial governor, Robert B. Mitchell, and territorial chief justice, John P. Slough, visited the district to confer with Maxwell about possible investment and land development schemes in the area. Simultaneously with their arrival, Lucien extended his claim to include all of the Moreno Valley. It is not unreasonable to presume that Maxwell discussed the matter with these men, who advised him to claim as much land as possible and worry later about demonstrating his ownership. By late November, Maxwell's new policy was announced in an article that for the first time introduced the term "Maxwell Land Grant" to identify what had previously been known as the "Beaubien and Miranda Land Grant" or the "Rayado Grant" and that suggested the vastness of the grant. Reported the *Santa Fe Weekly Gazette:*

Mr. Maxwell, the owner of the immense tract known as the "Maxwell Grant," some sixty miles square, desirous of encouraging settlement of the country, with his usual liberality, has proposed to the miners to give them leases to their claims at merely nominal rates. The mines thus far discovered are entirely upon the "Grant."[12]

Early in 1868, Maxwell employed former Cimarron Indian agent Jack Henderson as his representative to issue "leases to the miners, and thereby settling all disputes in regard to jumping." The "nominal rates" which had been promised turned out to be two dollars per month per claim of two hundred feet.[13]

Assertions that Maxwell's proposals met with "universal satisfaction," were clearly exaggerated. A letter from Elizabethtown, the new Moreno Valley mining town, early in March, 1868, reported that the miners in the valley were angry at having been betrayed by Maxwell and his Santa Fe advisors. They had begun their work "with the understanding from Mr. L. B. Maxwell" that they would not "be disturbed in their work." They had begun mining "with a good will; put in their work; spent what little money they brought with them." Those forced by water shortages to stop work "held over their claims until next spring, and started for different parts to gain subsistence during the winter."

The trouble had begun, the author reported, when Governor Mitchell visited the area, "satisfied himself that the mines were rich, and concluded that he ought to have his finger in them." At first the governor proposed leasing the entire district from Maxwell. Had this effort succeeded, the miners believed that he and his friends would have "made their own terms with the miners, or in other words, would have turned them into peons." Instead, Maxwell had decided to lease mining rights himself, and the governor agreed to send in troops to force compliance with his demands if necessary.[14] Whether these accusations are entirely true or not, Lucien began collecting rent wherever he could, and he initiated a series of business ventures which included not only Mitchell and, until his death soon after, Chief Justice Slough, but also two leading Colorado capitalists, Charles P. Holly and Henry Hooper, both important in the ultimate sale of the grant.

The town that Lucien and his business associates proposed to establish was located near the spot where the Cimarron River flowed out of the Moreno Valley. It was named Virginia City, in honor of Lucien's eldest daughter.

An announcement in the November 30, 1867, issue of the *Santa Fe Weekly Gazette,* the mouthpiece of the governor's political faction, noted that "Lucian [*sic*] Maxwell, having laid out a town at the entrance to the rich gold mines . . . located in what is known as the Maxwell grant" would auction off a total of four hundred lots. "We have no doubt," an accompanying editorial proclaimed, "that 'Virginia City' is destined to become one of our leading cities. Enterprise, capital, and energy backed with population, rich mines, and extensive pastoral and agricultural lands must succeed."[15]

The town project was, nevertheless, doomed to failure. Despite generally positive publicity and claims that Maxwell's landholdings were so large that they "precluded the establishment of a rival city," most miners preferred to settle at Elizabethtown, a village founded by Fort Union interests and located several miles north of Virginia City.[16] What is especially revealing about Maxwell's power is that, even though he claimed title to the land where Elizabethtown was located, he could do nothing to prevent its establishment or growth, apparently made no attempt to collect rent from those who lived there, and even purchased lots there himself. In fact, the miners' preference for "E-town," as it was popularly known, may have reflected, at least in part, a desire by the miners to establish their independence from Maxwell or their opposition to his leasing efforts.

Whatever the reasons, six months after it had been established, Virginia City still had fewer than fifty residents and lacked the hotels, restaurants, shops, and other amenities found at E-town. By mid-summer, a newspaper article reported, only partially in jest, that the village had "played out." "Virginia City moved up here yesterday," reported a writer from Elizabethtown, "came up on a burro; says it is too lonesome down there and can't stand it; had to go three miles just to speak to anyone."[17] Even Maxwell, recognizing the advantages of E-town, purchased from V. S. Shelby a store located there.[18]

The ill-fated Virginia City project was but one in-

Elizabethtown flourished, even though it had been established over Maxwell's objections and in competition with his Virginia City project. Courtesy Seton Museum, Cimarron, New Mexico.

stance of Maxwell's joint participation with other capitalists. The placer mines that had opened in the Moreno Valley depended for their operation entirely on the availability of water. Each year when the few small streams running off Baldy dried up, all mining activity halted. During the fall of 1867, Maxwell hired Captain Nicholas S. Davis, a former officer under Carleton, to explore the feasibility of constructing an elaborate ditch system to transport water from Red River, west of the Baldy district, into the Moreno Valley. By December the *Denver News* reported that "Mr. Maxwell" had begun construction which would provide the district with needed water. The project soon became too expensive and technically complex for Maxwell to handle alone, and he incorporated the Moreno Valley Water and Mining Company, whose directors and stockholders included Davis, Fort Union promoters William Kroenig and William H. Moore, stageline owner V. S. Shelby, and merchants John Dold and Morris Bloomfield. Maxwell apparently contributed much of the initial $115,000 capital.[19]

The project was immense, stretching more than forty-one miles and requiring the construction of three miles of aqueducts and side-hill flumes. Work began in May, 1868, continued until November of that year, and began again the following spring. More than four hundred men were employed; total costs exceeded $200,000. July 8, 1869, the first water reached Humbug Gulch on Baldy's western slope above Elizabethtown.[20] Unfortunately, despite its impressive size and cost the "Big Ditch" failed to produce expected results. It had been planned to carry from seven hundred to twelve hundred inches of water, but leaks reduced actual production to only one hundred inches. It failed to earn significant profit for Maxwell or to solve the persistent water problems that beset the Moreno Valley mines.[21]

While neither the Virginia City or Big Ditch projects profited Maxwell, they did introduce him and his grant to some of the leading, most imaginative, and most aggressive capitalists in the Rocky Mountain West. Previously, few if any potential developers recognized either the extent or the richness of the Beaubien and Miranda grant; seldom had outsiders seen much more than Lucien's famed Cimarron home. Now, as men like Mitchell, Slough, Hooper, and Holly traversed the property, learned of the rich mineral deposits being discovered, saw its vast cattle ranges, forests, and farmlands, and learned how vague its boundary descriptions were, these entrepreneurs began to dream of the potential profits that might be reaped from such a vast estate.

Meanwhile, Lucien's other mining endeavors proved infinitely more successful. The initial focus of Baldy Mountain mining had been on removing loose gold from sand and gravel deposits in the Moreno Valley. Lucien, however, must have suspected that the eastern or Ute Creek side of the mountain also contained gold and that mines dug into the rock itself might prove productive. In May, 1868, perhaps following previous prospecting trips a year before, three prospectors—Tim Foley, Matthew Lynch, and Robert Dougherty—probably acting with Lucien's permission or even on his behalf, began exploring the Ute Creek Valley. Upstream they panned until they no longer found gold. At an elevation of nearly 10,000 feet, high above the valley, they began to scour the ridges looking for the source of the gold. What they discovered was a thirty-foot-wide depression full of rotted quartz, in which three well-defined veins of gold were visible.[22]

Maxwell quickly learned of the discovery, presumably through the three prospectors, and began to develop a mine he called the Aztec. Just as he had in the Virginia City and Big Ditch enterprises, he formed a corporation, dividing ownership into twelve parts. Foley dropped out of the project. Dold and Dougherty each received two shares; Dougherty later sold his interest to Dold and to stageline owner V. S. Shelby. Shelby, Matt Lynch, and E. H. Bergmann, who managed the property, each owned one share, and Maxwell controlled the remaining five. When the profits were divided, however, Lucien took half, probably because he put up the capital required to develop the Aztec.[23]

Just how profitable the Aztec could be soon became apparent. Maxwell dispatched a sample of ore to the Untied States Mint in Denver for evaluation. The report assayer O. D. Munson sent him June 18, 1868, brought the good news. The quartz sample from the Aztec had yielded $19,455.37 in gold and $189.88 in silver, "being the very handsome sum" of $19,645.25.[24] Very handsome, indeed, responded the editor of the *Santa Fe New Mexican,* when he saw the report. Doubtless, he concluded, the Aztec was the richest mine "that has ever been discovered in the world," and if perchance there were only one hundred tons of ore at this value, Maxwell would have made nearly two million dollars. "But there is no reason to doubt that this great lode is extensive," he went on, "and that Mr. Maxwell will in a short time be known as the greatest gold producer on the globe."[25]

Lucien quickly set about developing the property. He knew little if anything about the technical or mechanical aspects of mining, so he hired E. H. Bergmann, a recently retired army officer, to purchase the needed equipment and superintend its installation and operation. Soon a 15-stamp mill, whose 435-pound stamps pounded onto an iron base thirty-three times a minute to pulverize the rock, arrived from Denver. The stamp mill and a twelve-horsepower steam engine were housed in a frame building which became the nucleus of a new settlement called Baldy Town, at the base of Aztec Ridge. Meanwhile, eighteen men began sinking a shaft deep into the mountain and digging tunnels into the rich ore bodies they found. Not all the work was as carefully conducted as it could have been, for Bergmann complained that efforts at "making money 'fast,'" had resulted in improper developments with "no view to future mining." Bergmann reversed these policies. "I am glad to say," he reported early in 1870, "the work is carried on now more systematically."[26]

Bergmann's efforts produced impressive results for Maxwell. In the fourteen months between the time the mill opened in late October, 1868, and December, 1869, the Aztec yielded 8,741 ounces of gold valued at nearly $175,000. During only six days of work, it produced 120 ounces of gold worth $2,640. In one ninety-day period, nine hundred tons of ore yielded 1,696 ounces worth about $34,000. Expenses, however, were also high. With forty-eight men in the mine and mill receiving from $2.50 to $5.00 a day, the ninety-day payroll totaled $8,294. The men's subsistence cost another $4,320, and six mules, each rented for $1.50 a day and fed for fifty cents, cost $1,080. Other expenses were for wood, candles, blasting powder, fuses, and so forth. "Wear and tear" on the mill accounted for $900. Expenses totaled $15,844. But the overall result for only three months was a clear profit of $18,076 or nearly $20 for every tone of ore. These results, Bergmann argued, proved the "uncommon productiveness" of the mine, and the quality of the ore still being discovered was "the richest . . . found in any mining country," fine enough to "astonish the mining world."[27]

Reports of the mine's actual production resulted in a flurry of highly favorable publicity. The editors of the *Santa Fe Weekly Gazette*, confessing that they had been "incredulous" at the earliest reports about the Aztec, admitted their mistake. "Should the lead continue to produce at this rate, it will soon make a fortune for the proprietors and establish for New Mexico the reputation of possessing one of the richest gold mines in the world."[28] When predictions that Maxwell's annual profits might total $100,000 reached the editor of the *Colorado Chieftain*, he voiced the opinion that "no gentleman in the West better deserves his good fortune." "These mines will pay the national debt, yet," he added several months later.[29]

One Colorado miner who watched a weekly cleanup that produced more than $8,000 worth of gold reported an average daily yield of $1,000. He brought down a dozen of what the miners referred to as "Maxwell's eggs," chunks of processed gold the size of chicken eggs, worth $17 an ounce. "Maxwell was worth half a million before the mines were discovered," remarked the ever-enthusiastic editor of the *Colorado Chieftain* after seeing the report, "and now, with an income of a thousand dollars a day from one mill . . . it would go far towards placing him pecuniarily in quite easy circumstances."[30] The next week's recovery was even better, producing $15,000 in gold from ore which averaged $210 a ton. "They say Maxwell is getting rich from the proceeds of his quartz mills," the editor of the Santa Fe *Gazette* observed wryly, "and he has our sympathies."[31]

While few miners in the Moreno Valley agreed to negotiate leases with Maxwell, and Henderson's efforts there were apparently quickly abandoned, Lucien was able to exercise virtually undisputed authority along Ute Creek. Sometimes he retained partial ownership of a promising mine, sharing in both development costs and income. Such was the case with the Montezuma, located near the Aztec, which New Mexico's Supreme Court Justice John S. Watts labeled as "the best lode in America." The mine was discovered by someone named "Big Jack," but Maxwell owned most of the 3,000-foot claim, ordered and paid for a 30-stamp mill for the site, and was reaping profits of nearly $1,000 a day by November, 1869.[32] He took an even more direct interest in placer workings along Ute Creek between Baldy Town and the Cimarron River. He built a house alongside the lower Ute and personally supervised a thirty-man crew at work with powerful hydraulic hoses. During a single unusually productive week, the Ute placers produced $700 worth of gold; six weeks of work returned $1,700.[33] Maxwell also operated a sawmill on Ute Creek and opened a store to supply the miners who lived there. In at least one case, that of the Last Chance mine, Maxwell purchased claims from the Leavenworth Company for $8,000 in order to work the location himself—another obvious example of the futility of his claim to ownership of the whole district.[34] In still other situations, such as

162

the French Henry Mine on the South Ponil Creek north of Aztec Ridge, Lucien sold surface or mineral rights to prospective miners.[35]

While the immediate impact of gold discoveries was felt in the vicinity of Baldy, the arrival of hordes of people and the excitement that naturally accompanied the rush to northern New Mexico affected the surrounding region as well. What previously had been known as Maxwell's Ranch now became Cimarron City, a bustling little town catering to the needs of many miners. "The young city is growing at a very commendable rate," reported the *New Mexican* in mid-1868. Several new businessmen had arrived, Lucien apparently sold town lots to prospective builders, and several new structures were going up. The future of the town looked bright, a Santa Fe editor observed after a visit, "in exceedingly strong contrast to the mushroomism of Virginia City."[36] Shortly, A. J. Calhoun opened a hotel—"an admirable place to lie over and rest"—and the location of a telegraph office at Cimarron placed the entire region in direct and instant contact with the eastern United States.[37]

The discovery of gold also produced political change. Lucien Maxwell had exercised virtually unimpeded authority on the grant since the mid-1850s, though legally all of northeastern New Mexico east of the Taos Mountains had been part of Mora County since its separation from Taos County in 1860. But it was a long way from the county seat at Mora, some thirty miles south of Cimarron, to the new gold towns, and the largely Anglo-American miners had little in common with the Spanish-speaking farmers who dominated the county. As a result, late in 1868 residents of Elizabethtown submitted a "long and earnest" petition requesting the territorial legislature to create a new county. Noting that the proposal met with "the hearty approval of the whole community," the editor of the *Colorado Chieftain*, reflecting the anti-Hispanic prejudices of the day, noted that the establishment of the new entity would assure that New Mexico had "at least one thoroughly American county."[38] The legislature acted on

January 25, 1869, to create Colfax County, named in honor of Schuyler Colfax, vice president of the United States during the Grant administration.[39]

Elections to choose a probate judge, the chief elected official in the county, were scheduled for early March. The only two candidates were J. B. Sutton, apparently an Elizabethtown miner, and Lucien B. Maxwell. Maxwell received over 350 votes more than his rival. In the precinct that included Cimarron, his natural stronghold, Lucien counted 298 votes to Sutton's 3; and in Ute Creek, 47 men preferred Lucien and only 8 voted for Sutton. Even in Elizabethtown, where Sutton's support was centered, Lucien outcounted his opponent 111 to 91.[40]

As probate judge, Maxwell had broad administrative and judicial authority. There is evidence that he was a poor administrator, probably in part because he tried to mete out justice in the informal and often arbitrary fashion he had on his own ranch. Moreover, Maxwell was frequently away from the area on extended trips in his efforts to sell the grant. Several years later, Lucien's successor in the post announced his intention to "bring order out of the chaos which has heretofore existed in the management of the affairs of this county."[41] Other problems were caused by the fact that even though territorial law required that county officials reside and maintain offices at the county seat, Lucien refused to move to Elizabethtown, which had been so designated. Residents of the Moreno Valley were naturally upset at having to travel to Cimarron to record deeds or take care of other legal matters when their own town was the place where business was supposed to be conducted.[42]

The creation of Colfax County brought many of the territory's leading lawyers and politicians to the region on a regular basis. When the first session of the district court for Colfax County convened at Elizabethtown, April 5, 1869, for example, Judge John S. Watts presided. Probably the most important person attending was United States Attorney for New Mexico Stephen B. Elkins, whose subsequent relations with Lucien and his grant would be highly significant.[43]

Other somewhat more subtle changes ultimately had an even greater impact on Maxwell's life. Before the discovery of gold, the Cimarron region was primarily agricultural and pastoral. It was small enough that all residents could know each other, and the population was predominantly Mexican American, including many poor or landless farmers. Maxwell's domineering personality enabled him to control nearly everyone with whom he came into contact. Once gold was discovered, however, thousands of newcomers, nearly all Anglo-Americans from Colorado or former army employees from Fort Union, flocked into northern New Mexico. The character of the region began to change. In June 1868, the editor of the *Colorado Chieftain* predicted that the discovery of gold at Baldy would result in the "Americanization" of northeastern New Mexico. The paper argued that "the introduction of a large American element hardened into American habits of industry, with American inventions and appliance, and presenting . . . examples of wealth, thrift, and enterprise" would inevitably have a "salutary effect" upon the region and its population.[44] For a man like Maxwell, long accustomed to a society which he understood and dominated, the disruption of traditional lifestyles and challenges to authority represented unwanted change.

The discovery of gold only intensified the pressure on the Utes and Apaches at the Cimarron Indian agency to leave their traditional homes. As miners explored creekbeds and mountain slopes, the deer and other wildlife needed by the Indians for food disappeared, forcing them to still greater dependence on government handouts. Conflicts between miners and Indians grew more frequent, and as it became easier for the Indians to acquire liquor, drunkenness became a more serious problem.[45] Any hope that the Maxwell ranch could be purchased for use as an Indian reserve had to be abandoned. Because of his intimate association with the Indians, Maxwell found himself under constant, almost unbearable pressure to help them, and his personal resources often supplemented what the government provided. Yet it became apparent that there was little he or anyone else could do to solve an increasingly difficult problem.

The most immediate impact on Maxwell was the accumulation of great wealth. It is impossible to estimate reliably his income during most years. In 1867, however, he paid federal income taxes in the amount of $4,886.16, from which his income can be deduced as $53,211.60. The following year, still before the Aztec mine came into full production, his estimated income fell to $29,175.60.[46] Tax information is not available for the following year—undoubtedly Maxwell's most profitable—but published reports indicated that his "net profits" from the Aztec alone between April 12, 1869, and July 4, 1870, totaled $60,000.[47]

For a man of relatively humble origins, who had never before spent lavishly and who only a few years earlier had found it necessary to borrow money from Kit Carson, the sudden acquisition of enough money to make him one of the wealthiest men in the Southwest resulted in many personality changes, not all of them positive. He spent lavishly. It was probably at this time that he filled his house with fine furniture, including several pianos, and covered his tables with fine silverplate brought from the East at great expense. Lavish entertainment could be provided for guests without any concern for cost or expectation of payment. Lucien did not manage money well. Huge sums were left around the house without the protection even of a safe; there were no banks closer than Denver. "I have seen as much as thirty thousand dollars—gold, silver, greenbacks, and government checks" at Maxwell's, recalled Colonel Henry Inman, who noted that Lucien took no precautions to prevent its disappearance and even left the doors unlocked and the rooms open to everyone.[48]

Gambling had been a long-standing interest of Maxwell's, and now it became a major pastime. He loved poker and another game called "old sledge," Inman remembered, played mostly with friends, and frequently wagered heavily. Maxwell must have been a skilled card player, and he often won, insisting, despite his wealth, on every cent that was due him. More than once, however, the next morning he presented an unlucky opponent with a gift of $500 or $1,000—often more than he had won from the man.[49]

Maxwell also developed a keen interest in horse racing. He acquired a number of excellent mounts, the most famous the "Ennis mare," and hired jockey Squire Hart to race them. For a race on January 23, 1870, Maxwell matched his mare against Trinidad resident George Thompson's "Shawnee Bob." Each put up stakes of $2,000 for the 500-yard run. In addition, the Pueblo newspaper predicted that "a great deal of money" could change hands on the result.[50] Hart recalled that on one occasion Maxwell gave him $5,000 in gold to bet on a race.[51] Maxwell's mare won the contest by two feet, and presumably Lucien won a good deal more than the stakes. A rematch in March offered the same stakes, but the distance was shortened to 440 yards. The next month Maxwell ran his "Bogus Bess" against "Shawnee Bob."[52] Maxwell and his horses occasionally won, but Colonel Inman reported that he usually lost money and was often "outrageously defrauded of immense sums" by dishonest jockeys.[53]

Despite pleasures such as horseracing, it became obvious to those who knew him that Lucien Maxwell was growing increasingly restless and eager to get away from the pressures of Cimarron as the decade of the sixties grew to a close. "I am tired of this place," he told Marcus Brunswick and John Dold, "from the Indians and the new-comers on the land." He offered to sell them "everything I have got," including the mines and livestock, for only $200,000. Dold was not interested, since he lacked the money and believed the property was "not worth it."[54] Maxwell made similar statements to others, however, and soon he found individuals to whom his offer proved extremely attractive.

8

The Sale of The Maxwell Grant

By mid-1869, two years after the rush of miners to the Baldy country began to disrupt his quiet life along the Cimarron, Lucien Maxwell decided to dispose of what newspapers had by this time dubbed the "Maxwell Land Grant." Since he foresaw the legal complications of transferring the property, title to which was anything but clear, and the need to attract substantial capital from investors, Maxwell sought and received—no doubt for a price—advice from some of the leading capitalists in the region. He soon discovered, and it may have surprised him as much as anyone else, the possibility of claiming a vast tract of land stretching not only throughout northeastern New Mexico but into Colorado as well. He also learned that establishing clear title to the tract raised legal problems so serious and complex that they would not be fully settled for decades. By that time, however, Lucien would have received a princely sum for the land and moved to a new ranch halfway across the territory, where he spent his final days in semi-retirement.

The principal advisers upon whom Maxwell relied in selling the ranch were Coloradans, led by Jerome B. Chaffee, politician, mine owner, and entrepreneur, one of the best-known businessmen in the West. Chaffee's initial wealth came from nearly a hundred gold and silver mines he owned. In 1864 he established the First National Bank of Denver, and probably through handling the money of New Mexico's businessmen in banking affairs, he became acquainted with Maxwell and his grant. Chaffee's successes soon increased his annual income to more than $50,000, as he participated in "nearly every major mining, railroad, and land venture" in Colorado.[1] Several of Chaffee's younger associates provided day-to-day assistance and advice to Maxwell. Charles F. Holly was a lawyer and miner from Boulder who had served as speaker of the first and second sessions of the Colorado House of Representatives.[2] He had come to Baldy soon after the discovery of gold, associating with Maxwell in the promotion of Virginia City. He later moved to Cimarron, where he became Maxwell's principal confidant and leading adviser, while also serving as clerk in the probate court where Maxwell was judge. Holly had been interested in Mexican land grants in Colorado since the early 1860s and had schooled himself in the legal questions related to them. Joining Holly in Cimarron was Henry N. Hooper, a Boston native and Harvard graduate who had commanded a black regiment during the Civil War and had spent time in the Colorado mines before coming to New Mexico. Still only thirty-five years old in 1869, Hooper was an extremely energetic and aggressive individual whose speculative dreams seem to have affected Maxwell. Another Colorado adviser, George M. Chilcott, was a Pennsylvania native who had lived in Iowa and Nebraska. In Colorado he had engaged in mining and land speculation and had served as a land registrar for southern Colorado, gaining considerable knowledge of land grant questions.[3]

Maxwell also relied on several New Mexicans for legal and personal advice. The most important was John S. Watts, who had come to the Southwest as a territorial Supreme Court justice in 1851, had represented New Mexico in Congress during the Civil War, and had succeeded John P. Slough as chief justice in 1868. Watts more than anyone in the territory was familiar with land grant questions and knew the contents of the Santa Fe archives.[4] Two younger men played a growing role in the development of Maxwell's grant. Stephen B. Elkins, a native of Missouri, came

The only known photograph of Maxwell shows him (left) with Charles Holly (standing) and Jerome B. Chaffee (right) during negotiations to sell the grant. Courtesy Victor Grant, Taos, New Mexico.

to New Mexico in 1863 and established a law practice first in Mesilla, later in Santa Fe. His activities extended throughout New Mexico, and, as noted above, in his official capacity as United States attorney he had attended the first court session for Colfax County held in Elizabethtown in 1869.[5] A schoolmate of Elkins, also from Missouri, Thomas B. Catron arrived in New Mexico in mid-1866, and according to his own testimony, he and Elkins traveled across Raton Pass together, visited Maxwell's, and discussed the size and potential value of the property.[6]

The sale of the grant finally was made possible by the fact that during the five years preceding 1869, Maxwell had slowly increased his ownership of the tract. He had acquired Guadalupe Miranda's interest in 1858. Further opportunities developed in 1864 with the death in Taos of Lucien's father-in-law, Charles Beaubien. Beaubien divided his estate among his six surviving heirs, five daughters and one son. Almost immediately Maxwell began to buy up shares from his brothers- and sisters-in-law, most of whom lived in Taos and had little interest in the land across the mountains. April 4, 1864, he paid Theodora Muller and her husband, Frederick, $3,500 for their interest; the same day Juana and her husband, Joseph Clothier, agreed to sell their part of the estate for $3,500, half to be paid in August and the remainder in October of that year. In July, Eleanor and her husband, Vidal Trujillo, sold their rights for $3,000. It was three years later before Petra and Jesús Abreú, who lived on the Rayado and had a much greater interest in the property than the others, agreed to dispose of their interests for $3,500. Not for another three years—just as he was preparing to offer the entire grant for sale—was Lucien able to secure Paul Beaubien's share for the same price.[7] Actually, even though most people assumed that he owned the entire grant, Lucien held all the shares for only a few months.

Moreover, he contended with continuing problems from the heirs of Charles Bent. The suit originally filed in 1859 dragged on until 1865, when, during the territorial

171

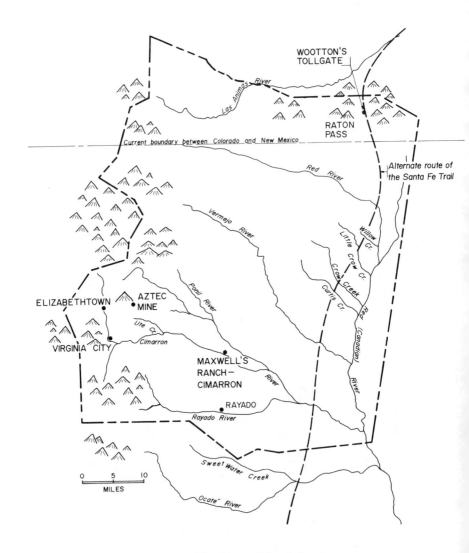

WOOTTON'S
TOLLGATE

Las Animas River

RATON
PASS

Current boundary between Colorado and New Mexico

Red River

Alternate route of
the Santa Fe Trail

Vermejo River

Willow Cr.

Little Crow Cr.

Crow Creek

Curtis Cr.

Ponil River

Red (Canadian) River

ELIZABETHTOWN ● AZTEC
MINE ●

Ute Cr.

VIRGINIA CITY ● *Cimarron*

MAXWELL'S
RANCH—
CIMARRON

River

● RAYADO

Rayado River

0   5   10
MILES

Sweet Water Creek

Ocaté River

The Maxwell Land Grant.
Map drawn by Kevin E. Coveart
© 1983 by the University of Oklahoma Press

court's spring term, Judge Kirby Benedict ruled that the Bent heirs had legal claim to a fourth of the entire grant and created a three-member commission to separate out that amount of the land for their use. Partly because the grant had never been surveyed, the division had never occurred, and in September, 1866, John P. Slough, New Mexico's chief justice and a friend and business associate of Maxwell, approved an arrangement whereby Lucien paid each of the Bent children $6,000 for their share of the grant. Payment was made to daughters Aloys and Teresina Scheurich, but the son, Alfred, died unexpectedly at the hands of Indians before the negotiations were concluded, initiating a long, complicated legal dispute not settled until the New Mexican Supreme Court issued a final ruling in 1895, long after Maxwell's death.[8]

Despite his failure to settle fully with the Bent heirs, in 1869, Maxwell initiated a series of steps aimed at the eventual disposal of the land. The first move came May 16, 1869, when Holly prepared a letter, in Maxwell's name, to New Mexico's surveyor general, T. Rush Spencer. Noting that almost a year earlier he had "arranged informally" with Spencer's predecessor to survey the exterior lines of the grant, but that the work had never been initiated, Maxwell asked that the necessary arrangements be completed "according to the law." He volunteered to make the required deposit and provide the surveyor with whatever animals and supplies would be needed. Maxwell chose not to mail the letter, but sent it with Chilcott, urging Spencer to come back with him to Cimarron "if by so doing it will facilitate the commencement of the work."[9]

Whether Spencer visited Cimarron is not known, but there appears to be a good deal more to this seemingly innocent letter than at first appears. Maxwell recognized the importance of the survey, for whatever initial interpretation was given to the vague Spanish documents would provide a basis for all future deliberations. He also knew the importance of securing the cooperation of the surveyor general in appointing a sympathetic surveyor. Spencer took charge of the land office only one day before Maxwell's letter was written, and he earned an almost instant reputation for unseemly cooperation with land claimants, usually in exchange for a personal interest in the property.[10] Exactly when, how, or if such an agreement was reached with Maxwell is uncertain, but at the time a corporation was established to manage Lucien's property for its new foreign owners, Spencer—supposedly a disinterested public official—was included as one of its officers. Moreover, he moved with inordinate haste in commencing the survey. By June 16, 1869, Spencer agreed to survey the grant boundaries, appointed Santa Fe engineer William W. Griffin as surveyor, and sent him, along with draftsman John Lambert, fifteen assistants, and sufficient wagons and pack animals for a three-months stay, north to Cimarron.[11]

Maxwell orchestrated the survey. He accompanied the party as it began along the southeast boundary. As work progressed, he explained to Griffin and his men where the lines should be drawn and how the vagaries of the descriptions should be interpreted. He ordered several poor Mexican Americans who had worked for him for decades to give evidence in support of his claims. Once when Faustin Jaramillo came to the Cimarron to pay Maxwell some money, for example, Lucien directed him to go to the head of the Uña de Gato, carrying a letter from Maxwell, and show Griffin's team the line that constituted the proper boundary.[12] Another time, when Griffin lost the line and came to Cimarron for help, Lucien sent Jesús Silva. Griffin asked Silva what his charge would be, and Maxwell had told him to say "five dollars a day." Silva recalled: "I did, and he paid it."[13] The guides Maxwell sent were not always reliable, Griffin complained, for the man who led him north from the Uña de Gato, perhaps Jaramillo, led him "very far astray," making it necessary to resurvey forty-two miles.[14]

Even before the survey had actually begun, Maxwell had formalized his decision to sell. On May 26, 1869, he and his wife granted Chaffee, Chilcott, and Holly an option to purchase their "Beaubien and Miranda or Rayado grant, containing about two million acres of land" or to induce "other persons to purchase it." Maxwell promised to provide a "good and sufficient deed." He must not have made a final decision to leave the area, however, for he reserved from the sale the "home ranch of cultivated land," about a thousand acres, his grain mill, and several mines. The total purchase price was set at $600,000.[15]

Efforts to sell the grant began almost immediately. Chaffee began work on a promotional brochure which he completed in New York on July 20. He outlined the history of the property, noting its confirmation by the United States Congress, and described its immense size—"over 3,000 square miles of territory, and over 2,000,000 acres of land—being larger than the State of Connecticut and some other States of this Union." The title, he continued, was "complete and perfect." More important than the grant's size, Chaffee continued, was its richness. It was "well watered," and from 300,000 to 500,000 acres were suitable for cultivation. The grazing land made it "the finest . . . stock-raising country in the world." There was enough coal yet to be discovered to operate a railroad "for hundreds of years." "This interest," the booklet assured prospective investors, "alone guarantees many millions of dollars to the value of this immense estate."

The most attention was devoted to the area's gold mines, although the fact that most claims were privately owned and that some were exempted from the proposed sale was omitted. The newly discovered field was at least twelve miles wide and twenty-five miles long, Chaffee reported, and enough work had been done to prove that the mines were "rich and extensive." The Aztec had already produced profits of $100,000, and "*many hundreds of thousands of dollars more are now disclosed, in ore in sight. . . .* The value of this mine alone—judging from what has been seen so far—is millions of dollars." There were also many placer mines, yielding another $1,000,000 a year, which could easily be "increased to several millions . . . with proper management."

Add to these mineral resources the availability of

timber and the presence of a flour mill, two sawmills, fifteen or twenty houses, and $50,000 invested in improving the land, Chaffee concluded, and you had one of the best properties in the United States. "It is accessible, it has a hospitable climate, it is in the immediate vicinity of large agricultural resources, immense beds of coal, and surrounded with never-ending quantities of wood and timber."

"The steady development of the 'Great West,'" he predicted, "will continue to enhance the value of this immense estate, until it will add one more to the many commonwealths of this nation, larger and richer in resources than many of them."[16]

Before copies of Chaffee's booklet could be distributed, however, news arrived from Washington which threatened the consumation of any sale. May 31, 1869, Surveyor General Spencer had written to his superior in Washington, commissioner of the general land office, Joseph H. Wilson, in order to report the initiation of the survey and forward Maxwell's deposit of $5,000 to pay the costs. A week later he mailed the contract he had entered into with Griffin to do the work. Wilson no sooner received these papers than he became suspicious of what was occurring in New Mexico, and on June 28, 1869, he countermanded everything Spencer had done. Initially Wilson's interest seems to have been sparked by a minor bureaucratic question: since a portion of the grant appeared to lie in Colorado, someone questioned whether or not Spencer, whose office was limited to New Mexican land matters, could initiate a survey. The investigation that followed raised enough more serious concerns that Wilson ordered the survey suspended "until further report is received from you in relation to the extent and locality of the claim." The descriptive boundaries were so vague, he explained, that it was impossible to determine exactly how much land might be included. "As near as we can form from them an idea," he wrote, they seemed to include "a much larger area" than the eleven square leagues that Mexican law had ever empowered governors to grant. Wilson instructed Spencer to notify Maxwell and his associates of the order, give them thirty days or longer to prepare documents showing the "true extent and locus" of the grant, and hold a hearing at which all relevant papers were to be examined. In the meantime, Wilson, obviously unaware that Griffin had begun his work ten days earlier, ordered Griffin to postpone commencing the survey.[17]

The mails moved slowly across the country, and it was the third week in July before Spencer received notice to postpone the survey. He ordered Griffin to cease his work and return to Santa Fe, which Griffin did after having surveyed seventy or eighty miles of boundary.[18] A copy of Wilson's letter soon reached Maxwell, who was instructed to appear at Spencer's Santa Fe office no later than August 18 to "make record or other authority, of what is claimed as the true extent and locus of the grant." Spencer suggested two possible alternatives: Lucien could choose to limit his claim to the maximum of eleven square leagues, in which case he would need to specify where that much land was located; or if he chose to claim more, documents were needed that would demonstrate his right to more than the stipulated maximum.[19]

In late July, obviously after considerable research and careful thought, Maxwell's advisers drafted a letter which Lucien signed. The argument they chose became the basis for all subsequent presentations: the grant included all lands within the natural exterior lines described in the Mexican documents, and regardless of what size limits might have been prescribed by Mexican statute, by its confirming act of June 21, 1860, Congress had in effect established a new grant which recognized no limit. What the government needed to recognize, their argument proceeded, was that "Congress had really meant what it had distinctly enacted in full council," and no federal agency had the authority to nullify an act of Congress. Moreover, ignoring past protests by miners, Indians, and others, the letter argued that for a quarter-century the grantees and their representatives had been "in quiet and peaceful possession" without having their title challenged.

Maxwell claimed total innocence. He had paid the grantees for what he considered "valid conveyances for the said entire estate," and he knew of no other claims to the same land. "Certainly," the letter continued in language which placed Lucien at a distance from a document he himself signed, "he had not expected that in advance of any individual claim adverse to these grantees, the government which had pledged to give faith to that of Mexico, and had by solemn legislative act *'quit claimed and relinquished'* all its right in the premises, should now after a quarter of a century of possession, itself call it in question." The letter argued further that it was senseless to ask, on one hand, for a precise indication of the "locus and extent" of the grant and, on the other hand, to suspend the very survey which was the only reasonable way of determining how much land was included or where it was located. Maxwell had applied for an official survey, he had deposited $5,000 to pay the expenses, a contract had been issued to undertake the work, and all he asked was "that the work so contracted and paid for be now carried to completion according to the law and his right in the premises."[20]

Maxwell's letter of July 29 avoided discussing what boundaries were claimed or how much land the total grant included, arguing only that if the survey were finished, this information would be available. Apparently, however, his advisers had a change of heart about this strategy, for, on August 16, John S. Watts telegraphed Spencer from Fort Union asking that the hearing set for August 18 be postponed until August 23. The same day, Lucien signed a second letter that for the first time detailed his claims. He estimated the distances between mounds that had allegedly been erected by Cornelio Vigil and supposedly still existed. It was only about a mile from the first to the second mound, he explained, but soon the distances grew to fifty, sixty, and even seventy miles. "The entire grant," Maxwell reported, "is supposed to contain about two million acres of land more or less." Most of the grant was in the newly established Colfax County, but it also extended as much as twelve miles into Colorado. Some persons might consider the boundaries vague, he went on, but in reality they were "fixed & immovable & definitely given." Mounds erected in the 1840s and still standing could be identified by "lawful witnesses as yet living in this vicinity;" the "mountains, mesas and rivers" named in the boundary descriptions were "well known to everybody in the vicinity and always have been." Moreover, everyone—from Mexican officials at the time of the donation, to Congress in approving the patent, to officials in the surveyor general's office—knew that the property included more than eleven square leagues. The commissioner had no right, therefore, to "assume jurisidiction of the question of title," he concluded, should respect contrary opinions long held, and order that the survey be completed.[21]

The hearing that convened in Santa Fe during August, 1869, served no purpose other than collection of materials to be forwarded to Washington, since by this time it was evident that neither Spencer nor Wilson but the secretary of the interior would rule in the case. August 18, Spencer mailed two sets of papers labeled A and B (either Maxwell's two letters or copies of documents from the Santa Fe archives), together with "an authenticated copy" of the original sketch map showing the grant boundaries, to Washington. Wilson acknowledged receipt two weeks later, on September 3, but he admonished Spencer not to re-start the survey until the secretary of the interior had rendered a formal decision that authorized the survey of the grant.[22] In the meantime, John S. Watts, Jerome M. Chaffee, and perhaps other Maxwell legal advisers worked for a favorable decision in Washington.[23]

Responsibility for rendering a decision rested with the secretary of the interior, Jacob D. Cox. The Canadian-born Cox had studied at Oberlin College, married the daughter of abolitionist Charles G. Finney, and adopted the radical political views that dominated the Republican party after the Civil War. As secretary of the interior in 1869 and 1870, he advocated civil service reform and eventually resigned in opposition to Grant's use of political patronage. In at least one other decision involving fraudulent mineral claims, Cox struck down effort by capitalists to accumulate extensive land holdings.[24]

Cox's opinion in the Maxwell case, rendered in a letter to Commissioner Wilson the last day of December, 1869, reflected his suspicion of big business. His attention was directed primarily to the claim that Congress had created a new grant without limiting its size. He himself had read the report of the congressional committee and found nothing either in it or in the act itself that gave any "clue whatever to the extent of the tract." On the other hand, there was evidence that the grantees had claimed title to no more than fifteen or eighteen leagues, whereas Maxwell was apparently trying to substantiate title to 450 or more leagues — over two million acres.

Cox used the Maxwell claim as an example and provided an interpretation of the congressional act not only for this case but for all similar ones. "In the absence of any other guide," he ruled, no more than eleven square leagues could confirmed. "There can be no hesitation," he instructed, "to determine that it was the purpose and intent of Congress to confirm to Beaubien and Miranda to an extent not greater than eleven square leagues to each claimant." This last phrase may signify an attempt at compromise, for neither Maxwell's letters nor the earlier correspondence from the Commissioner had suggested that the limit of eleven leagues might be applied separately to each grantee, thus doubling the allowable size.

Cox went on to issue what became the department's standard response in land grant cases. "It is therefore my opinion and you may receive it as the rule for this and all like cases," he directed the Commissioner that for any Mexican colonization grant which had been

*confirmed without measurement of boundaries or of distinct
specification of the quantity confirmed, either in statute or in
the report upon which confirmation was made, no greater quantity than eleven leagues to each claimant shall be surveyed and
set off to them, that such quantity shall be surveyed in tracts
of eleven square leagues each, the general position or place of
such tracts to be selected by the grantee and the tract to then
be surveyed as compactly as practicable.*

If Maxwell agreed to this ruling, he could have the money
already on deposit applied to the completion of the survey,
and any remaining would be returned. If, on the other
hand, he chose to reject the survey, the entire amount of
his deposit should be returned, in which case the Surveyor
General of New Mexico would take "no notice . . . of the
grant." The only other option, he concluded, was for Maxwell to take the case back to Congress for "a specific interpretation" of the 1860 confirming statute.[25]

The Cox decision appeared to place the plans of Maxwell, Watts, Chaffee, and the others to sell the grant in serious, perhaps fatal, jeopardy. Although a tract of twenty-two
square leagues would be immense and valuable, especially
since Maxwell could choose the richest lands, it could not
bring the amount of money Maxwell hoped to earn through
exercise of the Chaffee, Chilcott, and Holly option. Return
to Congress was too slow, expensive, and perilous an option
to receive serious consideration. Moreover, the Cox letter
received such widespread circulation, including publication in the *Santa Fe New Mexican,* that prospective buyers
might become aware of it and lose interest in the estate.[26]

The approach to these problems chosen by the would-
be sellers was, at best misleading: they ignored Secretary
Cox's decision entirely and proceeded as though it had
never been issued. The next working day after receiving
the secretary's letter, January 3, 1870, Watts wrote to the
commissioner of the general land office on behalf of Maxwell "in compliance with the permission given in the opinion of the Secretary of the Interior" and asked to withdraw

Maxwell's application to have the grant surveyed and requested return of the $5,000 deposit he had made.[27] Several months passed before the paperwork was complete, but Maxwell eventually received the entire amount.[28]

He then contracted privately with Griffin to complete the survey. The work was entirely unofficial and extralegal, although both contemporary reports and promotional booklets identified Griffin as a "United States Government Deputy-Surveyor" and avoided mentioning that Cox had canceled the official survey.[29] Like Spencer, Griffin was well paid for his cooperation; when Lucien and his colleagues formed the First National Bank of Santa Fe, he became its only paid employee, serving as teller and bookkeeper.[30]

Meanwhile, Watts and Chaffee remained on the east coast building a case for the validity of the grant to present to prospective buyers. Watts himself drafted a supporting letter, dated December 12, 1869, before the Cox decision but published several months afterward, long after Watts knew that serious questions had been raised about the extent of the grant. He described how he had resided in New Mexico for eighteen years, noted his service as associate supreme court justice, delegate to Congress, and territorial chief justice, and reported that he practiced law in all the courts of New Mexico. As part of his legal activities, Watts went on, he had reviewed "officially and legally" the Beaubien and Miranda grant and found it "good, valid, and perfect according to the laws of said territory." This was, of course, technically correct, since no one claimed the grant invalid according to New Mexico *territorial* law, citing only *Mexican* and *United States* laws limiting its size.

Moreover, Watts continued, again carefully skirting the edge of deceit, Congress had by the act of June 21, 1860, relinquished "all right, title and interest of the United states in and to the said estate" now owned by Lucien B. Maxwell. To add further credibility to his statement, Watts appended certificates from the clerk of the House of Representatives and from Secretary of State Hamilton Fish.

Neither referred to the grant, merely certifying that Watts had served as delegate and supreme court judge, but they could be interpreted as attesting to the truthfulness of his statements.[31]

To strengthen his case further, Chaffee approached William A. Evarts, a distinguished lawyer and political power in New York, who had served as attorney general during Andrew Johnson's administration and who, years later, would be secretary of state in President Rutherford B. Hayes's cabinet. Allegedly in exchange for the sum of $5,000, Evarts, who presumably knew nothing of the Cox letter and did nothing to find out about it, wrote Chaffee a letter dated March 2, 1870, that was published in several promotional brochures.[32] He had examined the document presented to New Mexico's Surveyor General William Pelham in 1857, Evarts reported, as well as the "authoritative confirmation" in the 1860 act of Congress. From these perusals, he ascertained that "there can be no doubt" of the "validity and efficacy" of the title. He wrote, "I am satisfied that the title of these lands has passed from the United States to the Mexican grantees, and is now vested in them or their assigns, and I am not aware that any question can be made of this complete and final disposition of the title of the United States."[33]

Judah P. Benjamin, who had served as attorney general in Jefferson Davis's Confederate government and subsequently fled to England where he became a respected attorney, prepared a similar opinion, allegedly for a $10,000 fee, as did other, lesser-known lawyers.[34]

Additional evidence collected by the promoters of the grant demonstrated its profitability. Isaah Rinehart, the Cimarron mill operator whose wife helped arrange Virginia Maxwell's marriage, attested to the quality of the flour he produced and estimated the mill's annual income at $26,440. Farm manager John Howell estimated that 400,000 acres could be brought to a "high state of cultivation" producing an annual income of several hundred thousand dollars. Edward H. Bergmann, manager of the

Aztec mine and mill on Baldy, presented statistics to show
how much money could be made from gold mining. Other
reports related the immense profitability of lumbering,
ranching, and other activities. To describe the countryside in a way that would enable foreigners unfamiliar with
the West to envision it, the promoters employed William
A. Bell, a Scottish traveler who had recently completed a
lengthy trip through the West. His report, published in
London in 1870 as *New Tracks in North America*, established
his reputation as an authoritative reporter. The profits already being earned were great, Bell wrote, but the arrival
of railroads in New Mexico foreshadowed an even brighter
future. "With the impetus given by the construction of direct railroad systems," he wrote, "conjoined with the introduction and judicious appliance of capital, the infusion of
energy and fresh ideas, assistance and encouragement to
immigration of the best class, and careful management,"
the Maxwell ranch would surely "yield, ere long, returns
in comparison with which its present revenues will appear
insignificant."[35]

The exact details of what transpired before the sale
of the grant cannot be fully reconstructed, and even Maxwell probably was not privy to them all. Early in 1870,
Maxwell agreed to a new option authorizing Chaffee, Chilcott, and Holly to buy the grant or transfer it to others,
again excluding the home ranch, several mines, and other
small parcels, for an increased price of $1,350,000.[36] Soon,
perhaps accompanied by New York land speculator Wilson
Waddingham, Chaffee sailed to England. There he joined
John A. Collinson, a London capitalist listed as co-author
with Bell of the booklet describing the grant, which had
been printed in England. Collinson was already putting
together an investment syndicate interested in the property. Utilizing the booklet, Chaffee and Collinson worked
during the spring of 1870 to raise the necessary money
and organize the Maxwell Land Grant and Railway Company. The deal for the sale of the ranch was complete by
late April, when Chaffee and Waddingham returned to
New York.[37]

One more detail needed to be taken care of. New Mexico had no law specifically authorizing foreigners to own land; and because of widespread anti-foreign sentiment in the United States, the English buyers were afraid that their purchase might provoke a reaction that would deprive them of the grant. To avoid complications, they chose three prominent New Mexicans, all of whom had been closely associated with Maxwell, to incorporate the company in Santa Fe: Governor William A. Pile, Surveyor General T. Rush Spencer, and attorney John S. Watts. Approval of the articles of incorporation May 12, 1870, removed the final impediment to completion of the sale.[38]

Summoned to New York to sign the necessary papers, Lucien spent several weeks consummating the sale. Marcus Brunswick, an Elizabethtown merchant to whom Maxwell owed $40,000, accompanied him East, where they met Chaffee, Chilcott, and Holly. There was considerable delay awaiting the arrival of the sale papers and money from overseas. April 30, 1870, Lucien signed the final documents, with Chaffee and Chilcott as witnesses. The money had not yet arrived. Brunswick, who acted as a messenger to bring the documents to Luz Maxwell for her signature, was instructed to await the arrival of a telegram from Lucien reading "New Mexico all right" before the signed deed was turned over to the company representative, a Mr. McFarland. The deeds were recorded in the Elizabethtown courthouse July 23, 1870.[39]

How much Lucien received for the grant is unclear. Chilcott, Chaffee, Holly, and perhaps Waddingham seem to have persuaded Maxwell that because of title questions raised by the government, he should accept a lower price than they had previously negotiated. They failed, however, to pass the reduction on to the English buyers, who appear to have been unaware of the Cox decision and the resulting shadow over the title. According to what Marcus Brunswick heard from both Maxwell and Chaffee, Lucien received $600,000, leaving the speculators with a tidy profit of $750,000. Other reports have Maxwell receiving $750,000.[40] Transporting such a large sum of money west posed a number of problems. According to a story repeated by Lucien's granddaughter, Maxwell returned with the cash in a handbag. The stagecoach in which he traveled stopped near Raton to water the horses. Nearby, the driver spotted two "mean men," who told him that they knew Lucien was carrying a huge sum but "they didn't care to try to get it" from him. Next day they robbed another stage of $20,000.[41]

As news of the sale spread westward, Maxwell's fame and that of his grant rose to new heights. "We congratulate Mr. Maxwell on so advantageous a sale," editorialized the *Daily New Mexican*, "and the company on the acquisition of a property which, under their judicious and skillful management will unquestionably yield a handsome return."[42] The editor of the *Colorado Chieftain*, who received a detailed report on the sale directly from Chilcott, was even more optimistic. "The sale will be a real benefit to the country, in as much as the wealthy company into whose hands the property goes will immediately set about improving and developing the wonderfully rich resources of the Colorado mines and the agricultural and pastoral lands of the domain . . . ."[43]

For Lucien Maxwell the sale of the grant marked another important turning point. His already substantial wealth increased further as a result of the sale, making him by far the richest man in the Southwest. Moreover, relief from the problems of managing so many diverse activities, coping with the thousands of miners who had immigrated to the area, and dealing with the seemingly impossible situation of the local Indians removed many daily burdens. It remained to be decided what Maxwell, who was still only 52 years old, would do with his immense wealth and how he would spend the remainder of his life.

9

Reflections on a Frontier Life

THE sale of his grant to English capitalists in mid-1870 marked the apogee of Lucien B. Maxwell's life. Never again would he assume the prominence or bear the heavy responsibilities he had known during the late 1860s. Rather than continuing to grow, his fortune now began to diminish. At Fort Sumner, where he established a new home, he lived in semi-retirement. Visits to Las Vegas, Santa Fe, or Cimarron occurred less frequently, and Maxwell seemed more interested in horse racing than in productive endeavors. It was, from all appearances, a time for looking backward, not ahead. By the time of his death July 25, 1875, many contemporaries had already begun to forget who Maxwell was or what he had accomplished along New Mexico's northern frontier.

Not everyone was pleased to learn that Maxwell had sold his ranch. The Moreno Valley mining community, speaking through the Elizabethtown *Press and Telegraph,* at first expressed skepticism, wondering whether the new company might be "a Wall Street speculative swindle, akin to those which have cursed Colorado, and other portions of the West, in the past few years."[1] By early September, when it was apparent that Maxwell would soon turn over control of the property to the English owners, a public meeting was convened in Elizabethtown to discuss the upcoming change. Although the discussion was conducted "calmly and dispassionately," the miners were adamant in contending that those who worked the mines and tilled the soil had stronger claims than either the English or the Indians. They demanded, moreover, that a United States patent be produced, an "authorized" survey be made, and the boundaries of the grant be clearly defined.[2]

The miners' opposition to the sale was passive by comparison with that of the Utes and Apaches at the Cimarron agency. During the preceding decades government agents had come and gone, and troops had alternately chastized and cared for the Indians. Lucien Maxwell, however, had always been there, often mediating between the agents, soldiers, or settlers, and providing food when no one else would. "He has so long acted as a sort of foster-father to them," reported veteran agent W. F. M. Arny, "they dislike the idea of losing him."[3] "This tribe has lived upon Maxwell's bounty so long," summarized the *Colorado Chieftain,* "that they have come to think that he is bound to feed them and let them loaf around his ranch the rest of their lives."[4]

Several of the chiefs threatened Lucien's life if he left, and said they would fight to prevent the transfer. Surveyor William Griffin recalled that one day while riding near Cimarron in a buggy, Lucien was stopped by several Indians and told that "if he sold that country, they would kill him." Maxwell managed to talk his way out of the touchy situation. "Was he alarmed?" asked a questioner. "No, Sir," Griffin replied, "Maxwell wasn't a man to be alarmed easily."[5] On yet another occasion, Indians went to Maxwell's house, where they met a new government agent, presumably either Arny or Charles F. Roedel, who succeeded A. S. B. Keyes. The Indians became so angry over the impending sale that they grabbed the man's beard and slapped him repeatedly. Lucien's daughter Paulita ran for her father, who ejected the troublemakers.[6] To assure Maxwell's safety and a peaceful transition to control by the new owners, the government once again ordered soldiers to Cimarron.[7]

In addition to mollifying the unhappy Cimarron Indians, Lucien faced a number of other problems, not the least of which was how to invest the fortune he had received for the grant. Cash was short in New Mexico, and there were relatively few opportunities for large-scale investment. One idea, probably initiated by Chaffee (who had established a pioneer Colorado bank), Watts, Holly, and Hooper, was to found a bank which would at once prove to be a profitable investment and provide a safe place for Lucien to store his money. On September 3, 1870, a meeting to organize what was to be called the First National Bank of Santa Fe convened in Cimarron. In addition to Maxwell, Holly, Hooper, and Watts were present, as well as Lucien's son Peter and surveyor W. W. Griffin, who had not yet completed his unofficial mapping of the grant.[8] Maxwell subscribed to and paid for 1,500 shares of stock valued at $100 each; he presented 200 shares to Holly and ten each to Hooper, Watts, and his son Peter. At the meeting it was voted to issue stock certificates bearing "impressions of the bank's president," Maxwell; when they arrived from the East, each bore a likeness of Maxwell smoking an enormous cigar.[9]

Three days later, Maxwell signed other, still more important documents. While the initial grant sale had reserved for Lucien and his family the "home ranch," mines, and other personal property, on September 7, 1870, he disposed of virtually everything he owned in Colfax County to the English company: the Cimarron mansion and surrounding land, a lot in Elizabethtown (presumably the store he had purchased from V. S. Shelby), mines on Willow Gulch and Ute Creek, an interest in the Montezuma mill and mine, and a one-twelfth interest in the Aztec mine. The merchandise in his Cimarron, Ute Creek, and Elizabethtown stores alone was valued at over $50,000, besides which the sale included two thousand sheep, two hundred cattle, a hundred horses and mules, farming equipment, twenty wagons, and other "personal property." He excluded only two family carriages and two pairs of the best horses and mules. The price was a bargain $125,000. Lucien agreed to take $75,000 in the form of a promisory

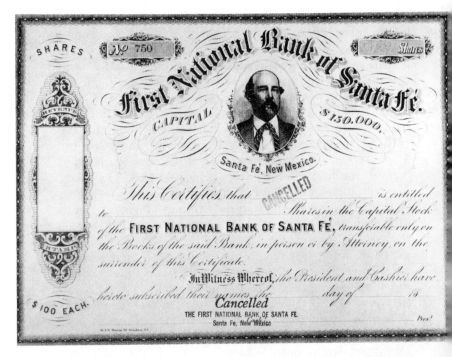

Stock certificates issued by the First National Bank bore the likeness of Maxwell smoking an enormous cigar. Courtesy First National Bank of Santa Fe.

note, suggesting that either he wanted very badly to leave or was already so wealthy that he had no interest in striking a better deal.[10]

Not for another month did Lucien and his family acquire a new home. October 10, 1870, the secretary of war telegraphed the news to New Mexico: "Accepted sum of $5,000 from L. B. Maxwell for buildings at Fort Sumner."[11] Lucien thus became the owner of facilities at a military post that, from the time it was established in 1862 until it closed seven years later, had become infamous as the site where the Navajo Indians were held following their defeat by Kit Carson's American army. The Fort Sumner reservation had proved disastrous. The Indians resented being moved across New Mexico from their traditional homes and refused to become dirt farmers. Furthermore, droughts, pestilence, and the same kind of erratic policy-making and mismanagement that characterized the Cimarron agency doomed the experiment to failure. As the costs of keeping the Indians at the fort increased and Indian reformers became increasingly vocal in their criticism, the government finally decided to return the Indians to the Four Corners country and abandon the fort, thereby making it available to Maxwell. Over the years Maxwell had sold the government considerable grain and beef for the Fort Sumner reservation, and visits in connection with these sales no doubt familiarized him with the area.[12]

The move from Cimarron to Fort Sumner was no simple undertaking. In addition to Maxwell and his immediate family, nearly forty other families, mostly Mexican Americans or Indians, chose to migrate southeast. When the government put mules up for auction at Fort Union, the sale stopped because a telegram arrived from Maxwell offering to take them all for $75 each.[13] He also resigned as probate judge—a post he must have conducted with considerable irregularity during the preceding year.[14] At the last minute there was fear that the Utes and Apaches would attack the party as it departed, but the Indians were falsely promised annuity goods and persuaded to go off on a hunt.[15] Soon a long train of migrants departed Cimarron, headed for the fort on the Pecos, where Maxwell set about moving into what had been the officers' quarters.

Lucien's departure from Cimarron revealed the fragility of order and the importance of Maxwell in preserving the peace there. Not for long could the serious legal questions raised by both the secretary of the interior and the local settlers or miners be glossed over. Within weeks after Maxwell's departure, riots by miners in Ute Creek and the Moreno Valley became so serious that Governor

William A. Pile, an official of the Maxwell Land Grant and Railway Company, sent in troops to put them down. The murder of an anti-grant preacher, the Reverend F. J. Tolby, galvanized local opposition to the grant company; soon another parson, O. P. McMains, began a long but futile effort to have what was always referred to as the Maxwell Land Grant invalidated. Ultimately, in 1887, the Supreme Court of the United States agreed with the argument first developed by Maxwell's advisers, that Congress had created a new grant by its confirmation, overturned Interior Secretary Cox's adverse New Year's Eve ruling, and thus confirmed that the land grant included 1,714,764 acres.[16]

Moreover, whereas Maxwell profited enormously from his entrepreneurial endeavors, his successors enjoyed so few profits that bankruptcy soon faced them. The Aztec Mine, which had been highly productive under Maxwell's ownership, closed down after a few years of operation, and most of the other hard-rock and placer mines ceased operation by the mid-1870s. So many ranchers and farmers came to the area that beef and grain could no longer be sold at elevated prices. The English Maxwell Land and Railway Company suffered from poor local management, inadequate knowledge of conditions in the Southwest, and the impact of the Panic of 1873. By 1875 the company was unable to pay local taxes or the salaries of its officers. The property was offered for sale at a public auction, and soon Dutch bondholders took it over under a new Maxwell Land Grant Company.[17]

For the Indians at the Cimarron agency, the departure of Maxwell constituted another step toward removal. Maxwell had sympathized with their plight, discouraged efforts to have them relocated to a permanent reservation, summoned the army when necessary to preserve the peace, and paid for feeding them when no one else would provide meat or flour. The English company, on the other hand, believed that the presence of the Indians discouraged farmers, railroad builders, and other capitalists from

Maxwell's Cimarron home in ruins, several years after he had moved to Fort Sumner. Courtesy J. W. Leitzell, Cimarron, New Mexico.

investing in their grant and encouraged their removal. A series of ineffectual and sometimes incompetent agents moved the Utes and Apaches from one hopeless situation to another until finally, in 1876, the Moache Utes were sent to the San Juan River country of southwest Colorado and the Jicarilla Apaches to the Dulce region of northwestern New Mexico.[18]

Moving did not entirely terminate Lucien Maxwell's relations with his old property. About a year after his departure, the Maxwell Land Grant and Railway Company, having finally discovered that they had been misled as to the extent and value of the grant, threatened to sue Lucien for $400,000, as Marcus Brunswick recalled, for "not having as many acres as he promised." Brunswick acted as mediator between Maxwell and the company manager, John L. Reed. Part of the payment for the home ranch had taken the form of a $75,000 promisory note, which Lucien offered to the English, along with a herd of horses, to settle the dispute. According to Brunswick, Stephen B. Elkins, who had been employed as the company's attorney, refused to take the horses, but agreed to take a promisory note from Maxwell for $10,000, which ended the case.[19] Nevertheless, company records show that on March 13, 1872, Lucien received final payment of principal and interest in the amount of $87,500 on the $75,000 note.[20]

Problems with securing title to the Fort Sumner land where Lucien was living were not settled so easily. Although the government had abandoned the fort and sold the buildings to Lucien, he had not secured title to the 13,645 acres that comprised the reservation. Soon after Maxwell's arrival, Eben Everett, the land register in Santa Fe, wrote to Commissioner Joseph Wilson requesting that the land be transferred from the War Department to the Interior Department so that it could be surveyed and sold, presumably to Maxwell. No action could be taken on the petition until Congress, as was usual when army posts were abandoned, on February 24, 1871, enacted a special

Ute Indians at their Colorado agency in the 1880s. Courtesy Colorado Historical Society.

act declaring the land for sale. Maxwell, hopeful that he could secure clear title, asked for permission to buy at a private, non-competitive sale for the federal minimum price of $1.25 an acre. Only then did he learn that an 1858 statute prohibited the preemption or homesteading of abandoned army posts; the land must be appraised and offered at public auction for no less than its estimated value. Arguments that Maxwell and more than a hundred settlers had moved to the fort before passage of the special act and had presumed that land title would result naturally from owning the buildings produced no sympathy or relief from Washington.[21]

Apparently Lucien abandoned hope that the issue would ever be resolved during his lifetime, for he turned the negotiations over to his son. In April, 1872, following the tactic adopted by his father in arranging the Griffin survey, Peter deposited $2,500 with the Santa Fe land office to have the ranch mapped. Nothing more happened until two years later, when young Maxwell proposed that the General Land Office sponsor a special bill in Congress to allow Maxwell and the other settlers special preemption and homesteading rights, thus guaranteeing them the right to purchase the land without competitive bidding. The commissioner refused to cooperate, arguing that the settlers had entered the reservation illegally and that since Maxwell, not the farmers, had made the deposit, only he was likely to benefit. Although the land was finally appraised in 1874, Lucien Maxwell died without ever owning any land at Fort Sumner. Indeed, complex legal technicalities, made worse by loss of the certificates of deposit, prevented Peter Maxwell from securing return of the $2,500 deposit until 1880, and it was 1884 before he was able to buy some of the Fort Sumner land at public sale.[22]

Failure to acquire title to the Fort Sumner ranch did not deter Maxwell from making improvements similar to those he had initiated at Cimarron. He dammed the nearby Pecos River with sandbags, for example, and dug irrigation ditches to carry the water onto the fields he brought into cultivation. He also introduced herds of blooded Merino sheep from the East and purchased a number of brood mares.[23] Unfortunately, the dangers that had imperiled ranching at Rayado and Cimarron a decade or more before, persisted on the Pecos. Already in the spring of 1871, Lucien reportedly had lost a thousand cattle to rustlers. Two years later, an epidemic of deadly epizootic infested the area, and Maxwell lost several horses and mules.[24]

Despite such setbacks, Maxwell's arrival on the Pecos stimulated the growth of an area previously known only for the unsuccessful Navajo experiment. By late 1870 the population had grown to the extent that residents demanded the creation of a new precinct.[25] There was no government mail service into the region either, so Maxwell joined stockmen Frank Wilburn and John Chisum to begin weekly service from Las Vegas at their own expense "for the accommodation of themselves and neighbors."[26]

Although Maxwell's later years were spent in semi-retirement, his business interests occasionally extended beyond Fort Sumner. Following the September, 1870, organizational meeting of the First National Bank of Santa Fe, Maxwell had signed a letter to the comptroller of the currency, applying for a federal charter. "This is the only bank in the Territory of New Mexico or within four hundred miles of Santa Fe," he wrote, "and it is our purpose to manage it in strict conformity with the law and your instructions . . . ." It was December 13, 1870, before Charter No. 1750 was issued to the bank and mid-April, 1871, before it opened for business.[27] The original plans to acquire a room in Santa Fe's historic Palace of the Governors, previously used as a federal depository had to be abandoned. Instead, business began on the west side of the plaza in a rented storeroom belonging to Fernando Delgado.[28] A meeting of the stockholders was scheduled for May 3, but when Maxwell failed to appear, it had to be postponed a week. What Lucien learned when the meeting finally convened was that business was languishing

Maxwell's home at Fort Sumner. Courtesy Museum of New Mexico.

because merchants and ranchers were reluctant to make deposits. Moreover, Maxwell's former associates, Elkins, Catron, and Griffin, together with José Perea, perhaps dubious of trusting a bank to Maxwell's control, had formed a rival National Bank of New Mexico. Holly favored selling out to the new enterprise. Lucien reportedly refused at first, but after a week of daily meetings, he agreed to transfer his shares to Elkins, Catron, and their associates. Rumor has it that he lost much of the $150,000 invested in the business, but there is little real evidence for this assertion, and the fact that most of the money had been invested in government notes makes it unlikely.[29]

Maxwell's other business ventures proved no more lucrative. The discovery in 1871 of what promised to be rich silver mines at Chloride Flat, near the town of Silver City, sparked a renewal of Maxwell's interest in mining. He made several visits to the region and must have acquired property sufficiently promising that he ordered a ten-stamp mill to work the ore. When fourteen wagons of machinery passed through Pajarito, a correspondent of the *New Mexican* asserted, in language reminiscent of what had been said when he was in Cimarron, "Had we a few more such men as Maxwell, the reserves of our territory would soon be developed." Such flattery proved unwarranted, for instead of reaping a new bonanza, the project faltered. Maxwell stopped the train several days short of Silver City because he decided to examine other mines near Socorro before determining exactly where to install the mill.[30] The equipment sat idle and unassembled at Fort Cummings for nearly a year. Maxwell hired Charles S. Bartholomew of Bosque Redondo to examine the Silver City mines for him. He seemed satisfied and reported that by early 1873 the mill would be "thundering away" on Silver City ore. Rumors suggesting that Maxwell was interested in selling the equipment seemed more accurate, and by early December, 1872, the mill had been bought by Maxwell's old acquaintance and frequent business partner V. S. Shelby. Thus ended Maxwell's mining activities.[31]

Little is known about what was allegedly Lucien's most disastrous investment. According to persistent but undocumented stories, he spent $250,000 on the bonds of a company organized to construct the Texas Pacific Railroad westward from Texas across New Mexico to Yuma, Arizona. The Panic of 1873 brought the company to bankruptcy, and Maxwell reportedly lost his entire investment.[32] The evidence is somewhat better that early in 1872 he signed a contract to build 150 miles of railroad on the Southern Pacific line "between two points in the State of Texas," for $40,000 a mile, or a total of $600,000.[33] Possibly he did lose money undertaking work for which he never received compensation, although there is no substantial evidence to support such a conclusion.

For the most part, however, Lucien's renown during the 1870s resulted from his horse racing interests. During the spring of 1871 Maxwell's fame spread throughout the West when he issued a "challenge to the world" to race his champion mare "Fly." The stakes might vary from $10,000 to $40,000. For a $20,000 stake Maxwell would allow $1,000 for travel expenses, doubled if it rose to $30,000. The race would be run in Las Vegas over a 400-yard course.[34] The challenge was reported by newspapers throughout the Southwest; someone who saw it in Kansas City and who knew that Lucien was also in banking pasted it to First National Bank stationery and tacked it in a local bank with the heading "banking in New Mexico."[35] Lucien's challenge was ultimately accepted by a man name Ben Dowell. Plans were laid for a race with stakes of three to four thousand dollars between Dowell's mare "Kit" and "Fly," scheduled for December 23, 1871, in El Paso, Texas. "There was great excitement," reported the *New Mexican*, and "people came from many miles in all directions to see the race." An estimated $25,000 in bets changed hands. In the featured race "Fly," who for some reason had a twelve-foot head start, lost to "Kit" by fifteen feet. Maxwell's "Nolan horse" did better in a second match, beating Dowell's stallion "Ned" by "a considerable distance."[36]

Interest in the El Paso race encouraged more challengers. Two men from Hamilton, Missouri, offered to race Maxwell for $5,000 over 400 yards, and $10,000 for 1,500 yards. "We will run any time, inside three months, on above terms," the men notified Maxwell, "and will meet you at any place agreed upon, to draw the agreement and put up the money."[37] The race, however, seems not to have come off. A rematch between "Fly" and "Kit," though, was scheduled for the spring of 1872, with Dowell putting up $5,000 against $4,000 from Maxwell and partner C. W. Kitchen. There is some hint that the previous results had been contested, for this time judges were to be "placed at the outcome," and care would be "taken to guard against jockeying." A second race rematched the Nolan horse against Dowell's stud.[38] Whether the race ever occurred is, unfortunately, not known. Kitchen became sufficiently interested in racing, however, that he soon afterward imported a new horse, "Walking John," that beat the famed "Fly" at Las Vegas early in December, 1872.[39]

By 1873, Maxwell's activities had virtually disappeared from the public record. He turned over most business

Peter Maxwell (left), *Lucien's only son, and Henry J. Leis. Courtesy Museum of New Mexico.*

affairs—even some horse racing—to his eldest son, Peter, who was in his mid-twenties. Little is known of Pete Maxwell, who became famous only because he was living in Lucien's old house at Fort Sumner when Sheriff Pat Garrett shot bandit Billy the Kid there. He reportedly married one Sadie Lutz, although they had no known children. He was nowhere near as successful as his father, and stories have it that he felt that he was wealthy enough that he need not work. He also developed serious drinking problems before his death June 21, 1898. Two other Maxwell children had died before the move to Fort Sumner: Maria Eleanore, born at Rayado in 1856, had died during a visit to Kaskaskia in 1858. Verenisa was born in Cimarron August 3, 1860, and died there March 20, 1864; she is buried near the old Maxwell house. Another child, whose name is unknown, was either stillborn or died very young.[40]

At least four of Maxwell's five surviving daughters moved with him to Fort Sumner, and the eldest, Virginia, who had married Captain Keyes shortly before the move, probably visited when her husband was stationed in the area. Sofia, who had been born at Rayado in 1854, eventually married Telesfor Jaramillo, probably after her father's death. Manuel Abreú married two Maxwell daughters; his first wife was Emilia, who was born at Rayado in 1852 and died in 1884. His second wife was Odile Berenice. Paula, probably the youngest daughter, married José Jaramillo. Maxwell's wife, Luz, outlived nearly all her children, dying July 13, 1900.[41]

Lucien's health slowly declined after he settled at Fort Sumner. He occasionally still visited the Cimarron country, traveling to Rayado as late as April, 1875, to sell his interest in the Big Ditch to Matt Lynch. In May of that year he ordered twelve men to travel on his behalf to Fort Sill, Indian Territory, to return horses that the Comanches had stolen from his ranch.[42]

Many persons have attributed his inactivity to a broken heart, contending that he was never happy after leaving

Sofia Maxwell Jaramillo. Courtesy of Victor Grant, Taos, New Mexico.

Paula Maxwell and José Jaramillo on their wedding day. Courtesy of Victor Grant, Taos, New Mexico.

his beloved Cimarron.[43] It is more likely, however, that progressive kidney failure caused his decline. His medical problems worsened during the summer of 1875, and he developed uremic poisoning. The nearest physician, Dr. J. H. Shout, was summoned by courier from Las Vegas, 150 miles from Fort Sumner. Relays of horses along the way enabled the physician to change mounts every twenty-five miles. July 25, 1875, Dr. Shout got as far as John Elkins's ranch on the Pecos, where he was turned back with the news that Lucien B. Maxwell was dead at age fifty-six.[44] He was buried in the officers' cemetery at Fort Sumner.[45]

Word of Maxwell's passing brought laudatory obituaries in the territorial press. "Against Lucien B. Maxwell, no man can say aught," editorialized the *Las Vegas Gazette,* "and he died after an active and eventful life, probably without an enemy in the world." The editor continued: "Of few words, unassuming and unpretentious, his deeds were the best exponent of the man." Maxwell was "hospitable, generous, and upright, and dispensed large wealth, acquired by industry and genius, with an open hand to the stranger and the needy."[46] In Cimarron, the town Maxwell had founded and that was his home for nearly fifteen years, the praise was even more generous. The editor of the Maxwell Land Grant and Railway Company's *Cimarron News and Press,* was certain that Maxwell's death "cannot fail to excite general, sincere, and deep regret throughout this Territory." Here was a man who had helped tame the frontier in the company of such heroes as the Bent brothers and Kit Carson. He was "universally respected and publicly esteemed," famous for "his patriotic acts rendered to his country, his self-sacrifices, his subsequent forecast, enterprise, energy, and constantly bestowed noble charities." Such a man, the long article continued, had been consecrated "with almost a sacredness of regard in the remembrance of the unprejudiced, the appreciative, and the grateful among our people." It was his destiny, the laudatory report concluded, "to endear himself to the popular heart, and even irrespective of race, to win common and universal approbation and respect."[47]

These obituaries failed, however, to assess the real historical significance of Lucien B. Maxwell to the settlement of the American frontier. He is best viewed as a transitional figure, who lived and worked on what historian Frederick Jackson Turner termed the "cutting edge" of civilization. First as a fur trader, trapper, and hunter, later in the company of Frémont, and finally along the edge of the Sangre de Cristo mountains of New Mexico, Maxwell was among the first Anglo-Americans to enter new regions and initiate the process of introducing civilization to an untamed region. For the first thirty years of his life, at least until the late 1840s, his role had been subordinate to that of others. Grandfather Pierre Menard, father Hugh Maxwell, Charles Bent, Kit Carson, and Charles Beaubien had all schooled young Lucien in the skills needed to prosper on the frontier. By the time he began to assert his independence, Maxwell had learned to operate successfully in a frontier environment.

Maxwell's success stemmed largely from his skill at using people more powerful or influential than himself to his own advantage. First at Rayado and later at Cimarron, he discovered how the menace of Indian attack — sometimes real, other times imagined or at least exaggerated — could be used to secure assistance and income from the United States army and the Office of Indian Affairs. A series of military commanders, notably William S. Grier, utilized their authority to help Maxwell, and nearly all the Indian agents at Cimarron fell under his direct influence. The Mexican-American farmers who followed Maxwell across the mountains to Rayado recognized his authority and apparently never objected, at least during his lifetime, to his patronizing, sometimes cruel and generally racist, treatment of them. Many followed him to Cimarron, and not a few eventually settled at Fort Sumner.

Maxwell's personality, as unbecoming as it may appear to those for whom the frontier is only a scholarly or a literary experience, precisely suited the needs of his day. He combined in his own psyche the elements of both barbarism and civilization that constantly interacted in frontier life.[48] His bravery was no less dominant than his arrogance. He obviously possessed skills not unknown to successful politicians, altering his behavior and attitude to coincide with changing situations and personalities—receiving Anglo travelers or military officers, for example, very differently from the way he received Indian chiefs or impoverished Mexican-American farmers. That he had a temper that sometimes erupted into savage violence there can be no doubt; equally important, however, was his generosity, and his erratic personal behavior seems never to have affected his success.

To some extent, Maxwell's financial success must be attributed to luck. The unique conditions which coincided with the American Civil War were not of his making, and he had little if anything to do with the discovery of gold, either in the gravel beds of the Moreno Valley or inside Aztec Ridge. Nor could anyone have predicted how fortuitous his marriage to Luz Beaubien would be in acquiring title to a large portion of northern New Mexico and southern Colorado. The tremendous increase in real estate values that made it possible for Maxwell to buy very cheaply and sell for a huge profit only a few years later was largely outside his control or influence.

Yet Lucien was uniquely able to turn admittedly fortuitous circumstances to his own advantage. He alone among the sons and sons-in-law of Charles Beaubien built his inheritance rather than dissipated it. Among the others, only Jesús Abreú played any significant role in the history of New Mexico, and his significance was minor when compared to Maxwell's. Lucien's own son, Peter, managed to squander away his inheritance. Few New Mexicans took as full advantage of the high prices and short supplies of the Civil War era to reap exceptional profits as Maxwell did, and no one in the Southwest was more skillful than he in turning the Indian menace to his own advan-

Luz Beaubien Maxwell,
Lucien's widow, in old age.
Courtesy of Victor Grant,
Taos, New Mexico.

tage or playing off the army against the Office of Indian Affairs. He even proved skillful at inspiring visiting writers and newspaper reporters to issue positive descriptions of his ability, generosity, and accomplishments.

That segment of frontier development in which Lucien Maxwell participated so skillfully was of very short duration. Less than a quarter-century separated Maxwell's arrival at Rayado and his sale of the grant, an incredibly brief period for so much development to have occurred. But while Maxwell's success in dealing with the earliest stages of frontier development was seldom surpassed, he soon confronted new factors with which he was unable to cope. As gold miners, eastern capitalists, and a crafty new breed of politicians refused to acknowledge his authority and, in some cases, manipulated him to their own advantage, Maxwell must have recognized that his era had ended. The transition from controlling to being controlled and the subsequent loss of power, prestige, and authority that it entailed occurred so rapidly that it must have been difficult for Maxwell to comprehend or accept. Yet this transition can be understood as one of the inevitable consequences of frontier development.

"Stand at Cumberland Gap and watch the procession of civilization, marching single file—the buffalo following the trail to the salt springs, the Indian, the fur-trader and hunter, the cattleman, the pioneer farmer—and the frontier has passed by." So wrote Frederick Jackson Turner in his seminal essay, "The Significance of the Frontier in American History."[49] Lucien Maxwell was a part of that march, playing several roles in succession, and in his own way he contributed like so many other frontiersmen to the bringing of civilization to the American West.

10

The Making of a Western Legend

THERE are in reality two Lucien Maxwells. The first is the frontiersman described from contemporary sources in the preceding chapters. A second has been created by the generations of amateur writers, novelists, and historians who have written about Maxwell in the decades since his death. In many ways the development of Lucien's popular image epitomizes the way in which legends about the West have grown: the image that has resulted bears so little relationship to his real life or personality as they can be known through reliable historical evidence that a new and mythical person has been created.

Like many frontiersmen, Maxwell left few materials that can be used to document his life. While he could read and write, his literary skills were rudimentary, and no more than a dozen letters in his hand, mostly short business notes, exist. He wrote no autobiography. During his lifetime only a handful of contemporaries described him or his life, and the only known obituaries reveal few details of his career. While diplomatic historian Thomas A. Bailey has argued that American presidents have grown in historical stature in correlation to the size and accessibility of their personal papers,[1] exactly the opposite seems to have held true for Maxwell. A lack of solid historical evidence has allowed imaginative authors nearly a hundred years freely to contribute tales about his life that constitute a Western myth.

The most significant contributor to the growth of the Maxwell legend was Colonel Henry Inman. During the late 1860s Inman served as an assistant quartermaster at Fort Union, forty-five miles south of the Cimarron, and visited Maxwell several times. Years later, after retirement from the army, Inman wrote *The Old Santa Fé Trail*, published in 1897 by the Macmillan Company in New York. Reprints appeared from New York, Topeka, and Minneapolis in 1898, 1899, 1909, 1916, and 1966.[2] While portions of Inman's book seem to give accurate descriptions of events in which he personally participated, he adopted such a romanticized, exaggerated, and erroneous view of the frontier that the book is most valuable, as Janet Lecompte has recently observed, "in determining where later writers obtained their misinformation."[3] Certainly this was the case with Lucien Maxwell, who, to Inman, epitomized the frontier. "Maxwell belonged to a generation and class almost extinct, and the like of which will, in all probability, never be seen again;" he wrote, "for there is no more frontier to develop them." Only comparisons with the feudal knights in Sir Walter Scott's *Ivanhoe* were adequate in describing the life Maxwell enjoyed. "He lived in a sort of barbaric splendor, akin to that of the nobles of England at the time of the Norman conquest," Inman continued. The Mexican-Americans who worked his land in a "feudal sort of way" were "as much his thralls as were Gurtha and Wamba of Cedric of Rotherwood, only they wore no engraved collars around their necks bearing their names and that of their master."

The life Inman described was indeed luxurious: tables covered with silver, lavish banquets presided over by "dusky maidens," and piles of money garnered from successful horse races and card games. Several stories revealed how trusting and brave Maxwell was: he frequently kept thousands of dollars in gold and paper in an unlocked bureau, for example, and once had his thumb amputated without the benefit of even a dose of whiskey. Here, he concluded, was a good and generous man, a builder of the West, "a representative man of the border of the same class as his compeers . . . ."[4]

Inman's descriptions became the basis for many subsequent histories, the authors of which seldom gave credit to their sources and sometimes were guilty of plagiarism. The closing of the frontier coincided with the production of many state and county histories published by midwestern or eastern printers and made profitable by the inclusion of commissioned biographies of "leading" citizens. In New Mexico, one of the first of these "mug book" histories appeared from the Pacific States Publishing Company in 1907. Although the principal author, George B. Anderson, added some background material on the Beaubien and Miranda grant and discussed the region's history after Maxwell departed, most of his material was drawn almost word for word from Inman, and he added his own embellishments and contributed several new "facts." To Anderson, Maxwell was "one of the most striking figures of the early mountain frontier, to found a successful American barony." He became wealthy enough to live "for pleasure alone," he continued, in an obvious rewrite of Inman, "in utter disregard of the expense of the necessities and comforts of life." Surrounding him were "native Mexicans" "as completely enslaved as the thralls of the ancient Norsemen." No previous author had identified Maxwell's middle name, and Anderson incorrectly guessed it must be Benjamin. He also reported erroneously that Maxwell became rich because "restrictions" on sheep grazing were removed. According to Anderson, wealth soon became Maxwell's principal problem. "Maxwell's sheep multiplied," explained Anderson, "and as the years rolled by his wealth increased so rapidly" that he was unable to spend it. "He tried gambling but, although it is said he never 'stacked the cards,' his poker playing served only to add to his accumulation of treasure."

Anderson's general conclusions differed little from those of Inman: Maxwell was "one of the best representatives of the undefiled frontier, before the days of the 'bad man,' a type which passed with the extinction of the frontier in its original purity."[5] In addition to the books that received wide distribution in New Mexico, Anderson contributed articles repeating the same information to such popular publications as *Out West* and *Santa Fe Magazine.*[6]

The attention devoted to Maxwell in these publications prompted others who had known him to include stories about Lucien in their memoirs. Thomas Harwood was the pioneering Methodist minister in New Mexico who married Maxwell's daughter Virginia to the army officer serving as Indian agent at Cimarron—a marriage against her father's wishes. Harwood's memoirs, published in 1908, told the story for the first time, and it reappears in most subsequent publications.[7] Both William H. Ryus, whose autobiography appeared in 1913, and Irving Howbert, whose *Memories of a Lifetime* appeared in 1925, also drew heavily from Inman.[8]

The first New Mexican historian to devote attention to Maxwell was Ralph Emerson Twitchell, a Las Vegas attorney closely tied to Santa Fe railroad and land grant interests.[9] His *The Leading Facts of New Mexican History,* published between 1911 and 1917, included a lengthy biographical footnote on Maxwell, mostly copied directly from Anderson or Inman. Maxwell was once again characterized as "one of the most striking figures on the early mountain frontier" and given the middle name Benjamin. In addition to passing along several of Inman's tales, Twitchell drew a more praiseworthy portrait than earlier writers had, perhaps reflecting his own biases or generally more positive attitudes toward land barons. "Maxwell was a man of unbounded generosity and possessed unlimited confidence in those whom he trusted," he wrote. "He was eccentric, improvident, liberal . . . . Though rough in manner there was nothing of the desperado about him."[10]

The vulnerability even of professional historians to the perpetuation of myths becomes evident in the pioneering work of William J. Ghent. Unlike his predecessors, Ghent was primarily interested in western exploration; Maxwell first appeared as an associate of John C. Frémont in *The Early Far West*, published in 1936. More important was the sketch of Maxwell that Ghent prepared for volume 12 of the authoritative *Dictionary of American Biography*, published in 1933. Ghent for the first time properly identified Maxwell's middle name as Bonaparte, and, unlike his predecessors, devoted nearly half his space to Maxwell's fur-trading and exploring activities. Ghent knew little about Lucien's life in New Mexico, however, and drew heavily on Twitchell and on information provided him by Maxwell's daughter Odile (spelled "Odila" in the publication) Abreú, who was still living. Ignorant of the problems Maxwell had faced in securing title to the grant or in having its extent recognized by the government and forgetting Mrs. Maxwell entirely, Ghent informed his readers that Maxwell became "the sole owner of the grant, a tract of 1,714,764 acres, the largest single holding in the United States." This overly-simplified and unsupported statement reappeared in most subsequent histories.[11] Ghent's general appraisal of Maxwell is somewhat more balanced than that of earlier writers. "He was improvident, and he seems to have had more than his share of eccentricities," he summarizes without providing any evidence, "but he was a kindly, generous, and dependable man, who was universally liked and whose friends were devotedly attached to him."[12]

The image of Maxwell became even more meritorious in materials related to his role in founding the First National Bank of Santa Fe. Following the sale of the grant, Lucien devoted some of his proceeds to establishing the first commercial banking company in the Southwest. He never participated in bank management, attended only a few board meetings, and gained fame primarily through garrish stock certificates on which his face was prominently featured. Nevertheless, he frequently became the central focus of bank advertising. "When the need arose in 1870 for a National Bank in the Spanish Southwest," a 1937 advertisement reported, "Lucien B. Maxwell provided

A portrait of Maxwell that reflects his popular image as developed by generations of later writers. Courtesy Seton Museum, Cimarron, New Mexico.

the capital and surplus. . . . The bank still flourishes. . . ."[13] This interest in history can be explained in part by the fact that Paul A. F. Walter, who served as bank president after 1933, was an amateur historian, who helped revitalize the New Mexico Historical Society, served as its president for many years, and co-edited the *New Mexico Historical Review.*[14] He became interested in Maxwell's relationship with the bank and published a series of semischolarly articles and booklets, all emphasizing Lucien's constructive activities as a banker and capitalist.[15]

Sharing many of the political, economic, and historical views held by Twitchell and Walter was William A. Keleher, the first person to undertake a serious historical study focusing primarily on Maxwell. Keleher was a prominent Albuquerque attorney who developed an interest in land grant law, about which he began speaking and writing articles in the 1920s.[16] He conducted research in newspapers, legal records, land office files, and other primary materials neglected by previous authors and interviewed two of Lucien's granddaughters, Mrs. Adelina Welborn and Mrs. Michel Nalda, who recalled many historical incidents, most of them occurring at Fort Sumner after Maxwell died.[17]

Keleher's *Maxwell Land Grant: A New Mexico Item* appeared in 1942 from the Rydal Press in Santa Fe. While the work suffers from a lack of careful documentation, Keleher produced a mass of new and generally accurate information, especially about the acquisition and sale of the grant, and he scrupulously avoided perpetuating the legends of earlier authors.[18] He focused almost no attention on Maxwell's personal life or character and did not cite Inman as a source.

For Keleher, Maxwell was at once a colorful pioneer and a successful capitalist. "Noted as a frontiersman, trapper and pioneer resident of New Mexico," he wrote to introduce a chapter titled "Maxwell, the Real Estate Man," "Lucien B. Maxwell was also somewhat of a businessman." Not only did he buy land cheaply and sell it for a substantial profit, but he parlayed government contracts into significant income. "Certainly," he concludes, "he was the most important individual real estate operator of his day . . . ."[19]

Keleher first drew attention to what seemed to him one of the worst historical injustices in the Southwest. Several years after Maxwell's death, Sheriff Pat Garrett killed bandit Billy the Kid in Maxwell's Fort Sumner home. Billy was subsequently buried in the same cemetery as Maxwell. But while thousands of tourists annually visited the grave of the famed outlaw, marked by a handsome headstone, Maxwell's grave bore no marker and Keleher guessed that "nine out of ten persons visiting the cemetery" would ask casually, "'Who was Lucien B. Maxwell?'" This, he observed, was "not too comforting a thought to his descendents or to those who appreciate the value of his contribution to the history of his adopted New Mexico."[20]

Nothing occurred to right this perceived injustice until a more popular article raised the same questions before a larger and more influential audience. In 1949, Joe Heflin Smith published "The Unmarked Grave" in *The Cattleman,* issued by the Texas and Southwestern Cattle Raisers Association and read by most ranchers in Texas and New Mexico. "In a lonely un-marked grave, that's lost to all but a few, in the little cemetery encircled by rotted posts and tangled rusty barbed wire," he lamented, "lies a man who was as constructive and kind as the outlaws were destructive and cruel." The biographical sketch of Maxwell which followed drew heavily on Ghent, Inman, and Keleher, and on interviews the author conducted with Maxwell's granddaughter Adelina Welborn. Following traditions established by Keleher and Walter, Smith emphasized Lucien's positive contributions to the development of the ranching industry in the West. "Perhaps," he concluded, "someday . . . there will be a monument erected to this great builder and developer of the West. Today, the outlaws hold the spotlight at Old Fort Sumner. Perhaps time will place the spotlight where it belongs."[21]

Smith's article and subsequent publicity about the ironies of the Fort Sumner cemetery soon produced substantial results. Herbert O. Brayer, a former University of New Mexico historian serving as Colorado State Archivist, headed the campaign to honor Maxwell. Brayer had recently written a book about William Blackmore, an English investor who bought up a great many Spanish and Mexican land grants in Colorado and New Mexico, and he sympathized with the argument that Maxwell ought to be honored.[22] "If you're a famous bandit they'll build a monument to you," he protested, "but if you're a builder they won't do a thing." He persuaded the Colorado State Historical Society to support the project and found a Denver monument company owner who was willing to donate a six-foot-high tombstone. "L. B. Maxwell To Be Honored Today as Empire Builder," headlined an Associated Press story published May 29, 1949, in the *El Paso Times* and other papers across the country. The dedication program was jointly sponsored by the New Mexico and Colorado historical societies, because as Brayer explained, "After all, Maxwell was as much a Coloradoan as he was a New Mexican."[23] The epitaph on the stone focused on the contributions Maxwell had made to the building of the West and perpetuated the myths of previous authors: "By industry, good fortune, and trading," it explained to tourists, he had become "the sole owner in 1864 of the largest single tract of land owned by any one individual in the United States . . . . Dynamic — Charitable — Lavish — one of the great Builders of the American West."[24]

The dedication of the Maxwell monument coincided with a flurry of interest in Lucien. Some of it centered in Cimarron, the village Maxwell had founded. The town had suffered decades of decline: conflict over the ownership of the Maxwell Land Grant produced violence that drove away many farmers and discouraged potential residents and investors;[25] the county seat moved elsewhere; and most of the gold mines that helped make Maxwell rich closed.[26] From the perspective of the twentieth century, Cimarron

A crude statue of Maxwell in the Cimarron town square. Photograph by the author.

perceived the era of Lucien Maxwell as the zenith of local history. Many Cimarron residents felt Maxwell deserved more recognition. An eccentric Spanish-American War veteran erected a statue of Maxwell in the town square. Unfortunately, it was so crude and awkward in design and execution that one author has termed it a "lasting insult to Maxwell." Others lamented the dilapidated state into which fire and neglect had brought Lucien's Cimarron home and proposed that it be restored as a pioneer museum.[27] Meanwhile, at the nearby Philmont Scout Ranch, officials renamed the old town of Rayado "Carson-Maxwell," restored Kit Carson's old house as a museum, and told campfire tales that recounted the heroism of Maxwell and his associates to boys from throughout the country.[28]

Cimarron has also produced a local historian. Francis Stanley Crochiola is a Catholic priest popularly known as Father F. Stanley. He has been assigned to parishes throughout New Mexico and West Texas for the last thirty-five years and has produced a series of more than a hundred distinctive, yellow-covered booklets of town history. His first major book, written while he was working in the Cimarron area, dealt with Lucien Maxwell and his grant.

The Grant That Maxwell Bought, published in a limited edition in Denver in 1950, portrayed Cimarron history as a vast and fascinating morality play wherein Lucien Maxwell becomes an "Everyman" striving for power and success in a godless world. "Maxwell was so strong, so extravagant, so certain, and so lost," preaches Stanley:

Living his life as a cattle-baron at Rayado, and again at Cimarron, he hurls that great massive shoulder of his as strength against spectral barriers like a wave whose power explodes in hidden mid-oceans under timeless skies because he wants all; feels the thrust and power for everything but gets nothing. Finally, he is destroyed by his own expansion, devoured by his hunger, tied down by his wealth that enslaves him, for he dies so poorly rich that his unhappiness is mistaken for material poverty.[29]

Stanley collected considerable new material from local sources, much of which is reprinted in the book, and he interviewed many individuals associated with Maxwell and his grant. With the discretion expected of a good priest, however, he was reluctant to pry too deeply into family secrets. "Several publishers have turned down this work," he explains, "because they wanted more of the family life and other such material." The addition of such personal information, he argued, would make the volume "too bulky" and was of little "consequence to the story." More important, Maxwell's descendants were entitled to "live their lives . . . without anyone like me coming along and saying: 'I am writing a book about the Grant—How did you get along with your dad?'"[30]

Nevertheless, Stanley told a great many undocumented and inaccurate stories about Maxwell. His knowledge of Lucien's youth, for example, was especially faulty, and he frequently filled in details, reported gossip, and added anecdotes which seemed probable. He initiated the incorrect story that Lucien's father died in a hunting accident, falsely reported that Maxwell was raised in his grandfather's mansion, and mistakenly claimed that he was educated by Jesuits. A typical Stanley tale recalls how as a boy Maxwell was given a gun "to hunt rabbits with, but he used it to practise [sic] marksmanship." He continues in his usual narrative form: "Target practice was such a mania with young Lucien that before long he was recognized as the best shot in Kaskaskia. Old Pierre [Menard] didn't like this too well for he had other plans for the boy that did not include trapping."[31]

Stanley's impact on the Maxwell legend was minor when compared to the effect of a novel published the same year. Harvey Fergusson was a native of New Mexico who spent most of his life in New York and California. He had visited the ruined Maxwell house in Cimarron, probably while working as a timber cruiser in the Taos area. Exploration of the vast adobe ruin sparked his fascination with Maxwell. "When I learned that a man had ridden into the wilderness where no human habitation had ever stood before," he reminisced, "had built that great house, founded a society and ruled it as long as he lived, my imagination was stirred." In the years that followed, he talked to old-timers, collected all the books and articles he could find, and considered writing a factual history of the grant. Eventually he decided to write a novel instead.[32]

Fergusson's *Grant of Kingdom*, published in 1950, is the definitive literary version of the Maxwell myth. It reconstructs "the struggle for power in a small but complete society." The hero, a thinly disguised Lucien Maxwell, is Jean Ballard, a midwesterner drawn to the Southwest by a desire to expand civilization and make a fortune. He meets Don Tranquilino Coronel, a wealthy Taos resident who owns a Spanish land grant, and falls in love with his daughter, Consuelo. Lack of familiarity with Mexican courtship customs and fear of family disapproval convince him that marriage may be impossible, but he engages a local lawyer to serve as a go-between, wins the acceptance of Consuelo's family, and settles with his new wife on his father-in-law's land.

Fergusson's primary interest is frontier settlement. The grant seems valueless to some, but Ballard recognizes "his destiny" and convinces himself that "if any man in the Southwest could go into the Dark River [Cimarron] Valley and stay there, he was that man." It is just this arrogant sense of daring which Fergusson admires.

What Jean Ballard proposed to himself, then, was a revolutionary move, a major feat in pioneering. He proposed to do what the Spanish government had intended, when it made those royal grants. He proposed to carry civilization across the mountains and plant it on the edge of the great plains, which must some day become a part of it.

Ballard proves to be an extremely successful pioneer. He negotiates with a Ute chief named Kenyatch (the actual name of a local Moache Ute with whom Maxwell frequently dealt), who agrees to allow him to settle on tribal lands and to see that no one else trespasses.[33] Soon a new settlement is flourishing. But Ballard has accomplished more than he at first recognizes:

For what had fallen into his hands was not merely a place to live and cultivate. It was the vital heart of a whole region, a place where men would gather as surely as he made it safe, a place to be ruled as well as owned, a means of power as surely as he had power in him. By chance almost beyond belief a king in Spain had granted him a kingdom.[34]

222

The device Fergusson utilizes to describe the "Ballard kingdom" is the fictionalized autobiography of James Lane Morgan, an easterner Ballard hires to provide him with legal advice, who is obviously drawn from Inman. The man Morgan meets when he first arrives in New Mexico is one of the giants of the West:

a heavy, powerful-looking man of middle height, a little too thick in the middle but limber and well carried, wearing a red woolen shirt, blue trousers and fine cowboy half-boots. His face was ruddy, his eyes dark blue, his black hair thick, curly and tipped with silver. His shirt was open at the neck to show a hairy chest which was also brightly grizzled. The effect was one of striking color and vitality, of slow-moving, soft-spoken confidence and power . . . he looked like a ruler, stood out in any group and commanded attention without trying.

Many of the scenes described by Inman and appropriated by earlier writers reappear in *Grant of Kingdom:* Mexican servants bring cold drinks, Ballard distributes huge black cigars to friends, lavish banquets are attended by dozens of guests, there are drawers full of money, and card games go on far into the night. Like others, Fergusson compares his hero to a medieval lord: "His dominion had grown out of frontier chaos just as the walled towns of Europe grew out of the Dark Ages." What he created was "as independent and self-sufficient as any principality in Europe."[35]

Not long after his arrival, Morgan learns that despite his apparent prosperity, Ballard is about to lose his kingdom because of excessive generosity. Fergusson explains his hero's decline not as a moral failure, as Stanley did, but as an inevitable consequence of changing times and demands. One day as he overlooks the Ballard mansion from a nearby hilltop, Morgan suddenly comprehends Ballard's predicament and visualizes the opening of a new era. "Ballard had taken the first step. He had created a walled town—walled by the wilderness, depending upon its isolation for its integrity." Now, however,

the wall had been breached, the turbulent vanguard of civiliza-
tion was pouring in. Someone must meet it and deal with it.
Someone must preserve the order he had created, extend his
conquest, master new forces of money and machinery which
were transforming the whole world.

Such a savior soon appears in the person of Major Arnold N. Blore, a former Confederate artillery officer modeled loosely after New Mexico entrepreneur Stephen B. Elkins, to whom Ballard sells his grant.[36]

Ballard's death provides Fergusson with a final opportunity to assess the significance of his hero. A fellow frontiersman and friend, Daniel Laird, delivers the eulogy in a cemetery overlooking the town Ballard had founded. "Here in the Dark River Valley there has been peace among men for many years," he explains, "and that peace was made and kept by him [Ballard]." No one ever went without food or lodging as long as he lived; there was no need for anyone to commit a crime. But now things were bound to change. "Now that he is gone we will learn that he was great," Laird continues, "and some of us will learn in pain and trouble."[37]

No publication, with the possible exception of Inman's *The Old Santa Fé Trail,* was more important in shaping popular views of Lucien B. Maxwell than *Grant of Kingdom.* It was aggressively promoted by Fergusson's publisher, William Morrow; it was certainly read by more people throughout the United States than all other books about Maxwell combined. It has remained almost constantly in print, and a new paperback edition appeared as recently as 1975. Moreover, the first section, which describes Ballard's courtship with Consuelo Coronel, was excerpted in the *Saturday Evening Post.*[38]

Nearly everyone who read it was impressed. Reviewer J. Frank Dobie predicted that it would endure as a work of art. "Of novels set in the nineteenth-century West," a more recent critic has concluded, "it is certainly one of the most suggestive and illuminating." Some consider it Fergusson's best work, noting that it is "longer, fuller, more complex, and extended in time" than his earlier novels; "it is epic rather than lyric."[39] Besides its literary qualities, *Grant of Kingdom* is so rich, well researched, and convincing that historians often consider it valuable in understanding the development of the Southwest. Texas historian Joe B. Frantz, for example, has argued that Fergusson's novel conveys "more truth than all the monographs put together that have been written about this area."[40]

Publication of Fergusson's novel did not end discussion of Lucien Maxwell. Agnes Morley Cleaveland, who had been born in the Maxwell mansion when her father was working for the English company that bought the grant from Lucien, published *Satan's Paradise* in 1952. It lies somewhere between history and fiction, like most works on Maxwell, drawing on personal memories, local gossip, and earlier writings to paint a picture of Cimarron "from Lucien Maxwell to [modern peace officer] Fred Lambert." The essence of the town, she argues, is wildness. "All the wildness of this wild land," explains the introduction,

> was rounded up and left to bellow in the tiny New Mexican town which Lucien B. Maxwell founded in the late eighteen-sixties and named Cimarron. It sprawled like a spent bullet whose fragments of native earth and rock fell into the shapes . . . of dwelling-places. . . .

Mrs. Cleaveland contributes a new aspect to the Maxwell legend by focusing upon his exploitation of Mexican-Americans. "Lucien Maxwell himself might have achieved a more unquestioned right to membership in that handful of men with scruples who defied men who had none if almost incredible prosperity had not blurred his vision." Cleaveland alleges that he had built his house with the labor of the Mexicans around him, collected rent from all within reach, and lived luxuriously to intimidate those who were poor. "He was," she concludes, "the perfect example of a benevolent despot—to his own immense profit, of course, but never killing nor badly frightening the geese who laid the golden eggs."[41]

Like all the pulp publications with which it shared shelf space, the cover of the November 1956 issue of *Men* magazine was designed to catch readers' attention. This number featured a single bare-chested man, his face defiant, holding a shotgun and wearing a brace of pistols. Challenging him from the bottom of the page were enough rifles, pistols, and knives to arm a small militia. The table of contents promised that in addition to discussions of whether southern girls were "lousy lovers" and information on how to secure employment as an undercover investigator, readers would find Noah Gordon's true story of New Mexico rancher Lucien B. Maxwell, "The Cowman They Called God."[42]

The story repeats in their most exaggerated form the myths about Maxwell that had developed over the eighty years since his death. Drawing heavily on Inman and Cleaveland, Gordon portrays Lucien as a man exercising absolute control over his environment and everyone within it. He forced peons to build him a magnificent house, Gordon wrote, while he rested in the shade, shirtless so passing "senoritas" [*sic*] could admire his physique. "For six days we toiled," the local Mexican-Americans reputedly said, "And on the Seventh day He [Maxwell] rested." Maxwell was a "dignified young God waiting for the rest of the world to be created so that he could begin to rule it." He was the law and the government; even hoodlums like Billy the Kid obeyed his commands. When one of his peons challenged Maxwell's authority, he knocked him in the mouth "crunching the white teeth and making pulp of the smiling lips."

Gordon invented numerous tall tales. He describes an event in which Maxwell won the respect of his mountain men colleagues when he fell to one knee and "drilled" a dangerous grizzly bear "through the left eye, killing it instantly." Kit Carson at first kids him because "Lucien ain't exactly a man's name," but soon admits Maxwell is "sure-as-hell a lot of man." He thought he was acquiring 32,000 acres from his father-in-law and is "stunned" when he discovers that he is "the largest individual real estate . . . [owner] in the United States, one of the largest in the entire world." Once again we learn how Billy the Kid was shot and buried near Lucien. A headstone has now been installed, we are told, but Maxwell's real monument becomes apparent when old Cimarron Mexicans show their children the place where blocks were cut out of the mountains to build Maxwell's house. "'El hombre did this,' they explain . . . . 'The Man did this when He made this land.'"[43]

Myth making never ends, and recent years have witnessed the continuing production of books and articles about Lucien Maxwell. Most have merely transmitted past tales rather than created new legends. New Mexico magazine editor George Fitzpatric contributed "The Baron of the Cimarron" to Westward, the monthly publication of Kaiser Steel Corporation; Jack D. Rittenhouse's "The Man Who Owned Too Much" first appeared in the monthly magazine of the National Lead Company's Baroid Division.[44] Later Rittenhouse's Stagecoach Press issued the article as a tiny, limited-edition book, the first volume devoted exclusively to Maxwell.[45] A similar article, repeating most of the traditional tales, is Hank and Toni Chapman's "Midas of New Mexico," published in the popular American West in 1971.[46] Some of the Maxwell myths worked their ways into Jim Berry Pearson's scholarly business history of the Maxwell Land Grant and my own popular history of Philmont Scout Ranch, both issued by university presses.[47]

The development of the Maxwell legend reveals how easily the personal views of authors work themselves into history. Romantics caught up in visions of feudal splendor, lawyers defending land grant and railroad interests, a minister of the gospel, a bank president, and several authors eager to sell a good story used Maxwell to strengthen interpretations that reflected their own preconceptions and vested interests more than historical reality. Too frequently unwary writers have repeated these stories, often embellishing them or inventing new tales. With each rewriting the distance between truth and myth increases. Equally troublesome is the temptation to create heroes who bear little resemblance to real human beings. Maxwell quickly became, depending on the author's perspective, either a super-hero or an arch-villian. Perhaps future generations of historians, whether their interest is in Lucien Maxwell or any other frontiersman, will be more perceptive of the distortions that have resulted from such carelessness, seek out primary sources, evaluate other writers more critically, and seek to produce more authentic portraits. Myth making can then be left, where it appropriately belongs, to novelists and screenwriters.

Notes

CHAPTER 1

1. *The Illinois Intelligencer* (Kaskaskia), September 2, 1818.

2. William V. Morrison, "Lucien Bonaparte Maxwell," manuscript in the Morrison papers, Illinois State Historical Society, Springfield.

3. The best recent biographical sketch is Richard E. Oglesby, "Pierre Menard," LeRoy R. Hafen, ed., *The Mountain Men and the Fur Trade of the Far West*, 10 vols., 6:307–18. Also Paul D. Spence, ed., *Guide to the . . . Pierre Menard Collection in the Illinois State Historical Library*, esp. pp. 1–5. Emile J. Verlie, ed., *Illinois Constitutions*, p. 46. *The Illinois Intelligencer*, September 2, 23, October 7, 1818.

4. John Reynolds, *Pioneer History of Illinois*, p. 291.

5. John Drury, ed., *Old Illinois Houses*, pp. 7–9. John W. Allen, *Legends and Lore of Southern Illinois*, pp. 6–7.

6. Drury, *Old Illinois Houses*, p. 9. For excellent photographs, see C. William Horrell, Henry Dan Piper, and John W. Voight, *Land Between the Rivers: The Southern Illinois Country*, p. 46.

7. Eugene Fodor et al., eds., *Fodor's Mid-West*, p. 80; *Brevet's Illinois Historical Markers and Sites*, p. 76.

8. Edward G. Mason, *Early Chicago and Illinois*, pp. 145, 162–65.

9. Anton J. Pregaldin, "Genealogy of the Menard *Dit* Brindamour Family," in Spence, *Guide to the . . . Pierre Menard Collection*, pp. 27–28. Slightly different names are given in Mason, *Early Chicago and Illinois*, pp. 147–48.

10. Mason, *Early Chicago and Illinois*, p. 145. Oglesby, "Pierre Menard," p. 309.

11. Oglesby, "Pierre Menard," pp. 309ff.

12. Henry S. Baker, "The First Lieut.-Gov. of Illinois," in Mason, *Early Chicago and Illinois*, pp. 156–57.

13. Pregaldin, "Genealogy," p. 28.

14. Louis Houck, *History of Missouri*, 3 vols., 2:304–305. John Rothensteiner, *History of the Archdiocese of St. Louis*, 2 vols., 2:198–200.

15. Houck, *History of Missouri*, 2:305. Most relevant documents are printed in *Maxwell Claim. Application of the Heirs and Legal Representatives of Hugh H. and John P. Maxwell to the Commissioner of the General Land Office*. For Maxwell's original petition, see pp. 1–2.

16. Descriptions of the Maxwell settlement at the forks of Black

River are in *Maxwell Claim,* pp. 18, 21, 22, 26. According to Morrison, "Lucien Bonaparte Maxwell," Hugh and his brother John were placed in charge of the store and trading post. Hugh removed to Sainte Genevieve after two years, "against the will and desire of the uncle," returning two years later. What evidence Morrison had for this information is unknown.

17. *Maxwell Claim,* pp. 5–7.

18. The appointment document, November 21, 1805, is in the James Wilkinson papers, Missouri Historical Society Library, Saint Louis.

19. Rothensteiner, *Archdiocese of St. Louis,* 1:201–203.

20. Hugh Graham, "St. Genevieve Academy: Missouri's First Secondary School," *Mid-America* n.s. 4, no. 2 (October 1932):71–74. Houck, *History of Missouri,* 2:312.

21. *Maxwell Claim,* p. 21.

22. Baker, "First Lieut.-Gov. of Illinois," p. 160.

23. Francis S. Philbrick, ed., *The Laws of Illinois Territory, 1809-1818,* pp. 81, 180.

24. *The Western Intelligencer* (Kaskaskia), December 11, 1817; June 3, 1818.

25. Edmund J. James, ed., *The Territorial Records of Illinois,* pp. 33, 76–77.

26. Theodore C. Pease, *Illinois Election Returns, 1818-1848,* p. 3.

27. *The Western Intelligencer,* November 6, 1817. *The Illinois Intelligencer,* October 27, 1818. *Maxwell Claim,* pp. 9–16. Missouri Historical Records Survey, *Early Missouri Archives [Part I, Sainte Genevieve Archives]* (Saint Louis: Missouri Historical Records Survey, 1941), pp. 16, 21, 68.

28. *Maxwell Claim,* p. 31. Act of Congress, April 27, 1816, 6 *U.S. Statutes* 168.

29. *The Illinois Intelligencer,* February 17, 1819.

30. Spence, *Guide to the . . . Pierre Menard Collection,* pp. 4, 29.

31. A photograph of a pencil drawing of the house, by Julien Chenu, is in the William V. Morrison Collection, Illinois State Historical Library. For other, similar houses, see Gregory M. Franzwa, *The Story of Old Ste. Genevieve.*

32. Joseph-Amédée Menard to M. B. Menard, July 29, 1844, Pierre Menard Collection, Illinois State Historical Library, Roll 8, frame 557.

33. Margaret Cross Norton, *Illinois Census Returns, 1820,* p. 239.

34. *Kaskaskia Advocate,* January 24, 1823.

35. *Kaskaskia Republican,* April 13, 1824.

36. Graham, "St. Genevieve Academy," pp. 76–77. Franzwa, *Old Ste. Genevieve,* p. 141.

37. Stafford Poole, "The Founding of Missouri's First College: St. Mary's of the Barrens, 1815–1818," *Missouri Historical Review* 65, no. 1 (October 1970):1–21. Houck, *History of Missouri,* 2:325–27.

38. Poole, "Missouri's First College," p. 21. In a personal communi-

cation to the author, November 7, 1977, Father Poole noted that "the history of the lay college at Saint Mary's in the years following its foundation are [sic] very obscure." About 1844 it was transferred to Cape Girardeau, where Maxwell apparently sent his own children for instruction.

39. See letters from Joseph-Amédée, Louis-Cyprien, and Matthieu-Saucier Menard in the Pierre Menard Collection, Illinois State Historical Library. Spence, *Guide to the . . . Pierre Menard Collection,* pp. 102–103, 119.

40. Louis-Cyprien to Pierre Menard, September 19, 1834, Pierre Menard Collection, Illinois State Historical Library, Roll 5, Frame 256.

41. W. J. G[hent], "Lucien B. Maxwell," *Dictionary of American Biography* (New York: Scribners' Sons, 1933), 12:441–42. Harvey Carter, "Lucien Maxwell," in Hafen, *Mountain Men,* 6:299.

42. Morrison, "Lucien Bonaparte Maxwell," p. 2.

43. Solon J. Buck, *Illinois in 1818,* pp. 143–47. John L. Tavebaugh, "Merchant on the Western Frontier: William Morrison of Kaskaskia, 1790–1837" (Ph.D. diss.), discusses the changing business climate in the area.

44. *Kaskaskia Republican,* October 5, 1824.

45. Tavebaugh, "Merchant on the Western Frontier," describes the complex business practices of Morrison and other merchants.

46. Oglesby, "Pierre Menard," pp. 309–13.

47. Jack D. Rittenhouse, *The Santa Fe Trail: A Historical Bibliography,* p. 7. Tavebaugh, "Merchant on the Western Frontier," pp. 119–21.

48. *Kaskaskia Republican,* February 15, 1825.

49. Buck, *Illinois in 1818,* pp. 2–3.

50. A. Lavasseur, *Lafayette in America,* 2 vols., 2:150–51.

51. Ibid., pp. 151ff.

52. Buck, *Illinois in 1818,* p. 13. Oglesby, "Pierre Menard," p. 315.

53. Buck, *Illinois in 1818,* p. 15.

54. *Kaskaskia Republican,* January 4, 1825.

55. Oglesby, "Pierre Menard," pp. 315–16.

56. Ferdinand Ernst, *Travels in Illinois in 1819,* pp. 155–56. *Kaskaskia Republican,* February 15, 1825.

57. Ernst, *Travels in Illinois,* p. 156. *Illinois Intelligencer,* September 15, 1819.

58. *Sangamo Journal* (Springfield), September 14, 1833. Morrison, "Lucien Bonaparte Maxwell," p. 3. Pregaldin, "Genealogy," incorrectly dates his death as September 4. The frequently reported story that Hugh died in a hunting accident is erroneous.

59. *Maxwell Grant,* p. 22. In 1845, for example, Edmund Menard paid taxes on land owned by H. H. Maxwell's heirs. This tax receipt and other similar documents are in the William V. Morrison Collection, Illinois State Historical Library.

CHAPTER 2

1. J. C. Wild and Louis F. Thomas, *The Valley of the Mississippi Illustrated* (Saint Louis: Chambers and Knapp, 1841; repr. Saint Louis: Joseph Garner, 1948), pp. 8–9.

2. J. S. Buckingham quoted in William E. Lass, "Tourists' Impressions of St. Louis, 1766–1859," *Missouri Historical Review* 53, no. 1 (1958): 12–13.

3. Harold H. Dunham, "Lucien B. Maxwell: Frontiersman and Businessman," The Denver Posse Westerners *Brand Book, 1949,* ed. Don Bloch (Denver: Privately Printed, 1950), p. 271, erroneously claims that Maxwell accompanied Frémont on this expedition. The vouchers do not include his name, and he may have been confused with a voyageur named Maxime Maxwell. Donald Jackson and Mary Lee Spence, eds., *The Expeditions of John Charles Frémont* 1:145.

4. Allan Nevins, *Frémont: Pathmarker of the West;* more recent and detailed is Ferol Egan, *Frémont: Explorer for a Restless Nation.*

5. John Charles Frémont, *Narratives of Exploration and Adventure,* ed. Allan Nevins, p. 23.

6. Henry Nash Smith, *Virgin Land,* pp. 23ff.

7. Louise Barry, *The Beginning of the West,* pp. 451ff; William H. Goetzmann, *Exploration and Empire,* pp. 240ff., provides needed perspective.

8. See vouchers in Jackson and Spence, *Expeditions of Frémont* 1: 42–46.

9. Egan, *Frémont,* p. 60.

10. John C. Frémont, *Memoirs of My Life* 1:73.

11. Dunham, "Lucien B. Maxwell," p. 271, says Maxwell "seems to have come West about 1837 in the employ of the American Fur Company," while Harvey L. Carter, "Lucien Maxwell," in LeRoy R. Hafen, ed., *The Mountain Men and the Fur Trade of the Far West* 6:299, says that "reports that he worked for the American Fur Company or that he kept a store in the Hardscrabble are erroneous."

12. William A. Keleher, *Maxwell Land Grant: A New Mexico Item,* p. 27.

13. Harvey L. Carter, *'Dear Old Kit': The Historical Christopher Carson,* p. 79.

14. R. L. Duffus, *The Santa Fe Trail,* p. 78.

15. Janet Lecompte, *Pueblo, Hardscrabble, Greenhorn: The Upper Arkansas, 1832-1856,* p. 20.

16. Carter, "Lucien Maxwell," pp. 299–300. George B. Grinnell, "Bent's Old Fort and Its Builders," Kansas State Historical Society *Collections* 15 (1923):57.

17. Hiram M. Chittenden, *A History of the American Fur Trade of the Far West,* 2 vols., 1:309ff.

18. David Lavender, *Bent's Fort,* esp. pp. 134ff.; David J. Weber,

NOTES

The Taos Trappers: The Fur Trade in the Far Southwest, 1540-1846, p. viii.
19. Lavender, *Bent's Fort, passim.* Grinnell, "Bent's Old Fort," pp. 31-44.
20. Lavender, *Bent's Fort*, pp. 182-93.
21. Grinnell, "Bent's Old Fort," p. 57.
22. L. R. Hafen, "The Early Fur Trade Posts on the South Platte," *Mississippi Valley Historical Review* 12, no. 3 (1925-26):340-41. LeRoy R. Hafen, "Fort St. Vrain," *Colorado Magazine* 29 (1952):241-55.
23. Harvey L. Carter, "Marcellin St. Vrain," in Hafen, *Mountain Men* 3:273-75.
24. Elinor Wilson, *Jim Beckwourth: Black Mountain Man and War Chief of the Crows*, esp. p. 101; Lavender, *Bent's Fort*, p. 197.
25. Hafen, "Early Fur Trade Posts," pp. 335-36. Ann W. Hafen, "Lancaster P. Lupton," in Hafen, *Mountain Men* 2:207-13.
26. B. F. Rockafellow, "History of Fremont County," in *History of the Arkansas Valley* (Chicago: O. L. Baskin & Co., 1881), p. 546. For an alternative view of Lupton's activities during this period, probably more correct, see Lecompte, *Pueblo, Hardscrabble, Greenhorn*, p. 133.
27. Weber, *Taos Trappers*, pp. 2-11.
28. George Frederick Ruxton, *Life in the Far West.*, ed. LeRoy R. Hafen, p. 182.
29. Lawrence R. Murphy, "Charles Beaubien," in Hafen, *Mountain Men* 6:23-29.
30. *Transcript of Title of the Maxwell Land Grant Situated in New Mexico and Colorado*, pp. 5-6, 16-17.
31. Ibid., pp. 6-17. For background, see Ward Allen Minge, "Frontier Problems in New Mexico Preceding the Mexican War, 1840-1846" (Ph.D. diss.), pp. 159ff.
32. Morrison, "Lucien Bonaparte Maxwell," p. 3.
33. Lewis H. Garrard, *Wah-to-yah and the Taos Trail*, p. 177, says that young Beaubien returned from college in 1846 after five years absence. Also Stafford Poole to the author, November 7, 1977.
34. Fray Angelico Chavez, "New Names in New Mexico, 1820-1850," *El Palacio* 64, nos. 9 and 10 (1957):317. Many sources give the date as June 3, 1844, including Pregaldin, "Genealogy," p. 33; Keleher, *Maxwell Land Grant*, p. 25; and Carter, "Lucien Maxwell," p. 301.
35. Edwin L. Sabin, *Kit Carson Days* (Revised ed., 2 vols.); M. Morgan Estergreen, *Kit Carson: A Portrait in Courage;* and Bernice Blackwelder, *Great Westerner: The Story of Kit Carson*, are standard. For a bibliographical essay, see Carter, *'Dear Old Kit,'* pp. 3-36.
36. Carter, *'Dear Old Kit,'* p. 5.
37. Virtually all historians agree on this date; the church records are translated in Sabin, *Kit Carson Days*, pp. 313-14. Chavez, "New Names," p. 300, gives January 28, 1843.
38. Barry, *Beginning of the West*, p. 449.
39. Morrison, "Lucien Bonaparte Maxwell," pp. 3-4.

40. Carter, *'Dear Old Kit,'* p. 64. Also Bernard De Voto, *Across the Wide Missouri.*

41. John C. Frémont, *Report of the Exploring Expedition to the Rocky Mountains in the Year 1842 . . .* , p. 9; John Charles Frémont, *Memoirs of My Life* 1:73–74; Jackson and Spence, *Expeditions of Frémont* 1:151.

42. Carter, *'Dear Old Kit,'* p. 81.

43. Frémont, *Report of Exploring Expedition,* p. 10.

44. Ibid., pp. 10–11. Charles Preuss, *Exploring With Frémont; The Private Diaries of Charles Preuss . . .* , pp. 6–7.

45. Frémont, *Report of Exploring Expedition,* pp. 18–19.

46. Ibid., pp. 19–20.

47. Ibid., pp. 23–24. Preuss, *Exploring with Frémont,* p. 19.

48. Frémont, *Report of Exploring Expedition,* pp. 27–30.

49. Ibid., pp. 31–32.

50. Ibid., pp. 35–36, 39–40.

51. Ibid., pp. 43–50.

52. Preuss, *Exploring With Frémont,* p. 30; Frémont, *Report of Exploring Expedition,* p. 51.

53. Frémont, *Report of Exploring Expedition,* pp. 53–64.

54. Ibid., pp. 64–69. Preuss, *Exploring with Frémont,* pp. 39–45.

55. Frémont, *Report of Exploring Expedition,* pp. 69–70. Preuss, *Exploring With Frémont,* pp. 45–46.

56. Preuss, *Exploring With Frémont,* pp. 64, 70.

57. Frémont, *Report of Exploring Expedition,* pp. 77–79. Jackson and Spence, *Expeditions of Frémont* 1:144–48.

CHAPTER 3

1. Bernard De Voto, *The Year of Decision, 1846,* p. 39.

2. Carter, "Lucien Maxwell," in Hafen, *Mountain Men* 6:30; Dunham, "Lucien Maxwell," in the Denver Posse Westerners *Brand Book, 1949,* p. 273; Morrison, "Lucien Bonaparte Maxwell," p. 4.

3. Chavez, "New Names," p. 300.

4. Lawrence R. Murphy, "The Beaubien and Miranda Land Grant, 1841–1846," *New Mexico Historical Review* 42, no. 1 (1967):31–32, 43–44. For background, see Charles R. McClure, "The Texan-Santa Fe Expedition," *New Mexico Historical Review* 48, no. 1 (January 1973):45–56.

5. No adequate biography exists. Lavender, *Bent's Fort,* pp. 191–92; Janet Lecompte, "Manuel Armijo's Family History," *New Mexico Historical Review* 48, no. 3 (July 1973):251–58; Minge, "Frontier Problems" are all incomplete or inaccurate. Elliot Arnold, *The Time of the Gringo,* is fictionalized.

6. Murphy, "Beaubien and Miranda Grant," pp. 32, 44.

7. David J. Weber, "Stephen Louis Lee," in Hafen, *Mountain Men* 3:181–86.

NOTES

8. Murphy, "Beaubien and Miranda Grant," pp. 32, 44. Morris F. Taylor, "A New Look at an Old Case: The Bent Heirs' Claim to the Maxwell Grant," *New Mexico Historical Review* 43, no. 3 (July 1968): 213-28.

9. L. C. Menard to Pierre Menard, May 21, 1843, Pierre Menard Papers, Illinois State Historical Library, Roll 8, Frame 189.

10. Frémont, *Report of Exploring Expedition*, p. 106. Egan, *Frémont*, pp. 122ff; Preuss, *Exploring with Frémont*, p. 81; Thomas L. Karnes, *William Gilpin: Western Nationalist*, pp. 77-79.

11. Frémont, *Report of Exploring Expedition*, pp. 105-106.

12. Egan, *Frémont*, p. 128.

13. Frémont, *Report of Exploring Expedition*, p. 107.

14. Ibid., pp. 111, 116.

15. Carter, *'Dear Old Kit,'* pp. 87-88.

16. E. K. Francis, "Padre Martinez: A New Mexican Myth," *New Mexico Historical Review* 31 (1956):265-89. Murphy, "Beaubien and Miranda Grant," pp. 32-33.

17. Murphy, "Beaubien and Miranda Grant," p. 33.

18. G. D. Robinson et. al, *Philmont Country: The Rocks and Landscapes of a Famous New Mexico Ranch.*

19. Agreement between Maxwell and Sibille and Adams, Fort Platte, September 27, 1843, Adams Papers, Missouri Historical Society, Saint Louis.

20. Murphy, "Beaubien and Miranda Grant," pp. 33-34.

21. Ibid., p. 24.

22. Garrard, *Wah-to-yah*, p. 156. Harvey L. Carter, "Richard Owens," and "John Hatcher," in Hafen, *Mountain Men*, 5:283-85 and 4:125-27. Carter, *'Dear Old Kit,'* p. 95. Estergreen, *Kit Carson*, p. 126, erroneously locates the settlement on the Rayado.

23. Dunham, "Lucien B. Maxwell," p. 274. Carter, *'Dear Old Kit,'* p. 98.

24. James J. Webb, *Adventures in the Santa Fe Trade, 1844-1847*, ed. Ralph P. Bieber, pp. 63-65.

25. Lecompte, *Pueblo, Hardscrabble, Greenhorn*, pp. 133-35.

26. Frémont, *Memoirs* 1:424. Lecompte, *Pueblo, Hardscrabble, Greenhorn,* pp. 150, 304, cites accounts from the expedition to demonstrate that Maxwell was not hired until Frémont reached Hardscrabble. This may be true, demonstrating an error in Frémont's memoirs, written many years later, or he may have paid Maxwell what was already due him so the money could be sent to his family in Taos before they proceeded farther west.

27. Nevins, *Frémont*, pp. 198-207. Allan Nevins, ed., *Polk: The Diary of a President, 1845-1849*, p. 19.

28. Frémont, *Memoirs* 1:426-27. Carter, *'Dear Old Kit,'* pp. 95-96.

29. Frémont, *Memoirs* 1:432-33. Carter, *'Dear Old Kit,'* p. 99, adds

Basil Lajeunesse (not mentioned by Frémont) to the party.
30. Egan, *Frémont,* pp. 300–308.
31. Frémont, *Memoirs* 1:445–46.
32. Printed in Jackson and Spence, *Expeditions of Frémont* 2:81.
33. Otis A. Singletary, *The Mexican War,* pp. 8ff. is a convenient summary.
34. Jackson and Spence, *Expeditions of Frémont* 2:112–13. Carter, *'Dear Old Kit,'* pp. 103–104.
35. Jackson and Spence, *Expeditions of Frémont* 2:120–21; Carter, *'Dear Old Kit,'* p. 106.
36. Charles L. Camp, "Kit Carson in California," *California Historical Society Quarterly* 1 (1922–23):134–35. Sabin, *Kit Carson Days* 2:463–64. Sabin doubts the story from T. J. Schoonover, *The Life and Times of Gen. John A. Sutter,* p. 109. Estergreen, *Kit Carson,* pp. 141–42 accepts its accuracy.
37. Egan, *Frémont,* pp. 360–69. Jackson and Spence, *Expeditions of Frémont* 2:196; Carter, *'Dear Old Kit,'* pp. 111–12. Barry, *Beginning of the West,* p. 656.
38. Carter, *'Dear Old Kit,'* pp. 111–12.
39. Ibid., p. 112. W. H. Emory, *Lieutenant Emory Reports,* ed. Ross Calvin, p. 87. Charles Ruhlen, "Kearny's Route from the Rio Grande to the Gila River," *New Mexico Historical Review* 32, no. 3 (July 1957): 214–15.
40. Singletary, *The Mexican War,* pp. 55–60. Dwight L. Clarke, *Stephen Watts Kearny: Soldier of the West,* pp. 101–66.
41. Clarke, *Kearny,* pp. 166ff.
42. Barry, *Beginning of the West,* p. 656.
43. Garrard, *Wah-to-yah,* pp. 117–19.
44. Ibid., pp. 123, 132, 134, 143–46.
45. Ibid., pp. 176–77. Also Howard L. Conard, *Uncle Dick Wootton,* pp. 153–60; and E. Bennett Burton, "The Taos Rebellion," *Old Santa Fe* 1, no. 2 (October 1913):177, 180–85.
46. Adelina Abreú Valdez, interviewed by Harry G. McGavran, M.D., 1958, tape recording in E. T. Seton Library, Cimarron, N.M.
47. Ibid.
48. Burton, "Taos Rebellion," pp. 178–79. Francis T. Cheetham, "The First Term of the American Court in Taos, New Mexico," *New Mexico Historical Review* 1, no. 1 (1926):23–41.
49. Cheetham, "First Term," pp. 28–29. Garrard. *Wah-to-yah,* pp. 171–73, 181–83.
50. Garrard, *Wah-to-yah,* pp. 190–91; Cheetham, "First Term," p. 29.
51. Garrard, *Wah-to-yah,* p. 173.
52. Cheetham, "First Term," pp. 33–37.
53. Murphy, "Beaubien and Miranda Land Grant," pp. 38–47.
54. Pregaldin, "Genealogy," p. 33. Corrections and additions by William Morrison are in his papers, Illinois State Historical Library, Springfield.

NOTES

CHAPTER 4

1. Susan S. Magoffin, *Down the Santa Fe Trail and Into Mexico*, ed. Stella M. Drumm, p. 88; Emory, *Lieutenant Emory Reports*, p. 43.
2. T. M. Pearce, *New Mexico Place Names*, p. 130.
3. Carter, *'Dear Old Kit,'* p. 124.
4. Dolores A. Gunnerson, *The Jicarilla Apaches: A Study in Survival*, p. 206.
5. David L. Caffey, *Head for the High Country*, p. 73.
6. George A. McCall, *New Mexico in 1850: A Military View*, ed. Robert W. Frazer, p. 150.
7. DeWitt C. Peters, *The Life and Adventures of Kit Carson*, p. 33.
8. McCall, *New Mexico in 1850*, p. 150.
9. Ibid.
10. Gunnerson, *The Jicarilla Apaches*, pp. 149ff.; Morris E. Opler, "Jicarilla Apache Territory, Economy, and Society in 1850," *Southwestern Journal of Anthropology* 27, no. 4 (1971):309–15.
11. Gunnerson, *The Jicarilla Apaches*, pp. 166–234.
12. Opler, "Jicarilla Apache Territory," pp. 315–18.
13. Ibid., pp. 319–27.
14. James Jefferson, Robert W. Delaney, and Gregory C. Thompson, *The Southern Utes: A Tribal History*, pp. vii–viii, 1–13. Morris F. Taylor, "Ka-Ni-Ache," *Colorado Magazine* 43, no. 4 (1966):275–76.
15. Ernest Wallace and E. Adamson Hoebel, *The Comanches: Lords of the South Plains*, p. 245.
16. Rupert N. Richardson, *The Comanche Barrier to South Plains Settlement*, pp. 159ff.
17. Taylor, "Ka-Ni-Ache," p. 276. Albert H. Schroeder, "Shifting for Survival in the Spanish Southwest," *New Mexico Historical Review* 48, no. 4 (1968):302–304.
18. Quoted in Opler, "Jicarilla Apache Territory," p. 320.
19. Charles L. Kenner, *A History of New Mexican-Plains Indian Relations*, p. 117.
20. Lawrence R. Murphy, "Rayado: Pioneer Settlement in Northeastern New Mexico, 1848–1857," *New Mexico Historical Review* 46, no. 1 (1971):38. Karnes, *William Gilpin*, pp. 201–202.
21. Murphy, "Rayado," p. 38.
22. Carter, *'Dear Old Kit,'* p. 136.
23. William V. Morrison to the author, May 17, 1977, p. 4.
24. Murphy, "Rayado," p. 38. Harvey L. Carter, "Calvin Jones," in Hafen, *Mountain Men* 6:207–12. Carter, *'Dear Old Kit,'* p. 127. William V. Morrison's corrections to the Maxwell genealogy, Illinois State Historical Library, Springfield, Illinois.
25. Murphy, "Rayado," p. 38.
26. Garrard, *Wah-to-yah*, pp. 144–45.
27. Jones's testimony is in *The United States vs. the Maxwell Land*

Grant Company et al. No 974, Transcript of Record, p. 72. The only known copy is filed with manuscripts related to the case in RG 267, National Archives. Hereinafter cited as *Transcript of Record.*

28. Janet Lecompte, "The Manco Burro Pass Massacre," *New Mexico Historical Review* 41, no. 4 (1966):309, 316.

29. Ibid., p. 309.

30. Ibid., pp. 309–10. Lawrence R. Murphy, "The United States Army in Taos, 1847–1852," *New Mexico Historical Review* 47, no. 1 (1972): 35–36.

31. Quoted in Howard L. Conard, *Uncle Dick Wootton,* p. 199.

32. Ibid., pp. 199–202. Lecompte, "Manco Burro Pass," pp. 310–14. Barry, *Beginning of the West,* pp. 756–57.

33. Conard, *Uncle Dick Wootton,* pp. 200–201. Interview with Jesse Nelson, F. W. Cragin notebooks, 8:69.

34. *Santa Fe Republican,* July 7, 19, 1848.

35. *Report of the Secretary of the Interior Made in Conformity to Law Upon Claims for Depredations by Indians in the Territory of New Mexico. Senate Executive Doc. 55,* p. 11

36. John Frémont to Jessie B. Frémont, January 27, 1849, printed in LeRoy R. and Ann W. Hafen, eds., *Frémont's Fourth Expedition,* p. 206.

37. Frémont's notes on the expedition, ibid., p. 298.

38. See Egan, *Frémont,* pp. 406–63 for a recent survey.

39. Ibid., pp. 464–74. E. M. Kern to his wife Mary, February 10, 1849, in Hafen and Hafen, *Frémont's Fourth Expedition,* pp. 123–24.

40. Carter, *'Dear Old Kit,'* pp. 123–24.

41. Murphy, "Rayado," p. 40. Anna P. Hannum, ed., *A Quaker Forty-Niner: The Adventures of Charles Edward Pancoast on the American Frontier,* pp. 208–209.

42. Murphy, "U.S. Army in Taos," p. 37.

43. For Calhoun's reports, see Annie H. Abel, ed., *The Official Correspondence of James S. Calhoun,* pp. 63–66.

44. Carter, *'Dear Old Kit,'* pp. 124–26 & n.

45. Francis P. Prucha, *Broadax and Bayonet,* pp. 149ff.

46. Carter, *'Dear Old Kit,'* p. 126.

47. Murphy, "Rayado," p. 42–43.

48. Carter, "Bill New," in Hafen, *Mountain Men* 5:252–53; Carter, *'Dear Old Kit,'* p. 127.

49. McCall, *New Mexico in 1850,* pp. 146–48.

50. Ibid., pp. 150–52.

51. Ibid., p. 148; *Report of the Secretary of War, 1852. House Executive Doc. 1,* p. 78.

52. Interview with Jesse Nelson, Cragin notebooks, 8:69.

53. *Transcript of Record of Charles Bent et als. vs. Guadalupe Miranda et als.,* pp. 166–68. Hereinafter cited as *Bent vs. Miranda.*

54. Quinn and Maxwell claim in *"Report . . . Upon Claims for Depre-*

dations," p. 441. Murphy, "Rayado," p. 44.
55. Murphy, "Rayado," pp. 44–45.
56. Ibid., p. 48. Also Chris Emmett, *Fort Union and the Winning of the Southwest,* pp. 14–18.
57. Emmett, *Fort Union,* p. 14.
58. Carter, *'Dear Old Kit,'* p. 132. Carter, "Kit Carson," in Hafen, *Mountain Men* 6:124.
59. Emmett, *Fort Union,* p. 120.
60. Conard, *Uncle Dick Wootton,* pp. 234ff. Alvar Ward Carlson, "New Mexico's Sheep Industry," *New Mexico Historical Review* 44, no. 1 (1969):28. *Santa Fe Weekly Gazette,* May 21, 1853.
61. *Santa Fe Weekly Gazette,* December 31, 1853. Carter, *'Dear Old Kit,'* pp. 132–33.
62. Interview with John O. Boggs, F. W. Cragin Notebooks, 8:80.
63. William H. Ryus, *The Second William Penn,* pp. 110–11.
64. Antoine Leroux's statement, March 1, 1853, in Gwinn H. Heap, *Central Route to the Pacific,* p. 33.
65. Pregaldin, "Genealogy," p. 33, and William V. Morrison corrections and additions to the Menard genealogy.
66. Chavez, "New Names in New Mexico," p. 317.
67. Peters, *The Life and Adventures of Kit Carson,* p. 332.
68. Morris F. Taylor, "Campaigns against the Jicarilla Apache, 1854," *New Mexico Historical Review* 44, no. 4 (1968):271–76.
69. *Santa Fe Weekly Gazette,* April 8, 1854.
70. Carson to Acting Governor Messervy, March 21, 1854, quoted in Bernice Blackwelder, *Great Westerner: The Story of Kit Carson,* p. 271.
71. Morris F. Taylor, "Campaigns Against the Jicarilla Apache, 1854," pp. 277–86.
72. Morris F. Taylor, "Campaigns Against the Jicarilla Apache, 1855," *New Mexico Historical Review* 45, no. 4 (1970):119–31.
73. *Santa Fe Weekly Gazette,* September 15, 1855.
74. Ibid., May 3, 1856.
75. Quoted in Sabin, *Kit Carson Days* 2:632–33.
76. Kenner, *New Mexican-Plains Indian Relations,* p. 121.

CHAPTER 5

1. Keleher, *Maxwell Land Grant,* p. 6. Victor Westphall, "Fraud and Implications of Fraud in the Land Grants of New Mexico," *New Mexico Historical Review* 49, no. 3 (1974):190–91.
2. "Notice to the Inhabitants of New Mexico," January 27, 1855, *Santa Fe Weekly Gazette,* March 3, 1855.
3. The petition is printed in *Transcript of Title,* pp. 3–4.
4. *Santa Fe Weekly Gazette,* February 7, July 4, 1857.
5. *Transcript of Title,* pp. 23ff.

6. Pelham's report on Claim No. 48, September 17, 1857, Ibid., pp. 25–26.

7. Miranda to Beaubien, February 24, 1858, in the unpublished *Transcript of Record*. The letter is printed in Keleher, *Maxwell Land Grant*, pp. 40–41.

8. L. Pablo Miranda to Lucien B. Maxwell, April 7, 1858, in *Transcript of Title*, pp. 31, 35–36.

9. Kenyon Riddle, *Records and Maps of the Old Santa Fe Trail*, Sheet 4.

10. J. Frank Dobie, *The Longhorns*, pp. 4, 9, 43. Pearce, *New Mexico Place Names*, p. 35.

11. Agnes Morley Cleaveland, *Satan's Paradise*, p. 1.

12. John G. Parke to L. M. Laws, April 14, 1851, in Letters Received, 9th Military Department.

13. William V. Morrison, "Lucien Bonaparte Maxwell," manuscript in the Morrison Collection, p. 4.

14. Ibid.; *Transcript of Title*, pp. 33–34; Pley to Abreú, February 22, 1860, manuscript in the collection of Harry G. McGavran, Jr.

15. Beaubien and Miranda to Bent, March 2, 1843, Day Book A, Register of Land Claims Under the Kearny Code, 1847, U.S. Bureau of Land Management Archives, Santa Fe.

16. Morris F. Taylor, "A New Look at an Old Case: The Bent Heirs' Claim in the Maxwell Grant," *New Mexico Historical Review* 43, no. 3 (1968):214ff.

17. Henry Inman, *The Old Santa Fe Trail*, p. 374.

18. Irving Howbert, *Memories of a Lifetime in the Pike's Peak Region*, p. 169. *Daily Rocky Mountain News*, February 15, 1866.

19. Compare, for example, the etching in Inman, *Old Santa Fe Trail*, p. 388, with the photographs in Horrell, Ryan, and Voight, *Land Between the Rivers*, p. 46.

20. Inman, *Old Santa Fe Trail*, p. 374; Howbert, *Memories of a Lifetime*, p. 169.

21. Inman, *Old Santa Fe Trail*, p. 375.

22. Cleaveland, *Satan's Paradise*, pp. 7–8. Her son Norman Cleaveland (with George Fitzpatrick) in *The Morleys—Young Upstarts on the Southwest Frontier*, speculates that the most elaborate furnishings were purchased by Maxwell's English successors in the house.

23. Howbert, *Memories of a Lifetime*, pp. 169–70.

24. Inman, *Old Santa Fe Trail*, p. 375.

25. *The New Mexican*, August 12, 1864.

26. E. B. Denison to A. B. Norton, September 4, 1867, Records, New Mexico Superintendency, RG 75, National Archives.

27. *Bent vs. Miranda*, p. 359.

28. Ibid., p. 125. *The New Mexican*, March 27, 1869.

29. Manuscript Census, Mora County, New Mexico, 1860, RG 29, National Archives. John Collinson and W. A. Bell, *The Maxwell Land Grant, Situated in Colorado and New Mexico, United States of America*, p. 7.

30. *The New Mexican,* August 12, 1864.
31. *Daily Rocky Mountain News,* February 15, 1866.
32. Collinson and Bell, *Maxwell Land Grant,* p. 7. *Bent vs. Miranda,* pp. 342, 394.
33. *Bent vs. Miranda,* p. 191.
34. Ibid., pp. 101, 255.
35. Ibid., p. 157. Manuscript Census, Mora County, 1860.
36. Howbert, *Memories of a Lifetime,* p. 169.
37. *Bent vs. Miranda,* pp. 341–42.
38. Collinson and Bell, *Maxwell Land Grant,* pp. 6–7.
39. Inman, *Old Santa Fe Trail,* p. 374.
40. *Bent vs. Miranda,* p. 93.
41. Collinson and Bell, *Maxwell Land Grant,* pp. 6–7.
42. Manuscript Census, Taos County, 1850; Mora County, 1860; Colfax County, 1870, RG 29, National Archives.
43. Keleher, *Maxwell Land Grant,* p. 35.
44. Pearce, *New Mexico Place Names,* p. 35; Sheldon H. Dike, *The Territorial Post Offices of New Mexico.*
45. Morris F. Taylor, *First Mail West: Stagecoach Lines on the Santa Fe Trail,* p. 78.
46. *Colorado Chieftain* (Pueblo), July 23, 1868.
47. Inman, *Old Santa Fe Trail,* p. 378.
48. *The New Mexican,* April 23, 1864; *Bent vs. Miranda,* p. 190.
49. *Daily Rocky Mountain News,* February 15, 1866.
50. William A. Bell, *New Tracks in North America,* 1 vol. ed., p. 108; *Daily Rocky Mountain News,* February 14, 1866.
51. Howbert, *Memories of a Lifetime,* p. 169.
52. *Bent vs. Miranda,* pp. 122–23.
53. *Colorado Chieftain,* January 13, 1870; *The Daily New Mexican,* March 28, 1870.
54. *Daily Rocky Mountain News,* February 15, 1866. *The New Mexican,* April 23, 1864.
55. Joe Heflin Smith, "The Unmarked Grave," *The Cattleman* 34, no. 12 (1949):66.
56. *Bent vs. Miranda,* pp. 117, 255.
57. William H. Ryus, *The Second William Penn,* p. 113.
58. *Bent vs. Miranda,* p. 157.
59. Thomas Richter, ed., "Sister Catherine Mallon's Journal," *New Mexico Historical Review* 52, no. 2 (1977):140–41.
60. *Bent vs. Miranda,* pp. 122–23.
61. Ryus, *Second William Penn,* p. 113; Interview of Narciso M. Abreú, July 1960, by Harry G. McGavran, M.D., tape recording in the Seton Library, Cimarron, N.M.; *Cimarron News and Press,* August 19, 1880.
62. *Daily Rocky Mountain News,* February 16, 1866; *The New Mexican,* April 23, 1864.
63. *Bent vs. Miranda,* pp. 255–56.

64. Ibid., p. 343.

65. Interview with Octave Geoffrion, F. W. Cragin Notebooks, 7: 36–38.

66. Inman, *Old Santa Fe Trail,* pp. 377–78.

67. *Bent vs. Miranda,* pp. 255, 117.

68. Ibid., pp. 375, 248.

69. Ibid., p. 158.

70. Ibid., p. 118.

71. Ibid., pp. 158–59.

72. Ibid., pp. 159–60.

73. Ibid., p. 159.

74. Ibid., p. 133.

75. Interview with Fred Demorais, F. W. Cragin Notebooks, 7:32.

76. *The New Mexican,* February 6, 1864. Inman, *Old Santa Fe Trail,* p. 374.

CHAPTER 6

1. Estergreen, *Kit Carson,* pp. 202–228.

2. Ibid., p. 225.

3. W. F. M. Arny to James L. Collins, September 1, 1862, in *Report of the Secretary of the Interior, 1862. Senate Executive Document No. 1,* pp. 386–87. Carson to William Dole, October 17, 1862, in Letters Received, New Mexico Superintendency, RG 234, Roll 551. Hereinafter cited as LRNMS.

4. The petition signed by Watrous and many others is in LRNMS, Roll 551.

5. Lawrence R. Murphy, *Frontier Crusader: William F. M. Arny.*

6. Arny to Dole, January 3, 1862. Lease between Arny and Maxwell, March 10, 1862, in Records, New Mexico Superintendency, RG 75, Roll 5. Hereinafter cited as RNMS. Arny to Dole, April 26, 1862, LRNMS, Roll 551.

7. The receipt, signed by Maxwell August 6, 1862, is in LRNMS, Roll 551.

8. Arny to Dole, March 17, 1862; Maxwell to Levi J. Keithly, December 21, 1862; James L. Collins to Dole, December 21, 1862; accounts of the Cimarron agency for the half-year ending December 31, 1862, all LRNMS, Roll 551.

9. Maxwell to Edmond Menard, November 11, 1862, Pierre Menard Collection, Illinois State Historical Library, Roll 9, Frame 35.

10. J. P. Usher to Charles E. Mix, July 29, 1862, LRNMS, Roll 551. Mix to Collins, July 29, 1862, and Collins to F. Maxwell, October 24, 1862, RNMS, Roll 5.

11. Michael Steck to F. Maxwell, August 17, 1863; F. Maxwell to Steck, December 3, 1863, RNMS.

12. Arny to Carleton, October 25, 1862; Carleton to Arny, October 31, 1862, LRNMS, Roll 551.

13. Inman, *Old Santa Fe Trail*, pp. 383–84.

14. *Bent vs. Miranda*, pp. 343–44.

15. Bell, *New Tracks in North America*, p. 109.

16. *Bent vs. Miranda*, pp. 430–32.

17. Usher to Dole, February 1, 1864; Steck to Keithly, January 25, 1864, and to F. Maxwell, January 26, 1864, RNMS, Roll 6.

18. Steck to F. Maxwell, September 15, 1865, January 18, 1864[5], RNMS, Roll 6. F. Maxwell to F. Perea, January 22, 1865, LRNMS, Roll 552.

19. Steck to Keithly, February 20, 1865, RNMS, Roll 6.

20. Salazar to Delgado, February 26, 1866, LRNMS, Roll 553.

21. Graves to Salazar, February 27, 1866, LRNMS, Roll 553.

22. Norton to D. N. Cooley, June 24, 1866, LRNMS, Roll 553. Norton to Maxwell, June 24, 1866, RNMS, Roll 7.

23. Cooley to Norton, July 19, 1866, RNMS, Roll 7.

24. Maxwell to Norton, August 7, 1866, RNMS, Roll 7.

25. Arny to Cooley, August 28, 1866, LRNMS, Roll 553. Norton to Cooley, September 12, 1866, RNMS, Roll 7.

26. Carleton to George Campbell, August 25, 1866, LRNMS, Roll 553.

27. A. J. Alexander to Cyrus H. DeForrest, October 2, 1866, LRNMS, Roll 553.

28. *Santa Fe Weekly Gazette*, December 1, 1866.

29. Carson to Capt. C. Pews, October 5, 1866, LRNMS, Roll 553. *The New Mexican*, October 13, 1866.

30. Norton to Henderson, October 9, 1866, RNMS, Roll 7. Henderson to Norton, November 27, 1866, in *Santa Fe Weekly Gazette*, December 1, 1866.

31. Norton to Maxwell, October 12, 1866; Maxwell to Norton, October 29, 1866, RNMS, Roll 7.

32. Norton to D. N. Cooley, September 28, 1866, in *Annual Report of the Commissioner of Indian Affairs, 1866. Senate Executive Document No. 1*, pp. 144–45.

33. Maxwell to Norton, October 29, 1866, RNMS, Roll 7.

34. Inman, *Old Santa Fe Trail*, pp. 379–80.

35. A. G. Taylor to Norton, May 3, 1867, RNMS, Roll 8. Carson to Norton, June 21, 1867; and Norton to Taylor, July 27, 1867, LRNMS, Roll 554.

36. Carson to Taylor, February 16, March 11, 1867, LRNMS, Roll 555.

37. Estergreen, *Kit Carson*, pp. 272–78.

38. Denison to Norton, September 4, 1867, RNMS, Roll 8.

39. *Santa Fe Weekly Gazette*, June 27, 1868.

40. Ibid., July 18, 1868.

41. Charles McClure to DeForrest, September 25, 1867, LRNMS, Roll 554.

42. *Colorado Chieftain,* October 29, 1868.

43. Arny to Denison, and Denison to Arny, December 12, 1868; Arny to Taylor, December 26, 1868, LRNMS, Rolls 555 and 556.

44. *Daily New Mexican,* December 2, 1868. Original bids are in LRNMS, Roll 556. E. S. Parker to William Clinton, November 23, 1869, RNMS, Roll 9.

45. Keyes to Clinton, August 31, 1869, RNMS, Roll 9.

46. Keyes to Clinton, September 15, 1869, RNMS, Roll 9.

47. Keyes to Clinton, October 31, 1869, RNMS, Roll 9.

48. Parker to Clinton, November 3, 1869, RNMS, Roll 9.

49. Maxwell to Grier, December 4, 1869, RNMS, Roll 10.

50. Getty to Grier, December 13, 1869, LRNMS, Roll 557.

51. Parker to Clinton, December 16, 1869, LRNMS, Roll 556.

52. Unaddressed excerpts from the letter, dated February 17, 1870, are in LRNMS, Roll 557.

53. Thomas Harwood, *History of New Mexico Spanish and English Missions,* 2 vols., 1:89–91.

54. Ibid., pp. 100, 106.

55. Ibid., pp. 108–10.

56. Pregaldin "Genealogy," p. 37.

CHAPTER 7

1. *Bent vs. Miranda,* p. 364.

2. Ibid., pp. 92–93.

3. Fayette A. Jones, *New Mexico Mines and Minerals,* p. 141. *History of New Mexico: Its Resources and People,* 3 vols. (Chicago and New York: Pacific States Publishing Company, 1907) 2:954. Darlis A. Miller, "Carleton's California Column: A Chapter in New Mexico's Mining History," *New Mexico Historical Review* 53, no. 1 (1978):10–11.

4. Rossiter W. Raymond, *Statistics of Mines and Mining in the States and Territories West of the Rocky Mountains, 1869,* p. 388. *Santa Fe Weekly Gazette,* June 20, 1868.

5. Jim Berry Pearson, *The Maxwell Land Grant,* p. 17.

6. *Santa Fe Weekly Gazette,* June 8, 1867.

7. *The New Mexican,* June 8, 1867.

8. *Transcript of Title,* pp. 5–6, 16–17.

9. Testimony of Phillip Mould, September 12, 1878, *Transcript of Record,* p. 235.

10. Bell, *New Tracks in North America,* p. 110.

11. *Santa Fe Weekly Gazette,* July 13, 1867.

12. Ibid., November 30, 1867.

13. Ibid., January 18, 1868.

14. *The New Mexican,* March 21, 1868.

15. *Santa Fe Weekly Gazette,* November 30, 1867.
16. Jones, *New Mexico Mines and Minerals,* p. 144. *Santa Fe Weekly Gazette,* July 13, 1867.
17. *Santa Fe Weekly Gazette,* June 27, 1868. *The New Mexican,* June 23, July 14, 1868.
18. *The Daily New Mexican,* March 27, 1869.
19. *Mining and Scientific Press* (San Francisco), January 11, 1868; *Santa Fe Weekly Gazette,* June 20, 1868; Jones, *New Mexico Mines and Minerals,* p. 144. Incorporation papers for the company (No. 0370) are in the New Mexico State Records Center and Archives, Santa Fe.
20. *Santa Fe Weekly Gazette,* June 20, 27, 1868. Raymond, *Statistics of Mines... 1869,* p. 391–93.
21. Raymond, *Statistics of Mines... 1869,* p. 391.
22. *Santa Fe Weekly Gazette,* November 28, 1868.
23. *Daily New Mexican,* September 23, 1870. Deed Book A, p. 3, Colfax County Records.
24. *Santa Fe Weekly Gazette,* August 8, 1868.
25. *The New Mexican,* June 30, 1868.
26. *The New Mexican,* July 21, 1868; *Colorado Chieftain,* July 23, 1868; *Santa Fe Weekly Gazette,* November 28, 1868; Raymond, *Statistics of Mines... 1869,* pp. 384–87. Collinson and Bell, *Maxwell Land Grant,* pp. 24–26.
27. Collinson and Bell, *Maxwell Land Grant,* pp. 27–28.
28. *Santa Fe Weekly Gazette,* November 11, 28, 1868.
29. *Colorado Chieftain,* December 17, 1868; March 11, 1869.
30. Ibid., May 13, 1869.
31. *Santa Fe Weekly Gazette,* May 22, 1869.
32. *Mining and Scientific Press,* November 20, 27, 1869; Raymond, *Statistics of Mines... 1869,* pp. 387–88.
33. Raymond, *Statistics of Mines... 1869,* p. 388.
34. *Weekly New Mexican,* June 22, 1869.
35. Maxwell to Buruel, Deed Book B, p. 151, Colfax County Records.
36. *The New Mexican,* July 21, 1868.
37. *Colorado Chieftain,* June 25, July 23, 1868.
38. Ibid., December 24, 1868.
39. Pearce, *New Mexico Place Names,* p. 38.
40. *Santa Fe Weekly Gazette,* March 13, 1869.
41. *Colorado Chieftain,* January 18, 1871.
42. *The Daily New Mexican,* March 15, 1870.
43. Ibid., April 1, 9, 13, 1869.
44. *Colorado Chieftain,* June 23, 1868.
45. *Annual Report of the Secretary of the Interior, 1868. House Executive Document 1,* p. 634.
46. *The New Mexican,* July 21, 1868; *The Weekly New Mexican,* May 25, 1869. The system for computing taxes is described in J. G. Randall and David Donald, *The Civil War and Reconstruction,* 2nd ed., p. 344.
47. *The Daily New Mexican,* September 23, 1870.

48. Inman, *Old Santa Fe Trail*, p. 378.
49. Ibid., pp. 375–76.
50. *Colorado Chieftain*, January 13, 1870.
51. Ibid., May 10, 1870. *The Daily New Mexican*, March 28, 1870.
52. *Bent vs. Miranda*, p. 128.
53. Inman, *Old Santa Fe Trail*, p. 376.
54. *Bent vs. Miranda*, p. 320.

CHAPTER 8

1. Howard R. Lamar, *The Far Southwest, 1846-1912: A Territorial History*, pp. 276–77.
2. Ibid., pp. 234–35.
3. Paul A. F. Walter, *Banking in New Mexico Before the Railroad Came*, pp. 16–17. Pearson, *The Maxwell Land Grant*, pp. 48–49.
4. Ralph E. Twitchell, *The Leading Facts of New Mexican History*, 5 vols., 2:392; Arie W. Poldervaart, *Black-Robed Justice*, pp. 72–83, describes Watts's judicial tenure.
5. Oscar D. Lambert, *Stephen Benton Elkins: American Foursquare*. Victor Westphall, *Thomas Benton Catron and His Era*, pp. 20ff.
6. For Catron's testimony, see *Bent vs. Miranda*, pp. 298–99. Westphall (*Thomas B. Catron*, p. 21), who had not seen this testimony, denounced it as "simply another of Mr. [William] Keleher's good stories."
7. *Transcript of Title*, pp. 37–47.
8. Ibid., pp. 48–49. Taylor, "New Look at an Old Case," pp. 213–25.
9. Maxwell ("per Holly") to Spencer, May 16, 1869, in Records, New Mexico Surveyor General, U.S. Bureau of Land Management, hereinafter cited as RNMSG.
10. Victor Westphall, *The Public Domain in New Mexico, 1854-1891*, p. 21.
11. *The Daily New Mexican*, June 22, 1869.
12. Testimony printed in *Transcript of Record*, pp. 62–64.
13. Ibid., p. 183.
14. Excerpts from Griffin's diary appear in Collinson and Bell, *Maxwell Land Grant*, pp. 16–24.
15. *Transcript of Title*, pp. 60–61.
16. J. B. Chaffee, *The Beaubien and Miranda Grant, in New Mexico and Colorado*, 8 pp.
17. Wilson to Spencer, June 28, 1869, RNMSG.
18. *Colorado Chieftain*, July 22, 1869.
19. Maxwell to Spencer, July 29, 1869, RNMSG.
20. Ibid.
21. Watts to Spencer and Spencer to Watts (telegrams), August 16, 1869; Maxwell to Spencer, August 16, 1869, RNMSG.
22. Wilson to Spencer, September 3, 1869, RNMSG.

23. Collinson and Bell, *Maxwell Land Grant*, pp. 30–31.

24. Edward T. James., ed., *The Dictionary of American Biography* (New York: Charles Scribners' Sons, 1930), 4:476–78.

25. Cox to "The Commissioner of the General Land Office" (Wilson), December 31, 1869, RNMSG.

26. *Santa Fe Daily New Mexican*, March 14, 1870.

27. Watts to Wilson, January 3, 1870, RNMSG.

28. Maxwell to Spencer, February 7, 1870; Wilson to Spencer, February 28, 1870; and Wilson to Spencer, March 25, 1870, RNMSG.

29. Collinson and Bell, *Maxwell Land Grant*, pp. 16–24. *Santa Fe Daily New Mexican*, August 4, 1870.

30. Robert R. Logan, "Early Banking in New Mexico," *New Mexico Business Review* 9 (1940):207.

31. Watts's statement dated at Washington, December 12, 1869, in Collinson and Bell, *Maxwell Land Grant*, pp. 30–31.

32. *Colorado Chieftain*, July 28, 1870.

33. Collinson and Bell, *Maxwell Land Grant*, pp. 31–32.

34. *Colorado Chieftain*, July 28, 1870.

35. Collinson and Bell, *Maxwell Land Grant*, *passim*.

36. *Transcript of Title*, pp. 62–64.

37. *Colorado Chieftain*, July 28, 1870. *Daily New Mexican*, July 22, 25, 1870.

38. *Daily New Mexican*, July 22, 1870. Pearson, *Maxwell Land Grant*, pp. 49–50.

39. *Transcript of Title*, pp. 64–65, 70–72. *Daily New Mexican*, August 5, 1870. Testimony of Brunswick, *Bent vs. Miranda*, pp. 321–33.

40. *Bent vs. Miranda*, p. 328. Cleaveland with Fitzpatrick, *The Morleys*, p. 62.

41. Smith, "The Unmarked Grave," p. 68.

42. *Daily New Mexican*, July 25, 1870.

43. *Colorado Chieftain*, July 28, 1870.

CHAPTER 9

1. Reprinted in the *Daily New Mexican*, August 5, 1870.

2. *Daily New Mexican*, September 15, 1870. Also see W. F. M. Arny to Joseph S. Wilson, September 12, 1870, in *Transcript of Record*.

3. *Weekly New Mexican*, September 20, 1870.

4. *Colorado Chieftain*, September 3, 1870.

5. Griffin's testimony is in *Bent vs. Miranda*, pp. 399–400.

6. Smith, "The Unmarked Grave," pp. 67–68.

7. *Weekly New Mexican*, September 20, 1870.

8. Walter, *Banking in New Mexico*, pp. 15–17.

9. Ibid., pp. 17–18. Logan, "Early Banking in New Mexico," p. 207.

10. Maxwell signed in the presence of Elkins and Holly, his wife

before Hooper. *Transcript of Title,* pp. 88–91.

11. Quoted in Lynn R. Bailey, *The Long Walk,* p. 1.

12. Ibid. Also Lynn R. Bailey, *Bosque Redondo: An American Concentration Camp, passim,* and Gerald Thompson, *The Army and The Navajo,* pp. 40–42, 73–75.

13. *Daily New Mexican,* August 25, 1870.

14. Ibid., September 12, 22, 1870.

15. Charles R. Roedel to Nathaniel Pope, September 1, 1871, in *Annual Report of the Secretary of the Interior, 1871. House Executive Document 1,* p. 811.

16. Pearson, *Maxwell Land Grant,* pp. 55ff. Also Morris F. Taylor, *O. P. McMains and the Maxwell Land Grant Conflict.*

17. The financial dealings of the companies and their representatives become extremely complicated. For a detailed discussion, see Pearson, *Maxwell Land Grant,* pp. 94–111. For a personalized view centering on one of the major participants, written by a descendent, see Cleaveland with Fitzpatrick, *The Morleys,* esp. pp. 61ff.

18. Murphy, *Philmont,* pp. 111–15.

19. Brunswick's testimony is in *Bent vs. Miranda,* pp. 327–30.

20. Pearson, *Maxwell Land Grant,* p. 54.

21. Westphall, *Public Domain,* p. 85.

22. Ibid., pp. 85–87.

23. *Daily New Mexican,* August 4, September 29, 1871.

24. Ibid., April 11, 1871, February 4, 1873.

25. *Colorado Chieftain,* November 30, 1871.

26. *Daily New Mexican,* January 12, 1871.

27. Quoted in Walter, *Banking in New Mexico,* p. 18.

28. Ibid., *Daily New Mexican,* April 15, 1871.

29. *Daily New Mexican,* May 10, 1871. Walter, *Banking in New Mexico,* pp. 19–20. Logan, "Early Banking in New Mexico," p. 209.

30. *Daily New Mexican,* December 27, 1870; April 12, 14, 15, 1871.

31. *Daily New Mexican,* May 6, 10, November 1, December 7, 1872.

32. Keleher, *Maxwell Land Grant,* p. 37; Pearson, *Maxwell Land Grant,* p. 53; Smith, "The Unmarked Grave," p. 69.

33. *Daily New Mexican,* February 18, 1872.

34. Ibid., April 20, 1871. *Colorado Chieftain,* April 28, 1871.

35. Logan, "Early Banking in New Mexico," p 207.

36. *Daily New Mexican,* January 12, 1872.

37. Ibid., May 15, 1871.

38. *Colorado Chieftain,* February 22, 1872.

39. *Daily New Mexican,* October 21, November 5, December 5, 1871.

40. Pregaldin, "Genealogy," pp. 33, 37. Morrison's corrections to the Maxwell genealogy in the Illinois State Historical Library. A photograph of Verenisa's headstone is in Tom Hilton, *Nevermore, Cimarron, Nevermore,* p. 10.

42. Keleher, *Maxwell Land Grant,* p. 37.

43. Ibid.; Smith, "The Unmarked Grave," p. 69. *The Republican Review* (Albuquerque), August 7, 1875.

44. Keleher, *Maxwell Land Grant,* p. 37.

45. Smith, "The Unmarked Grave," p. 69.

46. Quoted in Keleher, *Maxwell Land Grant,* p. 38.

47. *The Cimarron News and Press,* reprinted in *Republican Review,* August 7, 1875.

48. For a recent discussion, see Ray A. Billington, *America's Frontier Heritage,* ch. 4, pp. 69–95.

49. Turner's essay has been frequently reprinted. A convenient source is Frederick Jackson Turner, *The Frontier in American History.*

CHAPTER 10

1. Thomas A. Bailey, *Presidential Greatness,* pp. 54–56.

2. Jack D. Rittenhouse, *The Santa Fe Trail,* p. 133. Inman's importance may be measured by the fact that historian Herbert Howe Bancroft, whose *History of Arizona and New Mexico* appeared in 1889, mentions the "Maxwell Rancho" twice, but never refers to Lucien Maxwell.

3. Lecompte, *Pueblo, Hardscrabble, Greenhorn,* p. 355.

4. Inman, *Old Santa Fe Trail,* pp. 273–85.

5. [George B. Anderson], *History of New Mexico: Its Resources and People,* 3 vols., 1:177–83.

6. George Baker Anderson, "A New Mexico Baron," *Out West* 26 (1907):15–22; George Baker Anderson, "A New Mexico Baron," *Santa Fe Magazine* 4 (1910):65–68. A very similar article, copied almost word for word from Inman, is Edgar Forest Wolfe, "Ancient Days in New Mexico," *Los Angeles Sunday Times,* August 23, 1903. A copy is in Box 19, Will C. Barnes Collection, Arizona Historical Society.

7. Harwood, *History of New Mexico Spanish and English Missions* 1:89–91, 100, 106, 108–10.

8. Ryus, *Second William Penn,* pp. 169–70; Howbert, *Memories of a Lifetime,* p. 113.

9. Myra Ellen Jenkins, "Dedication to Ralph Emerson Twitchell," *Arizona and the West* 8 (1966):103–106.

10. Ralph Emerson Twitchell, *The Leading Facts of New Mexican History,* 5 vols., 2:415–16.

11. W. J. Ghent, *The Early Far West: A Narrative Outline, 1540-1850,* pp. 322, 344. It is impossible to determine precisely to whom the honor of owning the largest tract in American history should go, but names like William Penn, The Duke of York, and several other colonial personalities come to mind. Recently, Victor Westphall has identified Thomas B. Catron as the "largest individual landholder in the history of the United States. . . ." *Thomas B. Catron,* p. 72.

12. W. J. G[hent], "Lucien Bonaparte Maxwell," in Edward T. James,

ed., *The Dictionary of American Biography* (New York: Charles Scribners Sons, 1933) 12: 441–42.

13. *New Mexico Magazine,* June, 1937, p. 46.

14. Frank D. Reeve, "Paul A. F. Walter," *New Mexico Historical Review* 41 (1966):165–66.

15. Paul A. F. Walter, "New Mexico's Pioneer Bank and Bankers," *New Mexico Historical Review* 21 (1946):209–25. Walter, *Banking in New Mexico.*

16. William A. Keleher, "Law of the New Mexico Land Grant," *New Mexico Historical Review* 4 (1929):350–71. For the author's recollections of the project, see his *Memoirs: 1892-1969, A New Mexico Item,* pp. 250–54.

17. Keleher, *Maxwell Land Grant,* pp. ix–x.

18. See above, Chapter 8, Note 6.

19. Keleher, *Maxwell Land Grant,* p. 39.

20. Ibid., pp. 38–44.

21. Smith, "The Unmarked Grave," pp. 19–20, 66–69.

22. Herbert O. Brayer, *William Blackmore: The Spanish-Mexican Land Grants of New Mexico and Colorado, 1863-1878.*

23. *El Paso Times,* May 29, 1949, clipping file, El Paso Public Library.

24. A photograph of the stone appears in Jack D. Rittenhouse, "The Man Who Owned Too Much," *Baroid News Bulletin,* September-October 1957, p. 3. The text is reprinted in F. Stanley, *The Grant That Maxwell Bought,* p. 33.

25. Taylor, *O. P. McMains,* esp. pp. 33–347.

26. Pearson, *Maxwell Land Grant,* pp. 82ff.

27. For photographs of the sculptor, Dom Poglainni, completing his work, see Margaret Ward, *Cimarron Sage,* p. 46. The quotation accompanies a photograph of the statue in Hilton, *Nevermore, Cimarron, Nevermore,* p. 28. Hilton characterized Maxwell as "a Leviathan in a Land of Giants." *New Mexico Magazine,* June 1937, p. 36.

28. There were also "Lucien Maxwell Treks" into the mountains. Murphy, *Philmont,* pp. 218–20.

29. Stanley, *The Grant That Maxwell Brought,* p. 1.

30. Ibid., p. 29.

31. Ibid., p. 20.

32. Cecil Robinson, "A Dedication to the Memory of Harvey Fergusson, 1890-1971," *Arizona and the West* 15 (1973):311–13. Lawrence Clark Powell, *Southwest Classics,* pp. 65–66. James K. Folsom, *Harvey Fergusson,* pp. 1–5. Harvey Fergusson, *Grant of Kingdom,* p. v.

33. Morris F. Taylor, "Ka-Ni-Ache," *Colorado Magazine* 43 (1966): 275–302; 44 (1967):139–61.

34. Fergusson, *Grant of Kingdom,* pp. 66–67, 82–86, 87.

35. Ibid., pp. 94–95.

36. Ibid., pp. 107–108, 134–49.

37. Ibid., pp. 157–58.

38. Ibid., opposite p. v; Powell, *Southwest Classics,* p. 66.

39. William T. Pilkington, introduction to Fergusson, *Grant of Kingdom*, repr. ed., p. xi.

40. Joe B. Frantz, review of Lawrence R. Murphy, *Philmont*, in *History: Review of New Books* 1, no. 1 (October 1972):12. Ironically, the University of New Mexico Press's 1975 paperback reprint edition of *Grant of Kingdom* refers readers to my *Philmont*, p. vi, if they are "interested in learning more of the grant's history, incidentally, or possibly in making identifications between real-life personages and the cast of fictional characters."

41. Cleaveland, *Satan's Paradise*, pp. 1–2, 7–21. For family background, see Agnes Morley Cleaveland, *No Life For a Lady* (Boston: Houghton Mifflin, 1941) and Cleaveland with Fitzpatrick, *The Morleys, passim.*

42. Noah Gordon, "The Cowman They Called God," *Men* 5 (1956): 8, 46–48. One is tempted to wonder, because of the similarity of names, if this is a pseudonym for the Noel Gerson, whose biography of Kit Carson prompted Harvey Carter to term it "the worst book on Carson I have ever read." '*Dear Old Kit,*' p. 32.

43. Gordon, "The Cowman," p. 48.

44. George Fitzpatrick, "The Baron of the Cimarron," *Westward*, February–March 1961, pp. 4–9. Rittenhouse, "The Man," pp. 1–8.

45. Jack D. Rittenhouse, *The Man Who Owned Too Much. Maxwell's Land Grant, passim.*

46. Hank and Toni Chapman, "Midas of New Mexico," *The American West* 8 (January 1971):4–9, 62.

47. Pearson, *Maxwell Land Grant*, pp. 9–14, and Murphy, *Philmont*, pp. 57ff., contain errors from Stanley.

Bibliography

Manuscript Materials

Adams, David, papers. Missouri Historical Society, Saint Louis.
Barnes, Will C., collection. Arizona Historical Society, Tucson.
Colfax County records and deed books. County Courthouse, Raton, New Mexico.
Cragin, F. W., Early Far West Notebooks. Pioneers' Museum, Colorado Springs, Colorado.
El Paso Public Library, El Paso, Texas. Clipping files.
McGavran, Harry G., Interviews with Narciso Abreú and Adelina Abreú Valdez. Tape recordings. Ernest Thompson Seton Museum and Library, Cimarron, New Mexico.
McGavran, Harry G., Jr., collection. Los Alamos, New Mexico.
Menard, Pierre, collection. Illinois State Historical Library, Springfield.
Morrison, William V., collection. Illinois State Historical Library, Springfield.
Morrison, William, corrections to the Menard genealogy. Illinois State Historical Library, Springfield.
Morrison, William, letters to the author. Author's collection.
New Mexico Corporation Commission records. State Records Center and Archives, Santa Fe.
Poole, Father Stafford, letter to the author. Author's collection, Mt. Pleasant, Michigan.
U.S. Army. Letters Received, Ninth Military Department, RG 94, National Archives, Washington, D.C.
U.S. Bureau of Land Management. New Mexico Surveyor General records. Bureau of Land Management, Santa Fe.
U.S. Census. Manuscript census for Taos County, 1850; Mora County, 1860; Colfax County, 1870; RG 29, National Archives, Washington, D.C.
U.S. Department of the Interior. Office of Indian Affairs, Letters

Received, New Mexico Superintendency. RG 234, National Archives, Washington, D.C.

U.S. Department of the Interior. Office of Indian Affairs. Records, New Mexico Superintendency. RG 75, National Archives, Washington, D.C.

U.S. Supreme Court. *Transcript of Record,* United States vs. Maxwell Land Grant Company, et als., October term, 1886. RG 267, National Archives, Washington, D.C.

Wilkinson, James, papers. Missouri Historical Society, Saint Louis.

Newspapers

Cimarron News and Press, August 18, 1880.
Colorado Chieftain (Pueblo), June 23, 1868–February 22, 1872.
Daily New Mexican (Santa Fe), December 2, 1868–February 4, 1873.
Daily Rocky Mountain News (Denver), February 15, 1866.
The Illinois Intelligencer (Kaskaskia), September 2, 1818–September 15, 1819.
Kaskaskia Advocate, January 24, 1823.
Kaskaskia Republican, April 13, 1824–January 4, 1825.
Mining and Scientific Press (San Francisco), January 11, 1868–November 27, 1869.
The New Mexican (Santa Fe), February 6, 1864–March 27, 1869.
The Republican Review (Albuquerque), August 7, 1875.
Sangamo Journal (Springfield, Ill.), September 14, 1833.
Santa Fe Republican, July 7, 18, 1848.
Santa Fe Weekly Gazette, May 21, 1853–June 20, 1869.
The Weekly New Mexican (Santa Fe), May 25, 1869–September 20, 1870.
The Western Intelligencer (Kaskaskia), December 11, 1817–June 3, 1818.

Government Documents

Annual Report of the Commissioner of Indian Affairs, 1866. Senate Executive Document No. 1, 39th Cong., 2d sess.
Annual Report of the Secretary of the Interior, 1868. House Executive Document No. 1, 40th Cong., 2d sess.
Annual Report of the Secretary of the Interior, 1871. House Executive Document No. 1, 42nd Cong., 2d sess.
Report of the Secretary of the Interior Made in Conformity to Law

Upon Claims for Depredations by Indians in the Territory of New Mexico. Senate Executive Document No. 55, 35th Cong., 1st sess.

Report of the Secretary of the Interior, 1862. Senate Executive Document No. 1, 37th Cong., 3d sess.

Report of the Secretary of War, 1852. House Executive Document No. 1, 32nd Cong., 2d sess.

Dissertations

Minge, Ward Allen. "Frontier Problems in New Mexico Preceding the Mexican War, 1840–1846," Unpublished Ph.D. dissertation, University of New Mexico, 1965.

Tavebaugh, John L. "Merchant on the Western Frontier: William Morrison of Kaskaskia, 1790–1837," Unpublished Ph.D. dissertation, University of Illinois, 1962.

Articles

Anderson, George Baker. "A New Mexican Baron," *Out West* 26 (1907):15–22.

———. "A New Mexican Baron," *Santa Fe Magazine* 4 (1910): 65–68.

Burton, E. Bennett. "The Taos Rebellion," *Old Santa Fe* 1 (1913): 175–209.

Camp, Charles L. "Kit Carson in California," *California Historical Society Quarterly* 1 (1922–23):111–51.

Carlson, Alvar Ward. "New Mexico's Sheep Industry," *New Mexico Historical Review* 44 (1969):25–49.

Chapman, Hank and Toni. "Midas of New Mexico," *The American West* 8 (January 1971):4–9, 62–63.

Chavez, Fray Angelico. "New Names in New Mexico, 1820–1850," *El Palacio* 64, nos. 9, 10 (1957):291–318.

Cheetham, Francis T. "The First Term of the American Court in Taos, New Mexico," *New Mexico Historical Review* 1 (1926): 23–41.

Claussen, W. Edmunds. "Kit Carson's Hospitality Headquarters," *New Mexico Magazine* 28 (February 1950): 12–13, 37–39.

———. "Rayado Rancho," *New Mexico Magazine* 24 (March 1946): 11, 37, 39.

Clohisy, Matt. "Lucien Bonaparte Maxwell: Prince of the Wilderness," New York Westerners *Brand Book* 5 (1958):6–8, 14–15, 20.

Dunham, Harold H. "Lucien B. Maxwell: Frontiersman and

Businessman," The Denver Posse Westerners *Brand Book, 1949* (Denver: privately printed, 1950), pp. 269–95.

Fitzpatrick, George. "The Baron of the Cimarron," *Westward,* February–March, 1961, pp. 4–9.

Francis, E. K. "Padre Martinez: A New Mexican Myth," *New Mexico Historical Review* 31 (1956):265–89.

Frantz, Joe B. "Review of Lawrence R. Murphy, *Philmont,"* *History: Review of New Books* 1 (October 1972):12.

Gordon, Noah, "The Cowman they Called God," *Men* 5 (1956): 8, 46–48.

Graham, Hugh. "St. Genevieve Academy: Missouri's First Secondary School," *Mid-America* 15 (1932):65–79.

Grinnell, George B. "Bent's Old Fort and Its Builders," Kansas State Historical Society *Collections* 15 (1923):28–91.

Hafen, L. R. "The Early Fur Trade Posts on the South Platte," *Mississippi Valley Historical Review* 12 (1925–26):334–41.

———. "Fort Jackson and the Early Fur Trade on the South Platte," *Colorado Magazine* 5 (1928):9–17.

———. "Fort St. Vrain," *Colorado Magazine* 29 (1952):241–55.

Jenkins, Myra Ellen. "Dedication to Ralph Emerson Twitchell," *Arizona and the West* 8 (1966):103–106.

Keleher, William A. "Law of the New Mexico Land Grant," *New Mexico Historical Review* 3 (1929):350–71.

Lass, William E. "Tourists' Impressions of St. Louis, 1766–1859, Part II," *Missouri Historical Review* 53 (1958):10–21.

Lecompte, Janet. "Manuel Armijo's Family History," *New Mexico Historical Review* 48 (1973):251–58.

———. "The Manco Burro Pass Massacre," *New Mexico Historical Review* 41 (1966):305–308.

Logan, Robert R. "Early Banking in New Mexico," *New Mexico Business Review* 9 (1940):198–214.

McClure, Charles R. "The Texan-Santa Fe Expedition," *New Mexico Historical Review* 48 (1973):45–56.

Merrell, William S. "Pierre Menard of Illinois," *Mid-America,* 3, n.s. (1931):15–38.

Miller, Darlis A. "Carleton's California Column: A Chapter in New Mexico's Mining History," *New Mexico Historical Review* 53 (1978):5–38.

Murphy, Lawrence R. "Rayado: Pioneer Settlement in Northeastern New Mexico, 1848–1857," *New Mexico Historical Review* 46 (1971):37–56.

————. "The Beaubien and Miranda Land Grant, 1841–1846," *New Mexico Historical Review* 42 (1967):27–47.

————. "The United States Army in Taos, 1847–1852," *New Mexico Historical Review* 47 (1972):pp. 33–48.

"Old Maxwell Home," *New Mexico Magazine,* June 1937, p. 46.

Opler, Morris E. "Jicarilla Apache Territory, Economy, and Society in 1850," *Southwestern Journal of Anthropology* 27 (1971):309–29.

Poole, Stafford. "The Founding of Missouri's First College: St. Marys of the Barrens, 1815–1818," *Missouri Historical Review* 65 (1970):1–21.

Reeve, Frank D. "Paul A. F. Walter," *New Mexico Historical Review* 41 (1966):165–66.

Richter, Thomas, ed., "Sister Catherine Mallon's Journal," *New Mexico Historical Review* 52 (1977):135–55.

Rittenhouse, Jack D. "The Man Who Owned Too Much," *Baroid News Bulletin,* September–October 1957, pp. 2–8.

Robinson, Cecil. "A Dedication to the Memory of Harvey Fergusson, 1890–1971," *Arizona and the West* 15 (1973):311–13.

Ruhlen, Charles. "Kearny's Route from the Rio Grande to the Gila River," *New Mexico Historical Review* 33 (1957):213–30.

Schroeder, Albert H. "Shifting for Survival in the Spanish Southwest," *New Mexico Historical Review* 48 (1968):291–310.

Smith, Joe Heflin. "The Unmarked Grave," *The Cattleman* 34, no. 12 (March 1949):19–20, 66–69.

Taylor, Morris F. "A New Look at an Old Case: The Bent Heirs' Claims in the Maxwell Grant," *New Mexico Historical Review* 43 (1968):213–28.

————. "Campaigning Against the Jicarilla Apache, 1854," *New Mexico Historical Review* 44 (1969):269–91.

————. "Campaigning Against the Jicarilla Apache, 1855," *New Mexico Historical Review* 45 (1970):119–31.

————. "Ka-Ni-Ache," *Colorado Magazine* 43 (1966):275–302; 44 (1967):139–61.

Walter, Paul A. F. "New Mexico's Pioneer Bank and Bankers," *New Mexico Historical Review* 21 (1946):209–25.

Westphall, Victor. "Fraud and Implications of Fraud in the Land Grants of New Mexico," *New Mexico Historical Review* 49 (1974):189–218.

Williams, Helen D. "Social Life in St. Louis from 1840 to 1860," *Missouri Historical Review* 31 (1936–37):10–24.

Books and Pamphlets

Abel, Annie H., ed. *The Official Correspondence of James S. Calhoun.* Washington: U.S. Government Printing Office, 1915.

Allen, John W. *Legends and Lore of Southern Illinois.* Carbondale: Southern Illinois University Press, 1963.

[Anderson, George B.] *History of New Mexico: Its Resources and People.* 3 vols. Los Angeles, Chicago, and New York: Pacific States Publishing Company, 1907.

Arnold, Elliot. *The Time of the Gringo.* New York: Alfred A. Knopf, 1954.

Bailey, Lynn R. *Bosque Redondo: An American Concentration Camp.* Pasadena, Calif.: Socio-Technical Books, 1970.

———. *The Long Walk.* Pasadena, Calif.: Socio-Technical Books, 1970.

Bailey, Thomas A. *Presidential Greatness.* New York: Appleton-Century, 1966.

Bancroft, Herbert Howe. *History of Arizona and New Mexico.* San Francisco: The History Company, Publishers, 1889.

Barry, Louise. *The Beginning of the West.* Topeka: Kansas State Historical Society, 1972.

Bell, William A. *New Tracks in North America.* 1 vol. ed. London: Chapman and Hall, 1870; repr. Albuquerque: Calvin Horn, Publisher, 1965.

Billington, Ray A. *America's Frontier Heritage.* New York: Holt, Rinehart, and Winston, 1966.

Blackwelder, Bernice. *Great Westerner: The Story of Kit Carson.* Caldwell, Idaho: Caxton Printers, 1962.

Brayer, Herbert O. *William Blackmore: The Spanish-Mexican Land Grants of New Mexico and Colorado, 1863–1878.* 2 vols. Denver: Bradford-Robinson, 1949.

Brevet's Illinois Historical Markers and Sites. Sioux Falls, S.Dak.: Brevet Press, 1976.

Buck, Solon J. *Illinois in 1818.* Springfield: Illinois Centennial Commission, 1917.

Caffey, David L. *Head for the High Country.* Nashville, Tenn.: Abington Press, 1973.

Carter, Harvey L. *'Dear Old Kit': The Historical Christopher Carson.* Norman: University of Oklahoma Press, 1968.

Chaffee, J. B. *The Beaubien and Miranda Grant in New Mexico and Colorado.* New York: n.p., 1869.

Chittenden, Hiram M. *A History of the American Fur Trade of The*

Far West. 2 vols. repr. ed. Stanford, Calif.: Academic Reprints, 1954.

Clarke, Dwight L. *Stephen Watts Kearny: Soldier of the West.* Norman: University of Oklahoma Press, 1961.

Cleaveland, Agnes Morley. *Satan's Paradise.* Boston: Houghton Mifflin Company, 1952.

Cleaveland, Norman, with Fitzpatrick, George. *The Morleys— Young Upstarts on the Southwest Frontier.* Albuquerque: Calvin Horn, Publisher, 1971.

Collinson, John, and Bell, William A. *The Maxwell Land Grant, Situated in Colorado and New Mexico, United States of America.* London: Taylor and Co., 1870.

Conard, Howard L. *Uncle Dick Wootton.* Chicago: W. E. Dibble and Company, 1890; repr. Chicago: Lakeside Press, 1957.

De Voto, Bernard. *Across the Wide Missouri.* Boston: Houghton Mifflin Co., 1947.

———. *The Year of Decision, 1846.* Boston: Little Brown and Co., 1943.

Dike, Sheldon H. *The Territorial Post Offices of New Mexico.* Albuquerque: By the author, 1958.

Dobie, J. Frank. *The Longhorns.* Boston: Little, Brown and Company, 1941.

Drury, John, ed. *Old Illinois Houses.* Springfield: Illinois State Historical Society, 1948.

Duffus, R. L. *The Santa Fe Trail.* London: Longmans, Green and Company, 1930.

Egan, Ferol. *Frémont: Explorer for a Restless Nation.* Garden City, N.Y.: Doubleday and Co., 1977.

Emmett, Chris. *Fort Union and the Winning of the Southwest.* Norman: University of Oklahoma Press, 1965.

Emory, W. H. *Lieutenant Emory Reports.* Ed. by Ross Calvin. Albuquerque: University of New Mexico Press, 1951.

Estergreen, M. Morgan. *Kit Carson: A Portrait in Courage.* Norman: University of Oklahoma Press, 1962.

Fergusson, Harvey. *Grant of Kingdom.* New York: William Morrow and Company, 1950; repr. with introduction by William T. Pilkington, Albuquerque: University of New Mexico Press, 1975.

Fodor, Eugene et al., eds. *Fodor's Mid-West.* New York: David McKay and Co., 1974.

Folsom, James K. *Harvey Fergusson.* Austin, Texas: Steck-Vaughn Company, 1969.

Franzwa, Gregory M. *The Story of Old Ste. Genevieve.* Gerald, Mo.: Patrice Press, 1967.

Frémont, John C. *Memoirs of My Life.* Chicago and New York: Belford, Clarke, and Company, 1887.

———. *Narratives of Exploration and Adventure.* Ed. by Allan Nevins. New York: Longmans, Green, and Company, 1956.

———. *Report of the Exploring Expedition to the Rocky Mountains in the Year 1842 . . . .* Washington: Gales and Seaton, 1845.

Garrard, Lewis H. *Wah-to-yah and the Taos Trail.* Norman: University of Oklahoma Press, 1955.

Ghent, W. J. *The Early Far West: A Narrative Outline, 1540-1850.* New York: Tudor Publishing Co., 1936.

Goetzmann, William H. *Exploration and Empire.* New York: Alfred A. Knopf, 1967.

Gunnerson, Dolores A. *The Jicarilla Apaches: A Study in Survival.* DeKalb, Ill.: Northern Illinois University Press, 1974.

Hafen, LeRoy R., ed. *The Mountain Men and the Fur Trade of the Far West.* 10 vols. Glendale: Arthur H. Clark Co., 1968–71.

Hafen, LeRoy R. and Ann W., eds. *Fremont's Fourth Expedition.* Glendale, Calif.: Arthur H. Clark Co., 1960.

Hammond, George P., ed. *The Adventures of Alexander Barclay: Mountain Man.* Denver: Old West Publishing Company, 1976.

Hannum, Anna P., ed. *A Quaker Forty-Niner: The Adventures of Charles Edward Pancoast on the American Frontier.* Philadelphia: University of Pennsylvania Press, 1930.

Harwood, Thomas. *History of New Mexico Spanish and English Missions.* 2 vols. Albuquerque: El Abogado Press, 1908.

Heap, Gwinn H. *Central Route to the Pacific.* Glendale, Calif.: Arthur H. Clark Co., 1957.

Hilton, Tom. *Nevermore, Cimarron, Nevermore.* Fort Worth: Western Heritage Press, 1970.

Horrell, C. William; Piper, Henry Dan; and Voight, John W. *Land Between the Rivers: The Southern Illinois Country.* Carbondale: Southern Illinois University Press, 1973.

Houck, Louis. *History of Missouri.* 3 vols. Chicago: R. R. Donnelly and Sons, 1908.

Howbert, Irving. *Memories of a Lifetime in the Pikes Peak Region.* New York: G. P. Putnam's Sons, 1925; repr. Glorietta, N.M.: Rio Grande Press, 1970.

Inman, Henry. *The Old Santa Fe Trail.* New York: The Macmillan Company, 1897; repr. Minneapolis: Ross and Haines, 1966.

Jackson, Donald, and Spence, Mary Lee, eds. *The Expeditions of*

John Charles Frémont. Urbana: University of Illinois Press, 1970.

James, Edmund J., ed. *The Territorial Records of Illinois.* Springfield: Illinois State Historical Library, 1901.

Jefferson, James; Delaney, Robert W.; and Thompson, Gregory. *The Southern Utes: A Tribal History.* Ignacio, Colo.: Southern Ute Tribe, 1972.

Johnson, Allen, and Malone, Dumas, eds. *The Dictionary of American Biography.* 21 vols. New York: Charles Scribner's Sons, 1928–37.

Jones, Fayette A. *New Mexico Mines and Minerals.* Santa Fe: New Mexican Printing Company, 1904.

Karnes, Thomas L. *William Gilpin: Western Nationalist.* Austin: University of Texas Press, 1970.

Keleher, William A. *Maxwell Land Grant: A New Mexico Item.* Santa Fe: Rydal Press, 1942; repr. New York: Argosy-Antiquarian Ltd., 1964.

————. *Memoirs: 1892–1969, a New Mexico Item.* Santa Fe: Rydal Press, 1969.

Kenner, Charles L. *A History of New Mexican-Plains Indian Relations.* Norman: University of Oklahoma Press, 1969.

Lamar, Howard R. *The Far Southwest, 1846–1912: A Territorial History.* New Haven: Yale University Press, 1966.

Lambert, Oscar D. *Stephen Benton Elkins: American Foursquare.* Pittsburgh: The University of Pittsburgh Press, 1966.

Lavasseur, A. *Lafayette in America.* 2 vols. Philadelphia: Carey and Lea, 1829.

Lavender, David. *Bent's Fort.* New York: Doubleday and Co., 1954.

Lecompte, Janet. *Pueblo, Hardscrabble, Greenhorn: The Upper Arkansas, 1832–1856.* Norman: University of Oklahoma Press, 1978.

McCall, George A. *New Mexico in 1850: A Military View.* Ed. by Robert W. Frazer. Norman: Univeristy of Oklahoma Press, 1968.

Magoffin, Susan S. *Down the Santa Fe Trail and Into Mexico.* Ed. by Stella M. Drumm. New Haven: Yale University Press, 1962.

Mason, Edward G. *Early Chicago and Illinois.* Chicago: Fergus Publishing Co., 1890.

Maxwell Claim. Application of the Heirs and Legal Representatives of Hugh H. and John P. Maxwell to the Commissioners of the

General Land Office. New York: Pelletreau and Raynor, 1875.

Missouri Historical Records Survey. *Early Missouri Archives [Part I, Ste. Genevieve Archives]*. Saint Louis: Missouri Historical Records Survey, 1941.

Murphy, Lawrence R. *Frontier Crusader: William F. M. Arny*. Tucson: University of Arizona Press, 1972.

————. *Philmont: A History of New Mexico's Cimarron Country*. Albuquerque: University of New Mexico Press, 1972.

Nevins, Allan. *Frémont: Pathmarker of the West*. Rev. ed. New York: Longmans, Green and Company, 1955.

———— ed. *Polk: Diary of a President, 1845–1849*. New York: Longmans, Green and Company, 1929.

Norton, Margaret Cross. *Illinois Census Returns, 1820*. Springfield: Illinois State Historical Library, 1934.

Pearce, T. M. *New Mexico Place Names*. Albuquerque: University of New Mexico Press, 1965.

Pearson, Jim Berry. *The Maxwell Land Grant*. Norman: University of Oklahoma Press, 1961.

Pease, Theodore C. *Illinois Election Returns, 1818–1848*. Springfield: Illinois State Historical Library, 1923.

Peters, Dewitt C. *The Life and Adventures of Kit Carson*. Boston: 1859; repr. Freeport, N.Y.: Books for Libraries Press, 1970.

Philbrick, Francis S., ed. *The Laws of Illinois Territory, 1809–1818*. Springfield: Illinois State Historical Library, 1950.

Poldervaart, Arie W. *Black-Robed Justice*. Santa Fe: Historical Society of New Mexico, 1948.

Powell, Lawrence Clark. *Southwest Classics*. Pasadena, Calif.: Ward Ritchie Press, 1974.

Preuss, Charles. *Exploring with Frémont: The Private Diaries of Charles Preuss, Cartographer for John C. Frémont . . . .* Tr. and ed. by Erwin G. and Elizabeth K. Gudde. Norman: University of Oklahoma Press, 1958.

Prucha, Francis P. *Broadax and Bayonet*. Madison: State Historical Society of Wisconsin, 1953.

Randall, J. G., and Donald, David. *The Civil War and Reconstruction*. 2nd ed. Boston: D. C. Heath and Company, 1962.

Raymond, Rossiter W. *Statistics of Mines and Mining in the States and Territories of the Rocky Mountains, 1869*. Washington: Government Printing Office, 1870.

Reynolds, John. *Pioneer History of Illinois*. Chicago: Fergus Printing Company, 1887.

Richardson, Rupert N. *The Comanche Barrier to South Plains Set-*

BIBLIOGRAPHY

tlement. Glendale, Calif.: Arthur H. Clark Co., 1933.

Riddle, Kenyon. *Records and Maps of the Old Santa Fe Trail*. Stuart, Florida: Southeastern Printing Company, Inc., 1963.

Rittenhouse, Jack D. *The Man Who Owned Too Much. Maxwell's Land Grant*. Houston: The Stagecoach Press, 1958.

――――. *The Santa Fe Trail: A Historical Bibliography*. Albuquerque: University of New Mexico Press, 1971.

Robinson, G. D., et al. *Philmont Country: The Rocks and Landscapes of a Famous New Mexico Ranch*. Washington: U.S. Geological Survey Professional Paper 505, 1964.

Rockafellow, B. F. "History of Frémont County." *History of the Arkansas Valley*. Chicago: O. L. Baskin & Co., 1881.

Rothensteiner, John. *History of the Archdiocese of St. Louis*. 2 vols. Saint Louis: Blackwell Wielandy Co., 1928.

Ryus, William H. *The Second William Penn*. Kansas City, Mo.: Frank T. Riley Publishing Company, 1913.

Sabin, Edwin L. *Kit Carson Days*. Rev. ed. 2 vols. New York: Press of the Pioneers, 1935.

Schoonover, T. J. *The Life and Times of Gen. John A. Sutter*. Sacramento, Calif.: Bullock-Carpenter Printing Co., 1908.

Segale, Sister Blandina. *At the End of the Santa Fe Trail*. Columbus, Ohio: Columbian Press, 1932.

Singletary, Otis A. *The Mexican War*. Chicago: University of Chicago Press, 1960.

Smith, Henry Nash. *Virgin Land*. Cambridge: Harvard University Press, 1950.

Spence, Paul D., ed. *Guide to the Microfilm Edition of the Pierre Menard Collection in the Illinois State Historical Library*. Springfield: Illinois State Historical Society, 1972.

Stanley, F. [Crochiola, Francis Stanley]. *The Grant That Maxwell Bought*. Denver: World Press, 1950.

Taylor, Morris F. *First Mail West: Stagecoach Lines on the Santa Fe Trail*. Albuquerque: University of New Mexico Press, 1971.

――――. *O.P. McMains and the Maxwell Land Grant Conflict*. Tucson: University of Arizona Press, 1979.

The United States vs. the Maxwell Land Grant Company et al. No. 974. Transcript of Record. Washington: Privately printed, 1886.

Thompson, Gerald. *The Army and the Navajo*. Tucson: University of Arizona Press, 1976.

Transcript of Record of Charles Bent et als. vs. Guadalupe Miranda et als. Las Vegas, N.Mex.: La Voz del Pueblo Print, 1894.

Transcript of Title of the Maxwell Land Grant Situated in New Mexico and Colorado. Chicago: Rand McNally and Co., 1881.

Turner, Frederick Jackson. *The Frontier in American History.* New York: Henry Holt and Company, 1920.

Twitchell, Ralph Emerson. *The Leading Facts of New Mexican History.* 5 vols. Cedar Rapids: The Torch Press, 1911–17; first 2 vols., Repr. ed. Albuquerque: Horn and Wallace, 1963.

Verlie, Emile J., ed. *Illinois Constitutions.* Springfield: Illinois State Historical Society, 1919.

Wallace, Ernest and Hoebel, E. Adamson. *The Comanches: Lords of the South Plains.* Norman: University of Oklahoma Press, 1952.

Wallace, William S. *A Journey Through New Mexico's First Judicial District in 1864.* Los Angeles: Westernlore Press, 1956.

Walter, Paul A. F. *Banking in New Mexico Before the Railroad Came.* New York: The Newcomen Society in North America, 1955.

Ward, Margaret. *Cimarron Saga.* Pampa, Texas: Pampa Print Shop, n.d.

Webb, James J. *Adventures in the Santa Fe Trade, 1844–1847,* ed. Ralph P. Bieber. Glendale, Calif.: Arthur H. Clark Co., 1931.

Weber, David J. *The Taos Trappers: The Fur Trade in the Far Southwest, 1540–1846.* Norman: University of Oklahoma Press, 1971.

Westphall, Victor. *The Public Domain in New Mexico, 1854–1891.* Albuquerque: University of New Mexico Press, 1965.

———. *Thomas Benton Catron and His Era.* Tucson: University of Arizona Press, 1973.

Wilson, Elinor. *Jim Beckwourth: Black Mountain Man and War Chief of the Crows.* Norman: University of Oklahoma Press, 1972.

Index

Abbreviation: Lucien Bonaparte Maxwell is shown as LBM in subentries.

boundaries of, 152–53;
known by capitalists,
158–59; size limited,
180–81; *see also*
Maxwell Land Grant,
Rayado Grant
Beaubien, Charles: ix,
31, 33–34, 53–61, 69,
71–73, 80, 84–85, 89,
93, 99, 103–106, 171,
206–207
Beaubien, Eleanor: 171
Beaubien family: 171
Beaubien, Juana: 171
Beaubien, Luz: *see* Max-
well, Luz Beaubien
Beaubien, Mrs. Charles:
71
Beaubien, Narciso: 35,
43, 70–71, 106
Beaubien, Paul: 171
Beaubien, Theodora:
171
Beck, Preston: 81
Beckwourth, Jim: 31
Bell, William A.: 113,
128–29, 153, 184
Benedict, Kirby: 115, 173
Benjamin, Judah P.: 183
Bennett, H. R.: 122
Benoist, Leonard: 22
Bent, Alfred: 173
Bent, Charles: ix, 27, 53–
55, 57, 61, 69–70, 73,
79–81, 103, 106, 171, 206
Bent family: 33, 106, 171,
173, 205
Bent, Maria Ignacia: 72
Benton, Jessie: *see* Fre-
mont, Jessie Benton
Benton, Thomas Hart:
21, 85
Bent, St. Vrain and
Company: 27, 29, 31,
53, 70, 90
Bent's Fort, Colo.: 27,
29, 57, 63, 69–70, 75,
80–81, 86
Bent, Teresina: 173
Bent, William: 27
Bergmann, Edward H.:

159–61, 183
Bernavette, John: 95
Beuthner, Soloman: 109
"Big Ditch": 158–59, 202
"Big Jack" (miner): 162
Billy the Kid: *see*
Bonney, William H.
Blackmore, B. M.: 110
Blackmore, William: 218
Black River, Mo.: 8–10,
22, 29–30
Bloomfield, Morris: 158
Blore, Arnold N.: 224
Boggs, John: 96
Boggs, Tom: 62, 81, 99,
139
"Bogus Bess" (race
horse): 167
Bonaparte, Lucien: 4
Bonaparte, Napoleon: 4
Bonney, William H.
("Billy the Kid"): 112,
202, 217, 226–27
Bosque Redondo,
N.Mex.: 130–31, 199:
see also Fort Sumner,
N.Mex.
Boston, Mass.: 110, 169
Brant, Randolph: 21
Brayer, Herbert O.: 218
Bridger, Jim: 27
Bronson, Larry: 151
Brown, John: 81
Brown, Mrs. John: 81–82
Brunswick, Marcus: 167,
185, 194
Burr, Aaron: 9

Cairo, Ill.: 18
Calhoun, A. J.: 111, 163
Calhoun, James S.: 88
California: 33, 52, 55, 57,
62, 64–68, 84, 85, 95,
96, 152, 221
California Battalion
(Mexican War): 67
California Column
(Civil War): 126, 151
California, Republic of:
66
California, Upper: 65:

see also California
Campbell, George: 135,
137, 140, 151
Campbell, Robert: 29
Canada: 179
Canadian River: 35, 59
Cape Girardeau, Mo.:
35, 231
Carleton, James H.: 126,
134–35, 151, 158
Carson, Christopher
("Kit"): ix, 25, 53, 84,
94, 104, 122, 130, 135,
136, 137, 166, 190, 205–
206; marriages of, 53;
on Frémont's second
expedition, 57; on
Little Cimarron, 61;
on Culebra River, 62;
on Frémont's third
expedition, 63–68; as
messenger for Fré-
mont, 68–69; lends
money to LBM, 84;
declines Frémont
offer, 86; at Rayado,
86–87; in California,
95–96; as Indian agent,
98, 121, 138; testifies
regarding Beaubien
and Miranda Grant,
102; aids LBM in
Washington, 138–39;
death of, 139; will of,
139; museum at
Rayado, 219
Carson family: 139
Carson, Josefa
Jaramillo: 53, 72;
death of, 139
Carson, Kit, Mesa: 104
Carson-Maxwell
(Rayado, N.Mex.): 219
Cashmere goats: 113
Catholic Church: in
Louisiana, 8, 13; in
New Mexico, 57, 96,
145; and Sisters of
Charity, 114–15
Catron, Thomas B.: 171,
198, 249

Menard, Marie-
Thérèse-Michelle
Godin: 6
Menard, Matthieu-
Saucier: 8
Menard, Modeste-
Alzire: 6
Menard, Odile: 6, 7, 10,
11; see also, Maxwell,
Odile Menard
Menard, Pierre: 10, 14,
35, 92, 107, 206, 221;
biography of, 4–8;
appearance of, 5;
mansion of, 6; as
lieutenant governor,
6; marriages of, 6–7;
children of, 6–7; as fur
trapper and trader,
15–16; and interest in
Indians, 17
Menard, Pierre, Jr.: 6
Menard, Sophie-
Angélique: 8
Menard, Thérèse-
Bérénice: 6
Men magazine: 226–27
Mercure, Henry: 95
Merino sheep: 113, 197
Meriwether, David: 99–
100
Mesilla, N.Mex.: 171
Metcalf, Archibald: 81
Mexican War: 9, 65, 68–
69, 73, 137
Mexico: 25, 34, 177–78
Militia, Illinois: 10
Mining: California, 95,
150; on Beaubien and
Miranda Grant, 136–
37; gold discoveries,
149–50; on Maxwell's
ranch, 150–67; publi-
cized, 162; value on
Maxwell grant, 175,
183–84; decline, 192;
Silver City, 189–99
Minneapolis, Minn.: 211
Miranda, Guadalupe:
34, 57, 59, 73, 79, 102–
103
Miranda, Pablo: 103

Mississippi River: 3, 4,
17–19
Mississippi River
Valley: 8
Missouri: 20, 68, 75, 81–
82, 169, 200; Maxwell
family in, 8–10;
education, 9, 13–14;
Territorial Council, 9;
interest in West, 16
Missouri Fur Company:
15
Missouri River: 15, 20,
25, 69
Missouri Stage
Company: 112
Mitchell, Robert B.:
154–55, 159
Montezuma Mine: 162
Montoya family: 111
Moore, William H.:
151–52, 158
Mora County, N.Mex.:
163
Mora, N.Mex.: 57, 96,
106, 111, 152, 163
Moreno Valley, N.Mex.:
59, 151, 153–55, 158–59,
164, 187, 191, 207
Moreno Valley Water
and Mining Com-
pany: 158
Morgan, James Lane:
223
Mormons: 68, 96
Moro River, N.Mex.: 94
Morrison, William: 14–
16
Mother Lode, Calif.: 151
Mould, Phillip: 153
Mount Vernon of
Illinois: 6; see also
Menard, Pierre
Muller, Frederick: 171
Muller, Theodora
Beaubien: 171
Murray, Luke: 124
Mystic Lode (copper
mine): 151

Nalda, Mrs. Michel: 216
Napoleon: see Bona-

parte, Napoleon
National Bank of New
Mexico: 198
National Lead
Company: 227
Navajo Indians: 97, 112,
130, 190–91, 197
Nebraska: 27, 169
"Ned" (race horse): 200
Nelson, Jesse: 91
New, Bill: 90
New Helvetia (Sutter's
Fort), Calif.: 64
New Mexican (Santa Fe):
113, 120, 152, 160, 163,
181, 186, 198
New Mexico Depart-
mental Assembly: 59
New Mexico Historical
Review: 216
New Mexico Historical
Society: 216
New Mexico magazine:
227
New Mexico Supreme
Court: 169, 173
New Mexico Surveyor
General: 173–74, 176,
181, 183
New Orleans, La.: 8, 20
New Park, Colo.: 95
New Tracks in North
America (W. A. Bell):
184
New York, N.Y.: 3, 21, 25,
148, 183–84, 211, 221
Nicollet, Joseph: 21
"Nolan" (race horse):
200
North Platte River: 29;
see also Platte River
Norton, A. B.: 132, 136

Oberlin College: 179
Ohio River: 15, 18
Old Park, Colo.: 95
Old Santa Fe Trail, The
(Inman): 211, 224
Oregon: 20–21, 52, 55,
57, 65–66
Oregon Trail: 96
Ortebus, Charles: 71

Ortiz, Tomas: 71
Osage Indians: 56
Out West magazine: 213
Owens, Dick: 61, 63–65,
85
Pacific States Publishing
Company: 212
Pajarito, N.Mex.: 198
Palace of the Governors
(Santa Fe): 197
Pancoast, Charles E.: 87
Panic of 1873: 192, 199
Parke, John G.: 94, 105
Pathfinder: *see* Frémont,
John C.
Pearson, Jim Berry: 227
Pecos River, N.Mex.:
191, 196–97
Pelham, William G.:
101–102, 183
Penn, William: 249
Pennsylvania: 87, 109,
169
Peonage: 111–12
Perea, Jose: 198
Perry County, Mo.: 13–
14
Perryville, Mo.: 13
Peters, DeWitt: 76,
96–97
Philadelphia, Pa.: 3–4
Philmont Scout Ranch:
219–20, 227
Pike's Peak, Colo.: 151
Pile, William A.: 185
Pittsburgh, Pa.: 20
Plains Indians: 78, 105,
132
Planters Hotel, Saint
Louis: 20
Platte River: 25
Pley, Benina Lee: 106
Pley, José: 106
Poglainni, Dom: 250
Poinsett, Joel R.: 21
Polk, James K.: 62, 65
Ponil River: 59, 61, 63,
70, 79–80, 94, 111, 123–
24; *see also* El Ponil,
South Ponil Creek
Pope, John: 94
Pope, Nathaniel: 16

Post at Rayado: 90–91, 94
Prarie du Chien, Wis.: 17
Press and Telegraph
(Elizabethtown,
N.Mex.): 187
Preuss, Charles: 22, 43,
46–50, 56
Price, Sterling: 70
Pueblo, Colo.: 31, 56–57,
62, 140, 167
Pueblo Indians: 31, 57,
59, 70–71, 121, 135

Quinn, James H.: 79–81,
83, 98
Racism: by LBM, 119; in
Southwest, 163–65
Railroads: Maxwell's
interest in, 199
Randolph County, Ill.:
6, 12; *see also* Kaskaskia
Raton Mountains: 70, 82,
135
Raton Pass: 69, 83, 98,
171
Rayado Canyon: 76
Rayado Grant: 102, 136;
see also Beaubien and
Miranda Land Grant
and Maxwell Land
Grant
"Rayado" Indians: 75
Rayado, N.Mex.: 75–95,
104–105, 107, 118, 132,
140, 197, 206, 209;
description of, 75–76,
87; origins of name,
75–76; Indians at, 76–
77, 99; sponsorship of,
79; settlers at, 79,
buildings of, 81;
Carson at, 86, 122;
U.S. Army at, 88–91;
post at, 90–91, 94;
Maxwell family at, 96;
LBM leaves, 100, 104;
and Rayado Ranch
(Abreú's), 106; sale by
Maxwell, 106
Rayado River, N.Mex.:
ix, 35, 59, 62, 74, 76, 152
Red Cloud (Sioux

Chief): 31
Red River, N.Mex.: 133,
145, 158
Reed, John L.: 194
Rel (Sioux girl): 31
Religion: 114, 145;
baptism of Maxwell
children, 96; in
Maxwell myth, 220–21
Republican Party: 180
Revolts: *see* Bear Flag
Revolt and Taos
Uprising
Reynolds, John: 6, 17
Rinehart, Isaah: 110,
147, 183
Rinehart, Mrs. Isaah:
147
Río Grande: 65, 68–69,
153
Río Grande Gorge: 33
Río Grande Valley: 125
Rittenhouse, Jack D.: 227
Rocky Mountains: 20,
25, 150
Roedel, Charles F.: 188
Rotherwood, Cedric of
(fictional lord): 211
Royal (Sioux girl): 31
Rydal Press: 216
Ryus, William H.: 96,
114, 213

Sac Indians: 17
Sacramento, Calif.: 95
Sacramento River,
Calif.: 64
Sainte Geneviève, Mo.:
8–10, 13, 92, 230
Saint Louis, Mo.: 7, 18,
20–21, 27, 53, 62, 69
Saint Mary's of the
Barrens Seminary:
13–14, 19, 23, 35, 231
St. Vrain, Céran: 27, 29–
30, 71
St. Vrain, Marcellin: 29,
32
Salamanca, University
of: 8
Salazar, Manuel: 131–32
Salt Lake: *see* Great Salt

Lucien Bonaparte Maxwell: Napoleon of the Southwest,

designed by Sandy See and Edward Shaw, was composed
by the University of Oklahoma Press in 10- and 11-point
Baskerline, an Alphatype version of Baskerville, and 20-
point Goudy and printed offset on 55-pound Glatfelter,
with presswork by Cushing-Malloy, Inc., and binding by
John H. Dekker & Sons.